MIGHTY STORIES,
DANGEROUS RITUALS

MIGHTY STORIES, DANGEROUS RITUALS

Weaving Together the Human and the Divine

Herbert Anderson

Edward Foley

Jossey-Bass Publishers
San Francisco

Substantial discounts on bulk quantities of Jossey-Bass books are available to corporations, professional associations, and other organizations. For details and discount information, contact the special sales department at Jossey-Bass Inc., Publishers (415) 433–1740; Fax (800) 605–2665.

For sales outside the United States, please contact your local Simon & Schuster International Office.

Jossey-Bass Web address: http://www.josseybass.com

 Manufactured in the United States of America on Lyons Falls Turin Book. This paper is acid-free and 100 percent totally chlorine-free.

Chapter 1: Nussbaum quote from *Assembly*, vol. 21, no. 5, December 1995, copyright © by the Notre Dame Center for Pastoral Liturgy, P.O. Box 81, Notre Dame, IN 46556.

Chapter 3: Wiesel quote from *The Gates of the Forest* © 1966 by Elie Wiesel. (Reprinted by permission of Henry Holt & Co., Inc. and Georges Borchardt, Inc. for the author)

Chapter 7: Close quote from *Journal of Pastoral Care*. Quello quote reprinted with permission of Rev. Dan Quello.

Chapter 8: Brokering poems reprinted with permission of Herbert Brokering. Hymn stanzas text copyright © 1958 *Service Book and Hymnal*. Reprinted by permission of Augsburg Fortress.

Chapter 9: Lapsley quote from *New Theology Review*. Shea poem from *The Hour of the Unexpected* by John Shea. © 1977 Tabor Publishing, a division of RCL Enterprises, Inc.

Library of Congress Cataloging-in-Publication Data

Anderson, Herbert, date.
    Mighty stories, dangerous rituals : weaving together the human and the divine / Herbert Anderson, Edward Foley. — 1st ed.
      p. cm. — (The Jossey-Bass religion-in-practice series)
    Includes bibliographical references and index.
    ISBN 0-7879-0880-0 (alk. paper)
    1. Pastoral theology. 2. Storytelling—Religious aspects—Christianity. 3. Rites and ceremonies. I. Foley, Edward. II. Title. III. Series.
    BV4011.A488 1997   97–21075
    253—dc21

FIRST EDITION
HB Printing 10 9 8 7 6 5 4 3 2 1

CONTENTS

PREFACE

THIS BOOK WAS BORN in friendship and formed in diversity. One author is Lutheran, the other Roman Catholic; one teaches worship, the other pastoral care; one comes from a storytelling family, the other from a secret-keeping tradition; one is messy, the other is orderly. These superficial differences mirror deeper contradictions that are the paradoxical dimension of human life and relationships. Our common work in worship and pastoral care and our shared vision for this book are informed by those differences. When people acknowledge and appreciate the contradictions of living, the stories they tell and the rituals they enact are more likely to be authentic, even if they are seemingly contradictory. We hope this book reflects that same authenticity.

The Need to Link Narrative and Ritual

Narrative and ritual are different dimensions of human living that have gained popularity in recent years as discrete topics of intellectual inquiry. The study of ritual helps us understand both our patterns of interacting at home or at work and the religious practices of faith traditions. The narrative perspective has contributed to rethinking ethics, pastoral care, biblical studies, and preaching. Very little has been done, however, to explore the necessary and inescapable relationship between narrative and ritual.

Mighty Stories, Dangerous Rituals is about connecting the stories we tell with the rituals we enact. Ritual and story are common ways within a particular social context by which we order and interpret our world. They are necessary because storytelling and ritualizing together provide the vehicles for reconnecting God's story with our human stories. When easy commerce between the divine and human narratives occurs both in worship and in pastoral care, storytelling and ritualizing have the power to transform persons and communities of faith into signs of the presence of God.

The integration of worship and pastoral care is a critical agenda for the church's ministry for many reasons. First, there is an absence of ritual models for significant moments of crisis or transition. Life events such as leaving home, suffering a miscarriage, undergoing divorce, or (for a gay person) coming out of the closet, like so many other critical moments, are often devoid of ritual. The stories we tell about these moments often have the power to define difference or ascribe social failure, but still we have no rituals. The absence of appropriate rituals to help people through traumatic situations of change or loss is a palpable void.

Second, the standard public rituals in churches are often ceremonies without stories—ritual that has become disconnected from peoples' lives. In sermons, song texts, and the prayers that punctuate worship, the human narrative and the divine narrative seldom connect. The ceremony may be proper, but the rituals have no soul. Much of the current dispute about worship in this era of broad liturgical reform misses this point.

Third, standard rituals, such as those around birth and death, have radically new contexts that require rethinking. For example, how do we ritualize the end of a life when a person has been kept alive by artificial means? Who shall be present to witness a baptism if the child being baptized was born to a surrogate mother? Situations continue to emerge from medical and reproductive technology that have never been contextualized in story or ritual.

Fourth, the splintering of our social structures is so pervasive that they may no longer support healthy patterns of living. Even our neighborhoods hide lonely and disconnected people. The world in which we live is less likely to define who we are to be or tell us how we shall live. Shaping our identity or forging life patterns becomes an overwhelming psychospiritual quest without the ritual and narrative frameworks that would otherwise sustain us. As a result, we lack ways of telling stories that bind us together in community. Stories and rituals are not only necessary personal resources for growth and stability; they are the ways that faith communities frame our journeys in God.

Fifth, finding ways to weave the divine narrative with our human stories presumes that we know the stories of our religious traditions. One can no longer assume even the most general knowledge of the fundamental stories of the Judaic or Christian traditions. Those who regard themselves as practicing Christians today are biblically illiterate. They may know more about the life of an entertainer or sports hero than heroes of faith. As a result, we have a limited pool of metaphors and images to draw upon for interpreting our own story in a new way.

Finally, there is fragmentation in ministry itself. The general practice of ministry has been divided into various specializations such as social activist, pastoral psychotherapist, administrator, educator, or liturgist. There are necessary distinctions in ministry, but these distinctions need not and should not become separate ministries. Congregations of believers are *living communal webs* made up of interdependent parts. The integration of worship and pastoral care through linking ritual and narrative is one strategic alliance within a larger web of interdependent connections; it is also a way of creating community stories. The complexity of ministry for our time demands integration in order that the witness of faith communities will be marked by coherence and wholeness.

We experienced something of that coherence around the death of Joseph Cardinal Bernardin of Chicago, which occurred during the final stages of writing this book, in the fall of 1996. His death unified a city and deepened our understanding of the reciprocity of narrative and ritual. From the announcement that "the cancer has returned" until the day he died, Cardinal Bernardin invited the people of Chicago to walk with him and care for him. When we are ill, he said, we need not close in on ourselves. The stories and rituals of his dying and our grieving taught us another view of both death in life and living in the face of dying. His death was memorialized by Protestants, Jews, and Muslims alike because in his life he had sought to find common cause with people from different faith traditions. Although some of the rituals were public and others were private, and although some of the stories belonged to all the people and others did not, Bernardin's dying and our grieving together, with profound respect and enduring affection, momentarily changed a hard-driving, diverse city into a community with a common narrative and a unifying prayer. His dying helped us understand in new ways the power of both narrative and ritual to transform individuals and communities.

Myth and Parable and Other Contradictions

We fashion our narratives in many different ways. They are epics and mysteries, comedies and tragedies, adventures and character studies, myths and parables. It is this last distinction between myth and parable that we have found most helpful in understanding how and why we tell stories. In his book *The Dark Interval* (1975), biblical scholar John Dominic Crossan suggests that all stories are someplace on a continuum between myth and parable. *Myth,* as Crossan uses the term, mediates between irreducible opposites. It seeks to resolve contradiction and paradox. People spend great sums of money, for example, to create a mythic wedding in which all signs of human imperfection are covered and all personal conflicts are hidden. More than that, myth presumes the permanent possibility of reconciliation. *Parable,* by contrast, is about contradiction. Parables challenge our expectations of a world without blemish. In the parables of Jesus, the last are first, and the meek inherit the earth. The parabolic perspective creates contradiction in both narrative and ritual in order to reveal a truth that is otherwise hidden.

Both myth and parable are necessary in storytelling and in ritual making. That itself is a paradox. We need to believe that all things do work together for good for those who love God. That is a fundamental Christian myth that helps us endure the parabolic reality that wheat and weeds grow together, and God intends it so. Human beings are inclined toward the mythic, and because of that we need to keep the parabolic perspective alive, lest we believe that mythic weddings' will make happy marriages, lest we become trapped in mythic expectations of perfection. Although we might like to make our own story into a myth without contradictions, the parabolic approach is consistent with the Christian story. Parabolic stories invite transformation by opening us to the possibility of something new. The Jesus story is the ultimate parable—it challenges our mythic dreams of a life without suffering or contradictions.

In addition to myth and parable, there are other polarities or paradoxes that have helped us understand the reciprocity of worship and pastoral care. These polarities include moment and process, public and private, individual and communal. Each polarity illuminates some linkage between worship and pastoral care for the sake of ministry. Helping couples prepare for both the wedding event and the process of becoming married is enhanced when we are attentive to both the private and the public aspects of marriage. Coping with discontinuity in life has to do with discovering the inevitable threads of continuity hidden in our stories. These are contradictions that cannot be resolved but rather must be maintained in their contradictoriness.

For Whom Is This Book Intended?

Mighty Stories, Dangerous Rituals is written for a wide range of readers, religious and secular, professional and nonprofessional. Those who have a professional interest in exploring the relationship between narrative and ritual are invited to consider with us the inescapable reciprocity of narrative and ritual in both individual and communal life. Students preparing for ministry will find here a starting point for fostering connections between diverse aspects of the same pastoral work. Pastoral practitioners interested in furthering the relationship between worship and pastoral care can expect to discover new perspectives for their efforts to diminish fragmentation and foster coherence in religious communities. We are all practitioners who fashion stories and rituals to make sense of our lives. Anyone who wants to understand the relationship between human and divine stories in life and desires to weave them into a meaningful narrative will find this book a helpful resource. We particularly hope that our proposal be accessible for those who struggle to renew their awareness of the presence of God in their daily living.

Readers familiar with other literature on worship and pastoral care will find common themes in this book: the correspondence between life cycle rituals and agendas for human growth; ritual honesty and the need for authenticity in both story and ritual; the growing awareness that there are human situations that need ritualization; and the importance of keeping worship and pastoral care as distinct aspects of ministry while fostering reciprocity between them. Our perspective is distinguished by the possibility it presents of discovering ways to connect human stories with the stories of God by integrating narrative and ritual.

Naming the Ambiguity

Our title is ambiguous because the subject is complex. Stories and rituals are in fact both mighty and dangerous. Stories can take us on wondrous, unexpected adventures; they can also lead us astray. Sometimes we get trapped in narratives that are harmful, yet what we mean by *dangerous* is something different. The Christian ritual of baptism, for instance, is dangerous because not only does it promise God's presence and initiate each baptized person into a sustaining community of faith; it also marks an individual with the sign of Christ's cross—a reminder that living comes through dying. The cross is a dangerous symbol—challenging and contradictory, it upsets our desire for order or control. The invitation of baptism to live in the shadow of a cross makes it a dangerous ritual.

The book's subtitle, *Weaving Together the Human and the Divine,* reflects both the framework and the aim of our exploration. Although *narrative* and *story* are frequently used interchangeably, we distinguish between them to emphasize the transcendent dimension of divine narrative. Narrative and ritual are the larger vehicles by which we define meaning in life, communicate that meaning to others, and give order to individual and communal activity. Stories are like incident reports that particularize a narrative and also redefine it. Stories are often woven together to form a web of stories that then becomes a personal or collective narrative.

Narrative and ritual are not the only ways to define human existence, but they do provide a larger framework for reflecting on what holds us together and what keeps us apart. Each of us has stories to tell that allow the divine narrative to unfold, and all human stories are potential windows to the story of God. The more difficult task for pastoral practitioners is to connect the divine and human narratives so deeply that the stories and rituals diminish fragmentation and bind together believing communities.

Overview of *Mighty Stories, Dangerous Rituals*

Chapters One and Two explore the ways narrative and ritual are common to all experience. In Chapter Three, the connection between narrative and ritual is examined from a religious perspective. When Christians narrate and ritualize their lives, the Jesus story provides a transforming vision for expressing and creating meaning. Christian worship and ritual is a medium for discovering how God is always at work making something new of our personal stories. For that reason alone, we suggest that narrative, ritual, pastoral care, and worship are linked essentially and reciprocally. Among the many alliances that sustain the church's ministry and provide grist for pastoral theological reflection, the link between worship and pastoral care comes nearly to the core.

Chapters Four through Six examine the practice of pastoral care and worship at moments of birth, marriage, and death. The life-cycle milestones of baptism, weddings, and funerals each occur in the midst of a process that begins before and continues after the event. For example, baptism occurs in the midst of a welcoming process for the child that begins long before the birth and continues after the baptism. Although baptism has many other meanings, it is a ritual of hospitality by which a child is incorporated into the Christian community of faith. Each of these ritual events is enriched by taking seriously what we learn about the human story through pastoral care, which in turn will enhance the narrative process that frames the ritual.

In Chapters Seven through Nine we address three pastoral issues. Chapter Seven addresses stories in need of rituals. The effectiveness of pastoral practice is diminished at many transitional moments or crisis situations, such as leaving home or divorce, because there are too few ritual resources available. There are also rituals in Christian community life devoid of stories, which is the topic of Chapter Eight. The absence of narrative often makes worship a sterile formality. We know that religious rituals are devoid of stories when we cannot locate our place in the drama being enacted in the liturgy or even know the point of the drama. There is no point of contact between the divine narrative and our human experience of struggle and pain.

In Chapter Nine we develop a spirituality of reconciliation for coping with the tensions embedded in human living and that exist between worship and pastoral care. Worship and pastoral care are not the same, even though they are inescapably linked in the practice of religious communities. We propose a spirituality of reconciliation that neither fuses distinctions nor allows them to become the occasion for separation. Rather, it honors the contradictions in friendship and lives respectfully between polarities of ministry such as worship and pastoral care. Human wholeness is possible only when we are able to live with contradiction. That is because the deepest truths of life need paradox for their full expression.

Acknowledgments

We have had many conversation partners in the process of preparing this book. They have given us stories, critical response, and the encouragement necessary to develop this approach to worship and pastoral care. Gilbert Ostdick, OFM, a colleague at Catholic Theological Union, deserves special recognition for being the first collaborator with Herbert Anderson in developing a course on worship and pastoral care. We are grateful to the many participants in that seminar over the years, especially those who worked on a preliminary draft of this book.

Our approach to integrating narrative and ritual, pastoral care and worship, has been enriched by conversations with the following colleagues who constituted with us a working group on practical theology: Dianne Bergant, CSA; Gary Riebe-Estrella, SVD; and Robert Schreiter, CppS. They have helped us understand practical theology as a way of reflecting on Christian life and ministry that attends carefully and critically to both human experience and religious traditions as resources for developing more appropriate strategies for a ministry of transformation.

We are particularly grateful to Sarah Polster, Darren Hall, and the staff at Jossey-Bass for their interest in this project and their determination to make it a helpful book for pastoral practitioners and for anyone interested in exploring the wholeness of life through narrative and ritual.

---

o

The mighty part of writing this book together has been the wonderful company of folk whose personal stories and incidental conversations have helped form our perspective. Writing this book has changed us—that is the dangerous part.

Chicago   HERBERT ANDERSON
August 1997   EDWARD FOLEY

THE AUTHORS

HERBERT ANDERSON is professor of pastoral theology at Catholic Theological Union in Chicago. He is also an ordained pastor of the Evangelical Lutheran Church in America. He earned his M.Div. degree (1962) at Augustana Seminary and his Ph.D. degree (1970) at Drew University. Anderson's previous teaching experience includes Wartburg Theological Seminary (1975–1985) and Princeton Theological Seminary (1969–1975). He has also been a parish pastor, a campus minister, a hospital chaplain, and a pastoral counselor. He is married and is the father of two grown children.

Anderson has written and taught in the general areas of pastoral care, with special focus on grief and the family. He has written numerous articles and reviews and is author or coauthor of nine other books, including a five-volume series, Family Living in Pastoral Perspective, that includes *Leaving Home* (1993), *Becoming Married* (1993), *Regarding Children* (1994), *Promising Again* (1995), and *Living Alone* (1997).

Anderson is currently the president of the American Association of Practical Theology. He is a member of the International Academy in Practical Theology and the American Family Therapy Academy. He has lectured and conducted workshops throughout the United States and in Europe, Australia, Papua New Guinea, and Korea.

EDWARD FOLEY is professor of liturgy and music at Catholic Theological Union in Chicago. He is also an ordained Roman Catholic presbyter and a member of the Province of St. Joseph of the Capuchin Order since 1966. He earned his M.Div. degree (1975) from St. Francis School of Pastoral Ministry in Milwaukee, his M.M. degree (1975) in choral conducting from the University of Wisconsin at Milwaukee, and both his M.A. degree (1980) in liturgical research and his Ph.D. degree (1987) in theology from the University of Notre Dame.

A specialist in worship and the arts, Foley identifies himself as a practical theologian. He has published ten previous books, including *Ritual Music* (1995), *Developmental Disabilities and Sacramental Access* (1994), and *From Age to Age* (1991). He has also authored more than 150 scholarly and pastoral articles and reviews and sits on a number of editorial boards.

Foley is president of the North American Academy of Liturgy. A well-known speaker, he has lectured throughout the United States and in Canada, Ireland, and Europe. He presides and preaches at St. Mary's Catholic Church in Riverside, Illinois.

MIGHTY STORIES, DANGEROUS RITUALS

PART ONE

OF STORIES
AND RITUALS

THE POWER OF STORYTELLING

The stories we tell, whether human or divine,
mythic or parabolic, order experience, construct
meaning, and build community.

○

In the aftermath of the massacres that occurred in Rwanda in the early 1990s, a woman psychologist was asked to visit one of the many refugee camps of Rwandans in Tanzania. It seemed that the women of that camp, though safe from the slaughter, were not sleeping. During her visit to the refugees, the psychologist learned that the women, who had witnessed the murder of family and friends, had been told by camp officials not to speak of such atrocities in the camp. The women followed this instruction, but the memories of the carnage haunted them, and they could not sleep.

The psychologist decided that in response to this situation she would set up a story tree: a safe place for the women to speak of their experiences. Every morning she went out to the edge of the camp and waited under the canopy of a huge shade tree. The first day no one came. On the second day one woman appeared, told her story, and left. Another showed up the following day, then another and another. Within the span of a few days, scores of women were gathering under the tree each morning to listen and to share their tales of loss, fear, and death. Finally, after weeks of listening, the psychologist knew that the story tree was working. Reports confirmed that the women in the camp were now sleeping.

○

THIS STORY OF RWANDAN WOMEN is difficult to forget. Although most of us have never witnessed the horrors of civil war nor experienced the aftermath of genocide, we can visualize women gathering under a tree to remember. We may not understand the specter of family slaughter nor comprehend thousands of refugees living in squalor, but we do know about fear and sleeplessness. Part of the power of narrative is that it enables us to make deep human connections that transcend unfamiliarity in locale and experience. Stories transport us to times and places we do not know. Through narrative, we become spiritual travelers undaunted by time, distance, or new landscapes. It is as if stories have mystical power to invite us, willingly or unwillingly, to enter unknown worlds.

The Power of Story

Stories make claims on our minds and hearts, often before we know why or how. We may be reading a magazine or listening to the news when suddenly, without warning, some tale of heroism or tragedy grabs our attention. We had no intention of being emotionally hijacked during the news. Nor was there any expectation that empathy was required for reading a magazine. We simply happened to watch the news one night or randomly page through a magazine at the dentist's office, when suddenly we were hooked. We were drawn into a tale without permission, forethought, or desire to be involved. Stories, such as that of Rwandan women refugees, claim us with their power and sometimes carry us to remote places where we never intended to go.

The most compelling reason why stories have such power to engage us is the narrative form of human existence itself. Human experience is structured in time and narrative. We comprehend our lives not as disconnected actions or isolated events but in terms of a narrative. We conceive of our lives as a web of stories—a historical novel or a miniseries in the making. We think in stories in order to weave together into a coherent whole the unending succession of people, dates, and facts that fill our lives. The narrative mode, more than other forms of self-reporting, serves to foster the sense of movement and process in individual and communal life. In that sense, the narrative framework is a human necessity. Stories hold us together and keep us apart. We tell stories in order to live.

Stories are not simply heard or read or told; they are created. We use stories to construct meaning and communicate ourselves to another. Stories help us organize and make sense of the experiences of a life. Sometimes, however, we use stories to fashion a view of life for ourselves that avoids reality. We may also tell stories to reveal ourselves or conceal ourselves from others. Whatever the purpose, we construct stories to integrate the disparate elements of our lives. Family therapists Joy Friedman and Gene Combs (1996) conclude that "each remembered event constitutes a story, which together with our other stories constitutes a life narrative, and, experientially speaking, our life narrative is our life" (p. 32). For that reason, it is not exaggerating to say we are our stories.

Storytelling, as Dan McAdams (1993) has observed, also "appears to be a fundamental way of expressing ourselves and our world to others" (p. 27). Some of the stories we tell are passed down to us in our families or in the culture or in our religious traditions. Because of these stories, we ascribe certain meanings to particular life events and regard others as without significance. Other stories are our own creation. Still others are told about us after we die.

Because narrative is so essential for constructing the worlds we inhabit, sustaining the communities that hold us, and enlivening the rituals that shape us, we begin with a general discussion of the place and power of narrative in human life.

Constructing Meaning Through Story

Stories are privileged and imaginative acts of self-interpretation. We tell stories of a life in order to establish meaning and to integrate our remembered past with what we perceive to be happening in the present and what we anticipate for the future. We weave many stories together into a life narrative that conveys what we believe to be essential truths about ourselves and the world. Each story, as a fragment in the narrative, is not so much an exercise in objectivity or a reporting of events as it is an interpretation of them. Stories do not simply recount what happened but what happened from our perspective.

This self-interpreting function is readily apparent in the daily rehearsal of stories or story fragments. It may appear that we are offering a commentary on the world, relating some interchange with a co-worker, or trying to let our children know what childhood or family life was like thirty years ago. The primary, unspoken objective of our storytelling, however, is to provide an appropriate interpretation of our own life. The goal is not just to discover a world or provide an interpretation of the world that allows us to live in it but rather to discover and interpret a world that allows us to live with ourselves. We retell incidents, relate occurrences, and spin tales in order to learn what occurred, especially *to me*. Such an interpretive process makes the world more hospitable. By telling what had happened to them, for example, the Rwandan women were able to fashion a world that included their experience.

The creative and interpretative nature of the human narration is revealed in every story moment, but it becomes especially apparent in situations of disagreement or conflict. Although we may insist that we are arguing about the *facts* in the situation, the fundamental differences are often around the *interpretation* of the data or shared experience. Imagine seeing a Woody Allen movie with friends. In the conversation that follows, one friend may have been deeply moved, while another regarded the movie as mildly entertaining. Another friend may have experienced the movie as a mindless exercise in self-indulgence by the screenwriter-director-producer-star, while still another may have thought it to be profound. Although everyone saw the same movie, and although everyone may argue about which interpretation is more accurate or appropriate, from a narrative perspective, all views are "correct." Each interpretation of the story achieves its purpose—an authentic report of the experience of the movie from the viewpoint of the participant.

Suppose, however, one of the participants in the Woody Allen movie experience felt isolated by the conversation because no one seemed to share her point of view on the film's offensiveness. And when she returned home, she sent the following e-mail message to a friend in Spain:

> Sandy,
>   I have just had another lonely experience being with people. I am better off staying home. We saw a stupid Woody Allen film, and nobody else was offended by his sexism. I am tired of always being an outsider. I cannot remember the last time being with people made me feel less alone.
>
> Janet

Janet's effort to make sense of her experience at the movies with her friends was shaped by previous moments in her life narrative in which having a different perspective intensified her loneliness. Others might interpret that same experience of having a differing point of view as confirmation of personal uniqueness or as demonstration that most people are not autonomous thinkers. The meaning Janet found in this experience reinforced similar stories and was reinforced by similar stories from her narrative. We create stories and live according to their narrative assumptions.

Stories are mighty, however, not only because we shape our lives through them but also because they have the power to unsettle the lives we have comfortably shaped by them. In that sense, the narrative mode itself subverts our settled social realities. Our self-interpretation is not the last word, because our stories are not just our stories. When we weave together the human and the divine, we are attentive to another story that is not completely our own, a narrative that has the power to transform. When we are fully attentive to the stories of God, Brueggemann adds, "it becomes clear that we are in the midst of stories—valuing our own past, pushed by ruthless force, oddly visited by the one whom we dare to call God" (1990, p. 22). Weaving together the human and the divine enables us to hear our own stories retold with clarity and new possibility. And when our own stories are retold, our lives are transformed in the telling.

Because we live in the stories we create, we need to be sure that the stories we live are shaped, in large measure, by our own vision of life. Trying to live according to someone else's story is like wearing hand-me-down clothes all the time. Therefore, the life narrative we compose should be significantly shaped by the choices we make and the actions we take.

Communicating Through Story

Beyond being simply a character conveyed in the stories of others, each of us is the primary author of our own life narrative. We continuously and actively author and reauthor our lives through story, articulating for ourselves and others the choices we make and the things we have done. For this reason, it is important to understand a story from "inside" the author. When the stories we tell conceal rather than reveal our understanding of ourselves and our world, they isolate us from others. When, however, the aim of storytelling is to interact with others and identify common ground, stories have the potential to build authentic communities of shared meaning and values.

We interpret ourselves to others through story more often than we are aware and maybe even more often than we intend. Communicating through story frequently occurs when we attempt to teach a lesson or make a new friend or explain our behavior to someone in a narrative way. While the intention might be to impart a lesson to our children, we do so by compressing a series of tales from our childhood and shifting into storytelling mode. Along the way we reveal something of ourselves to our children. For example:

I don't know what the matter is with you kids. You are always in front of that tube. When I was your age, we didn't have a color television in our bedroom. There was only a black-and-white set in the living room, and we were only allowed to watch it at night. We spent much more time outside, playing ball or riding our bikes. Turn that thing off, and find some other way to occupy your time.

The social ritual arranged for meeting new neighbors or introducing ourselves to recently hired co-workers will often be filled with stories, some of which might be very revealing. Although the aim of telling the story is not personal sharing, we tell our story, or at least a part of it, to strangers. When we are looking for points of identification with someone we hardly know, we will tell a story. Sometimes we tell stories about ourselves because it is easier to talk than to listen:

I'm originally from San Jose, but I moved away for college. My first job took me to Dallas, but I always wanted to return to the Bay Area. My wife is from Dallas and always wanted to move up north. We came to San Jose in 1988.

In attempting to offer some cogent explanation to our daughter's sixth-grade teacher why our offspring is so giddy in the classroom or uninterested in learning anything that is not featured in her favorite teen magazine, we may shift into narrative mode. Before we know it, we have conveyed a great deal of information about ourselves through the stories in this process:

I had the same problem when I was in school. My friends and I pored over every page of *Tiger-Beat* magazine. It was the center of our life for a few months. It was just a phase that didn't last very long. . . . I was doing fine by the seventh grade. Kathy will get over it, too.

Telling a story from our experience is a common but often unhelpful response to a crisis. It is often more comforting to the teller than the person to whom the story is told. Simply telling our story may even be problematic, however, if it shifts the focus from the person in crisis to ourselves. Because of our anxiety or awkwardness or both, we try to comfort a friend whose mother has just been admitted to a hospital emergency room after an apparent heart attack by recalling a similar situation in our own family history:

It's going to be okay. Remember when this same thing happened to my dad a few years ago? He gave us quite a scare, but he pulled through just fine. You've seen him recently—healthy as a bear, and as ornery as ever. Don't worry. I'm sure your mom is going to be fine, too.

As the previous examples show, the external reason for telling a story may be to motivate our progeny, break the ice with a new acquaintance, resolve a family conflict, or maintain our equilibrium during a crisis situation. During the storytelling process, however, we externalize our internal interpretation of ourselves and the world. As a form of indirect speech, story reveals as much as it conceals even when self-revelation is not the intent. We may recount selected episodes, compress many stories into one, or sprinkle our speech with story-fragments. Storytelling is so much a part of everyday speech that we are seldom aware of communicating in the narrative mode.

When Stories Conceal

Stories, as such, are not fundamentally designed to provide essential facts or data about ourselves or our world, although that may sometimes be a purpose. Even so, it is important that our stories fit the understanding and interpretation of our life by others. Sometimes our storytelling is used only as a tool to develop an identity and offer a respectable self-interpretation of ourselves for ourselves. Thus we shape the events and circumstances of our lives into a story that reinforces our self-identity and worldview without attention to the interpretation of others. When our narrative does not square with the stories that others tell of us, we isolate ourselves.

Consider the following narrative as an exercise in self-deception. Chris believes that life owes him much more than he has thus far received. At thirty-two, he is likable and seemingly well-motivated but always in trouble financially or relationally. When confronted with one more loss of a job, end of a relationship, or arrest for public intoxication, Chris will explain his situation by reminiscing about his wonderful childhood.

---

o

The way he remembers it, Chris was raised in an idyllic family setting with indulgent parents, who gave him and his siblings whatever they wanted. His childhood home in rural Ohio was spacious and well-appointed on the inside and crowned outside with a huge swimming pool. Because his parents entertained a lot, there was always a party on the horizon, with more than adequate amounts of food, recreational drugs, and liquor. Chris began drinking in his early teens, about the same time he began smoking marijuana. Things began to fall apart when Chris was in his early twenties. The family business failed, the homestead was sold, the money disappeared, and the good life came to an end. After a falling out with his parents, Chris moved to Texas and took a job waiting tables. Now he is stuck in a trade that he hates.

Chris reports that he despises his life. He cannot understand why the family business failed. He is very bitter that his parents sold the home he loved so much. "It's not fair," he often complains. "I deserve better than this." The tragic symbol of his unhappy life is the ever-present lottery ticket in his pocket. "One day I am going to win a million bucks," he announces. "Then I'm going back to Ohio and buy back the old house. Everything will be as it should be."

O

This story, which Chris repeats with unflagging consistency after a few beers, illustrates how the privilege of self-interpretation can be abused. His narrative does not include any episodes about his drinking, his various arrests for driving while intoxicated, or the many demolished relationships that have unraveled in the midst of his drinking sprees. The most dominant force in his life—his alcoholism—is never mentioned. Rather, his carefully constructed tale is of a congenial childhood and a promise of a great future gone awry. What appears to Chris to be a matter of survival actually fabricates an identity that disconnects him from the present and traps him in a past that never was. The private interpretation of his story has led Chris into a cul-de-sac of only private meanings. We are in danger of being isolated in our life narrative whenever our storytelling conceals more than it reveals.

When Stories Reveal

When we tell stories about ourselves, we are often amazed to discover unknown commonalties that bond us quickly with strangers or deepen the affections of friends or family. Not every exercise of our narrative function is self-evading. When our autobiographical tales are self-effacing, disarming, or amusing, they reveal the kind of openness that is necessary for building community. Storytelling not only makes us human; it creates vulnerability. Melissa Musick Nussbaum admits that her autobiographical stories, which originated as stories told to her own children, have such a purpose. A particular favorite of hers—and her children—is titled "The Time I Wet My Pants at Sue Harris's Wedding":

I was Sue Harris's flower girl. I was dressed in a stiff full slip undergirding an explosion of pastel taffeta. The slip crackled when I sat. It was an outfit almost too gorgeous to bear, and the feel of it against my skin sent me into tremors of hopping on one leg in delight. My mother interpreted this as a full bladder hop. She was partly right. A few minutes before the wedding was about to begin my mother suggested, then demanded, that I go to the bathroom. Of course, I needed to go, but I couldn't bear to miss the various domestic dramas being performed around me in the vestibule. . . .

I have tried to remember as I mopped puddles over the years how it felt to want so badly to stay for the action and so badly to relieve one's bladder that one did both. Which is what happened to me at Sue Harris's wedding. I did need to urinate, and I did need to stay. So I let loose all over the solemn stone floor of the First Methodist Church in Tulia, Texas. I stepped away from the grown-ups, over to the side in a dark corner to urinate. A janitor happened by and, seeing the yellow stream trickling down the steps, asked me suspiciously, ... "Where did that water come from?" I looked him sweetly in the eye and said, "I don't know; it must be raining," and marched soggily down the aisle, strewing rose petals and savoring the interesting sensation of my lace-socked feet squashing in my Sunday shoes [Nussbaum, 1995, p. 696].

Nussbaum admits that this kind of storytelling reveals something about herself that is important for her children. Having them imagine her shamefaced before others, when they are so often shamefaced before her, allows her children "to imagine themselves as grown-ups" and to know that things will not always be as bewildering as they are in childhood. Nussbaum concedes, however, that such storytelling is not only important for her children; it is also important to her. In her words, "To tell the story allows me to remember how it was to be a child: noisy, sticky, curious, bold, clumsy, eager, cruel" (p. 696).

Telling stories or fashioning a narrative are not, at their root, just speech patterns but life patterns—not simply a way of talking to explain the world or communicate ourselves but a way of being in the world that, in turn, becomes the basis of our explanations and interpretations. Our stories are not so much a part of experience as they are the premise of experience. An amazing dynamic exists between our lives and our stories: each one shapes the other. Our collective life experiences are interpreted through a personal narrative framework and shaped into a master story that, in turn, influences subsequent interpretations. Each of us carries a personally constructed narrative framework into each situation we encounter. This framework becomes a key for interpreting reality and determines to what extent the stories we compose reveal and conceal.

Each of us is a storyteller, actively composing the story of our life. Chris, for example, is not simply mouthing stories about his life that deny his alcoholism; he is living a narrative that does the same. Even so, we do not shape this narrative alone. There are many outside influences over which we may have very little control. Chris's parents did indulge him and his siblings. The family business did fail, and financial stability deteriorated. Chris's alcoholism is a disease, traceable to his mother's drinking problem and socially traceable to a family that perpetually partied. Like the rest of us, Chris is more a coauthor than a solitary narrator of his life.

A life narrative is a joint product of person and environment. The reality that we coauthor our narrative with others parallels the idea that becoming a person is an ongoing process shaped by and shaping a wide range of agents and institutions. Fashioning stories is an act of creating one's life in ways that include these coauthors, whose influences should not be minimized or ignored. Theologian Rebecca Chopp has described this process in a way that bypasses old battles about determinism. "Our stories are related to but not determined by factors such as events beyond which we have no control, other actors to which we are in relation, and traditions that we appropriate or resist" (Chopp, 1995, p. 32). Although Chopp is using narrative agency to identify the new freedom women have to name their experience, women and men alike need to recognize that writing one's story is a complex process with more than one collaborator.

We will return later to the theme of coauthoring when we consider the connection between divine and human narratives. Understanding our story in relation to God's story is necessary for persons of faith. Nonetheless, even though others, including God, have a part in authoring our story, we are ultimately responsible for the narrative. For that reason, we need not be trapped in or by our story. Even Chris, while mired in a powerful tale of self-deception, has the capacity—although maybe not the will—to author a different life and craft a different narrative. The power of interpretation is always ours. It is therefore always possible to narrate our lives in another way. Consequently, storytelling is an act of hope, and even defiance, because it carries within it the power to change.

Mythic and Parabolic Narratives

As previously noted, we use stories to construct meaning and communicate ourselves to one another. Thus our storytelling could be envisioned as having an internal purpose (making sense of the world) and an external purpose (communicating ourselves to others). As the stories of Chris and Melissa illustrate, however, there are many ways to narrate our lives.

In some measure, this diversity exists because of the great differences in characters and events that distinguish one story from another. Each of us has different coauthors, different set designers, different choreographers, production managers, and supporting casts. Stories differ in content and complexity. The dissimilarities in our stories may also come from our different styles of developing them. Some storytelling has a didactic or apologetic character. Other stories amuse us, or they satirize or lampoon an event, a personality, or even ourselves. Apart from apology or satire, we also fashion stories as mysteries or romance, comedies or tragedies, adventures or character studies.

If understanding the ambiguity of life and communicating that understanding to others are basic reasons for the narratives we fashion, then we need to reflect upon which form of storytelling will most accurately convey our particular understanding. Of all the classifications possible for understanding how we fashion our stories, John Dominic Crossan's polar opposites of myth and parable are two of the most useful. In his classic study on parables, *The Dark Interval* (1975), Crossan argues that myth and parable define the limits of a story's possibilities. Crossan suggests that all narration can be understood as existing someplace along a continuum between these two binary opposite forms.

Myth for Crossan does not mean a pleasant story that is untrue, or what he calls sophisticated lying. Nor is it some type of legend populated with gods and goddesses. Rather, in the technical sense in which he employs it, *myth* refers mostly to mediation and reconciliation. Crossan draws upon the work of the French philosopher Claude Levi-Strauss, whose basic thesis, Crossan explains, is that "myth performs the specific task of mediating irreducible opposites" (Crossan, 1975, p. 51). Myth bridges the gap between apparently irreconcilable stances, individuals, or situations and demonstrates that mediation is possible.

The classic fairy tale *Beauty and the Beast* is a myth. In its simplest form, the story is about Beauty, the youngest and most beautiful daughter of a once-wealthy merchant. She is dedicated to her father, even though he has lost his fortune and has been abandoned by his other children. When the father becomes lost in a forest and accidentally wanders into the den of the fearsome Beast, he becomes the Beast's captive. Eventually the father is ransomed by his daughter Beauty, who exchanges places with him. In turn, the Beast falls in love with Beauty. When the Beast finally wins her over and she consents to marry him, the Beast is released from the spell that had possessed him and revealed to be a handsome and wealthy prince.

This fairy tale is a myth in Crossan's technical sense. It is a tale of many opposites: beauty/beast, poor/rich, commoner/royalty, woman/man, captive/free. In the conclusion of the story, however, all of these apparently opposing forces are reconciled. In the process, the core meaning of myth is revealed: mediation is possible. Crossan concludes, "What myth does is not just to attempt the mediation in story of what is sensed as irreconcilable, but in, by, and through this attempt it establishes the possibility of reconciliation" (Crossan, 1975, p. 53). The double function of myth is this: to resolve particular contradictions and, more important, to create a belief in the permanent possibility of reconciliation.

Parable, on the other hand, is not about mediation but about contradiction. It creates irreconcilability where before there was reconciliation. According to Crossan, parable has a double function that opposes the double function of myth. Parable not only introduces contradiction into situations of complacent security, "it challenges the fundamental principle of reconciliation by making us aware of the fact that we made up the reconciliation" (Crossan, 1975, p. 57). If the stories we create are to be authentic reflections of the lives we live, we need room for ambiguity and vulnerability. Parabolic narratives show the seams and edges of the myths we fashion. Parables show the fault lines beneath the comfortable surfaces of the worlds we build for ourselves. Myth may give stability to our story, but parables are agents of change and sometimes disruption. For that reason, parable is often an unsettling experience.

Flannery O'Connor was a novelist who excelled in parable. In her short story "Revelation," an upstanding Christian woman, Ruby Turpin, and an acne-scarred college girl named Mary Grace meet in a doctor's office. Ruby Turpin chatters away about her great gratitude to God for giving her such a blessed life. While others ignored Ruby or listened politely, Mary Grace was enraged. Finally, no longer able to bear Mrs. Turpin's public "thank you Jesus," Mary Grace hurled a book at Ruby and then leapt on top of her. Mrs. Turpin was stunned not only by the physical attack but by the girl's chilling words, "Go back to hell where you came from, you old wart hog."

While Ruby was not physically hurt, she could not shake the memory of the girl's hateful words. Why had she, a hardworking, churchgoing Christian, been singled out for this message? There were real trash in that same waiting room who really deserved those words. In her final confrontation with God, Ruby thought that if God liked trash so much she might just join their ranks, quit work, and spend her days lounging around. Ruby could be shiftless like the other trash. The thought of Mary Grace's insult seemed as though it was an insult from God. Anger rose strong and quickly inside of Ruby until she shook her fist to the heavens and shouted out to God, "Who do you think you are?"

It was at that point that Ruby Turpin had her "revelation," for as she looked toward the heavens she seemed to see a whole company of white trash, now clean for the first time, moving toward heaven. There were

> battalions of freaks and lunatics shouting and clapping and leaping like frogs. And bringing up the end of the procession was a tribe of people whom she recognized at once as those who, like herself and [her husband] Claud, had always had a little of everything and the God-given wit to use it right. She leaned forward to observe them closer. They were marching behind the others with great dignity, accountable as they had always been for good order and common sense and respectable behavior. They alone were on key. Yet she could see by their shocked and altered faces that even their virtues were being burned away [O'Connor, 1965, pp. 217–218].

Ruby Turpin's encounter with Mary Grace had shattered her vision of God's well-ordered universe and pulled the rug out from under her own secure place in that world. The vision she saw contradicted all of her tidy expectations. She was a hardworking, decent, Christian woman who had the world and God figured out. Everything was in its place. After her encounter with Mary Grace, however, Ruby Turpin found herself in a very different world, confronted with an unexpected kind of God. As we leave her at the end of "Revelation," stunned and vulnerable, it is unclear how well Ruby will navigate this new terrain. What is clear, however, is that her view of the world has been turned upside down by a parabolic vision of clean trash "rumbling toward heaven."

Living Between Myth and Parable

Mythic narrations comfort us and assure us that everything is going to be all right; parables challenge and dispute the reconciliation that our myths have created. Myths allow us to dream and to believe in a future better than the present; parables disallow us from living in a dream world, call us to confront the present, and deter us from trusting in any hope that does not face the hard reality of the present. The irony, of course, is that these are complementary narrative forms, and human beings need both of them.

If our narrative is out of touch with the parabolic, for example, there is the real danger that we will be trapped in a dishonest dream, as Chris's story demonstrates. Although his body is shutting down from years of alcoholic poisoning, and his personal life is crumbling, Chris continues to narrate the tale of his idyllic childhood. And with every purchase of a lottery ticket, he wagers that the dream can be recovered. The hope he lives, however, is more than simply false—it is destructive. His unwillingness and inability to demythologize his childhood and wager on something other than winning the lottery is figuratively and literally killing him. The problem is not that Chris has dreams; the problem is that in his mythic fashioning of life, he has nothing else.

A life devoid of mythic narration, on the other hand, is a life without the possibility of reconciliation and ultimate peace. It is true that parables challenge our myths and the reconciliations we have created. But parables can only subvert a world already created in and by myth. In doing so, parables give rise to a new reconciliation and therefore to a new myth. Melissa Musick Nussbaum's parabolic revelation of her childhood challenges the myth of the perfect parent who was once a perfect child. Her children love the myth-shattering pants-wetting story:

> Since their birth, I have been set up before them as the final arbiter in matters of morals and hygiene. . . . I'm the one who, to little children dribbling on the toilet and absentmindedly picking their noses, is Other, She-Who-Is-Always-Right. But to hear that story, and others like it, is to know that I, appearances and admonitions to the contrary notwithstanding, have walked a familiar road [Nussbaum, 1995, p. 696].

Nussbaum's parabolic narration debunks the myth of the perfect parent, the pure arbitrator and the unmoved mover. In doing so, it creates a new myth: that imperfect children can grow up to be lovable, imperfect adults. Thus parables are not about eliminating reconciliation; rather, they are about challenging the reconciliation with which we are comfortably living. The elimination of all myth, without the ultimate possibility for harmonizing all of those discordant strands in our lives, could leave us awash with meaninglessness or on the brink of despair.

While both mythic and parabolic stories are necessary for an authentic narrative, the parabolic story is more difficult to master. Human beings are much more inclined to revel in the world of the mythic. There are obvious reasons for this. The underlying message of mythic narration is that things are going to be all right. For example, in terms of the fairy tale *Beauty and the Beast,* one might imagine, "If things could work out for Beauty—who was separated from her poor and ailing father, and was the captive of a Beast—then they could certainly work out for me." Myth engages the natural optimism of the human spirit and the physiological instinct of the human organism. Our bodies struggle to live, and with every ounce of strength, they reject the ultimate parable of our own death. It is the death parable, however, which ultimately must be embraced in order to make the transition to the myth of eternal life.

When Stories Are Not Told

Parable is especially difficult for human beings because it has one great natural enemy: secret keeping. When communities such as families or parishes keep secrets, the consequences are extensive both for the individuals and the communities. Whether it be by explicit decision, implicit agreement, collusion, or a combination of these, communities sometimes decide never to tell the whole story and to keep some past event hidden at all cost. As a result the community is stuck in fixed patterns of interaction, roles are rigidly defined, and stories are closely monitored in order to keep the secret safe. Such secret keeping is deceptively mythic: prematurely announcing that reconciliation is possible without allowing participants in the story to name that which needs to be reconciled.

This kind of secret keeping as the enemy of the parabolic needs to be distinguished from our need to differentiate levels of intimacy through different types of self-disclosure. For example, rules of etiquette suggest that we do not divulge the intimate details of our lives to total strangers or passing acquaintances. Secret keeping also needs to be distinguished from the various levels of information sharing in which responsible people need to engage. Parents, for example, know that all of life's secrets are not shared with children. Employers also know that every bit of information about the workings of the office or personnel is not to be shared at the water cooler.

Secret keeping is more than differentiating levels of self-disclosure or making judgments about which information can be shared with children or employees. Rather, secret keeping is a pattern of deception that prevents people from accessing crucial segments of their own life story. We may not tell the whole story of our life when we prepare a resume to send to a prospective employer. Yet if we take seriously the challenge of narrating our lives as a way to discover and communicate our authentic selves, then such deception is not the way. The parabolic perspective helps us counter the impulse to present ourselves as a seamless robe, without blemish or flaws or even ordinary stitching.

There is no one rule about secrets. The complex ethical dilemmas embedded in community secrets do not yield to a simple formula. Our approach to secrets in our families, churches, or other communities must flow from the conviction that every secret-keeping situation is unique, even though most secrets are toxic. Secrets erode trust, tangle lines of communication, and disrupt communities by regularizing deception. The lingering danger of secrets to the well-being of intimate communities is clearer than the solution to that danger. Families and other human communities often are healed when old, corrosive secrets are revealed; sometimes, however, they are not.

The danger of secret keeping is highlighted when one reckons with the communal nature of human narration. Defining ourselves through story is both a personal and a communal act and thus a matter of psychological and social responsibility. In storytelling our personal autonomy is confronted by our social context, our primary authorship is challenged by a sea of coauthors. We are communal creatures; thus storytelling and storymaking are always psychosocial activities. They contribute mightily to the creation and maintenance of human communities.

Self-narration, therefore, it not simply an individual activity. Storytelling and storyliving is also a community activity. They build bonds, make identification possible, break down barriers, and enable us to recognize the commonality of our experience. In that sense, storytelling is dangerous. Through story we become aware that our lives are often more vulnerable than mighty. Narrating and discovering the common themes in our individual stories enables us to build community around shared vulnerability. When they are honest, stories express and create community.

We Are Our Stories

There are several implications for pastoral ministry from constructing meaning and communicating ourselves through story. The first is that people such as Chris need not be trapped in their stories. It is possible to find new stories for shaping meaning in our lives and by so doing bring forth new worlds of possibility. The task of pastoral care is to help people reframe their lives in the light of God's story for the sake of greater freedom and responsibility.

Second, it is more difficult to be absolute about any interpretation of reality from a narrative perspective. If all reality is socially constructed, constituted through narrative, and organized and maintained through stories, then we need to allow for the possibility of several meanings of the divine story as it has been mediated through the Bible and religious traditions.

Third, linking the human and the divine story becomes a creative but very complex activity that depends on respecting differences. Although we construct stories to organize the disparate elements of our lives and make sense of the world for ourselves, the stories we fashion will enhance or diminish the possibility of community. Stories that conceal more than they reveal are likely to foster isolation rather than intimacy. Therefore, since creating community is one aim of telling stories, honesty, authenticity, and a recognition of the parabolic in life should be part of every story. We will revisit this theme throughout this book.

Finally, it is important for the sake of Christian ministry to acknowledge that fashioning a narrative is a personal responsibility even though we are never the sole author of the story. Each life narrative is an individual creation achieved largely through improvising rather than pursuing a vision already defined or living out someone else's narrative. And yet each narrative is composed of many stories with many coauthors. For persons of faith, God is understood as one of those authors. One key way to increase our awareness of the enduring link between God's narrative and ours is to foster greater reciprocity between worship and pastoral care in the practice of ministry. Stories are mighty and dangerous, but so are rituals, especially those connected with religious expression. Ritual is one place in our regulated lives where we remember the stories of God that have the power to transform us and take us to a new place. As we will demonstrate throughout this book, worship and pastoral care are two complementary aspects of ministry that have a special capacity for respecting and merging the divine and human story.

What is most important about this theme is that we cannot and need not escape the narrative structure of human life. Telling stories is the way to be human. Even as we create our stories, we are at the same time being shaped by the stories we fashion. This narrative approach to life is risky, however. Authentic life as individuals and in community reveals more than it conceals. It keeps the tension between mythic and parabolic stories so that the stories we tell will reveal enough ambiguity and vulnerability to create and sustain human communities. Because we do not tell stories apart from rituals, we turn next to the role of ritualizing in human life.

RITUALIZING OUR STORIES

Rituals not only construct reality and make meaning; they help us fashion the world as a habitable and hospitable place.

○

Grandma Anna Lotti learned the tradition of making Easter pies, or *calzone,* at her home in Southern Italy. This process occupied the family for much of Lent: first stuffing and drying forty pounds of sausage, then chopping hundreds of pounds of ham, hard-boiled eggs, and cheeses. Ingredients were combined, seasoned, and baked on the Saturday before Easter. Consumed as they poured from the ovens, these hearty pies left no doubt in the stomachs of those who ate them that fasting had come to an end.

After Grandma died, her oldest boy, Tony, and her only daughter, Cecilia, continue the tradition. Their children and grandchildren each receive an assignment at the beginning of Lent and spend weeks cutting cheeses, acquiring spices, or boiling eggs. They all gather on the Saturday before Easter in Aunt Cecilia's huge kitchen to assemble and bake 125 pounds of pie: a modest amount according to the standard set by Grandma Anna.

Although recipes are written down, and many have participated in this ritual for over thirty years, the event inspires no small debate. Those doing the blending, up to their elbows in ingredients, argue about the mixture. Each step of cutting, mixing and baking requires exacting quality control. Unevenly chopped cheese, or limp parsley is unceremoniously rejected. When the right mixture is finally agreed upon, the first pies are assembled, sealed with a top layer of dough, and dispatched to the ovens. During the hour it takes for them to bake, a second batch is prepared. And so it continues through the morning and into the early afternoon until all the pies are made.

A few years ago one of Tony's daughters invited a close friend to the annual event. When Tony heard of this he was outraged and pressured his daughter into withdrawing the invitation. The presence of a guest could not be tolerated; it would violate the sacredness of the event. As he later explained to her, making *calzone* is a family affair.

o

TONY'S EFFORT to protect the family's *calzone*-baking tradition from outsiders may seem extreme to us. After all, it is only a ritual. Upon closer examination, however, Tony's concern may not appear that unusual. True, many believe that Americans have lost an appreciation of symbols or concern about ceremony. Joseph Campbell reiterated this view in his celebrated television series *The Power of Myth,* with Bill Moyers. Campbell's analysis, however, is not supported by the evidence. It is not that "ritual is dead" in this country, as Campbell asserted, but rather that, until relatively recently, ritual did not get much respect. It was often ridiculed, particularly by academics, and regarded as a vestige of more primitive and unsophisticated societies. Despite such denigration, however, ritual continued to thrive. The truth is that a whole range of Americans take their rituals just as seriously as peoples of other places and times. We do so because, like stories, rituals are a basic way by which we construct reality and make meaning. Thus for Tony Lotti and many others of that clan, making *calzone* is making family.

That Americans are as ritually fascinated and committed as peoples of other places and times is well illustrated by the masses of visitors who flock to Arlington National Cemetery every year for the changing of the guard—an eerie experience of standing in an open-air amphitheater before the tomb of the unknown soldier with hundreds of strangers in complete silence. The slap of military cleats and the clicking of cameras are the only sounds to be heard. Boisterous teenagers and gregarious tourists of every conceivable background are transformed into respectful witnesses to this highly choreographed ritual.

Such seriousness marks not only our military or public rituals but our domestic ones as well. Children, for example, often insist that bedtime rituals need to be followed with unvarying exactness. Thus the comic strip character Dennis the Menace reminds his parents that water for his bedtime drink must come from the kitchen faucet, not the one in the upstairs bathroom. Preschoolers act out domestic chores or replay their favorite television show with deadly seriousness. Errant playmates are quickly reprimanded when they do not follow the rules.

This ritual earnestness also exists among adults. Newly married couples develop intricate routines for going to bed and getting up, for being naked and making love, for reading the same morning paper or sharing the television remote control. Developing such ritual patterns often requires that each partner modify traditions brought from the respective home of origin. Sometimes, however, these ritual traditions are not easily accommodated. Trimming the Christmas tree, for example, can become an aesthetic battle of exaggerated proportions between those who insist on arranging each strand of tinsel and the "tossers" who heave handfuls of the shiny strips toward a listing pine. More than one family conflict has originated in such holiday rituals. Maybe, like Tony Lotti, we take our rituals more seriously than we admit.

The Ritual Imperative

Ritual activity can be found throughout the whole of nature. Certain birds employ flying patterns or stereotyped posturing to attract a mate, while male stickleback fish engage in a zigzag kind of mating procession to lure a female back to the carefully prepared nest. Reptiles and insects employ ritual patterns for organizing the hunt, caring for their offspring, and avoiding life-threatening conflicts.

Like other species on the planet, human beings take rituals seriously because, in a very real sense, they are essential for our survival. We too employ rituals for establishing courtship, organizing the hunt, caring for offspring, and avoiding life-threatening conflicts. In a nuclear world, for example, the ritualization of peace treaties and the ceremonial celebration of alliances can contribute much toward the avoidance of catastrophic conflict and the maintenance of peace.

This book, however, is not concerned so much with the contribution ritual makes to the biological survival of the human species; rather we are interested in ritual's importance for our psychological, social, and religious survival and advancement. It is our contention that rituals are essential and powerful means for making the world an habitable and hospitable place. They are a basic vehicle for creating and expressing meaning. They are an indispensable medium by which we make our way through life. In this respect, ritual is much like narrative. Both are fundamental and irreplaceable means for creating a socially, psychologically, and religiously habitable world. Furthermore, we believe that narrative and ritual have both a natural and an essential linkage in this meaning-making process.

Before exploring that linkage, however, it is helpful to describe briefly how and why rituals can be considered essential for our survival.

Unlike many other inhabitants of this planet, human beings are not genetically programmed with the sophisticated array of survival instincts present in so many other species. We do not automatically know which foods are good for us and who our natural enemies might be. Thus at birth human beings embark upon a long process of acquiring the skills and information that will help us survive: material that is already genetically encoded in a baby loggerhead turtle and in so many other newborns. Just as important, for human beings, as physical survival is social survival. We are social creatures, and negotiating relationships with other human beings is one of our most compelling, trying, and fulfilling endeavors. As social scientists such as Erik Erikson remind us, we enter into relationships and achieve this socialization in large measure through ritual.

As Erikson explains, each newly born human being could, in principle and within some genetic limits, fit into any number of what he calls "pseudo-species" and their respective habitats. Thus the same human child could theoretically survive in a family of computer-literate urban residents, a family of seal-hunting igloo dwellers, or a family of island-bound coconut harvesters. Because of this potential, Erikson contends that each child must be "coaxed and induced to become 'speciated' during a prolonged childhood by some form of family: [she or] he must be *familiarized by ritualization* with a particular version of human existence" (Erikson, 1977, p. 79). It is by means of this ritualization that each child not only becomes familiar with a particular form of society but identifies with a particular segment of the human race. Through ritualization, therefore, each child comes to share a particular sense of corporate identity and builds a foundation for developing an independent personal identity.

Through the many rituals of childhood and the stories that accompany these rituals, each of us forges an identification with some particular family, tribe, or other segment of humanity. It is also through these minute patterns of daily interplay between children and their social context that each begins the lifelong process of developing a personal awareness of the self as a differentiated individual within a particular social context. From this vantage point, we might begin to understand why the family patriarch, Tony Lotti, could be so vehement about excluding strangers from the *calzone*-making ritual that his family enacts each Saturday before Easter. This is not simply a pleasant or efficient means for producing a favorite food for the Lotti clan; this is an enduring way in which the Lotti family has shaped its identity for more than eight generations: from Italy to a Chicago suburb, from immigrant status to citizenship, from a family of uniform religious practice to one that tolerates the lax and the lapsed. The ritual also serves as an important setting for the various relatives to establish an independent and particular identity within the family.

One comes of age in the Lotti clan, for example, when the family agrees to bake a pie for that individual, and the honoree, in turn, is allowed to carve her or his initials in the crust or even within certain limitations request some variation in the pie mixture itself. Distancing oneself from the family during the year is tolerated, as long as one participates in this and a few other "sacred" family rituals. A family member's decision not to participate may be important for the well-being of that individual, but it is not perceived as contributing to the well-being of the family. Thus nonparticipation clearly jeopardizes one's standing in the family. And who would be surprised to learn that in the Lotti family, reconciliation after an extended absence can be achieved by showing up, unannounced, at Aunt Cecilia's on the Saturday before Easter with five pounds of neatly cubed Tuma cheese in tow.

Ritual has the capacity to create and express meaning, both on the familial and the individual level. Whether we are handing the car keys over to a newly licensed sixteen-year-old, celebrating twenty-five years of marriage, or moving an aging parent to a nursing home, ritual contributes to the shaping of relationships, meaning, and identity both for the family and the various individuals within that family. While the balance between these individual and communal meanings will vary from culture to culture, the rituals of English-speaking North Americans presume respect for both individual and communal meaning. As we will note in forthcoming chapters, our rituals—like our narratives—sometimes overemphasize one of these polarities to the detriment of the other. Thus the individual story or ritual role is sometimes overlooked for the sake of some communal meaning, and other times the larger communal or even ecclesial story is neglected or ignored for the sake of individual or private meaning making. Effective ritual—at least in the context of dominant U.S. culture—ordinarily presumes a healthy balance between the two.

Ritual's capacity for expressing and creating meaning also renders it a potentially dangerous endeavor. Like the stories that frequently accompany them, rituals can bring to light truths we would rather ignore or expose contradictions in our relationships that our we would rather not admit. It is ordinarily our hope, for example, that domestic gatherings at Thanksgiving and Christmas will be enjoyable moments that bring the family closer together. Often, however, these gatherings are uncomfortable situations in which the pretense of civility between certain family members is exposed in the required intimacy of the holiday dinner or gift exchange. Rituals often require such an unusual level of intimacy and physical proximity that, in the process, they unmask explosive feelings or long-simmering grudges. They are, indeed, both mighty and dangerous.

Tony Lotti's gatekeeping over the *calzone*-making gathering, for example, reveals real vulnerabilities within that family. His daughter is forbidden to invite a guest, although, on occasion, Tony has invited the local pastor—his best friend—to be present for the event. Tony explains away this apparent discrepancy by noting that priests have always had a special place within the family. For the daughter, however, this ritual contradiction raises the question of whose family is this anyway and points to a real difficulty that many of the children have with their father's patriarchal ways. Despite whatever intentions or explanations one brings to such a ritual, the expressive and creative capacity of ritual renders it a powerful and dangerous human activity. In future chapters we will examine how the powerful and dangerous facet is further magnified when rituals extend beyond human relationships or stories and mediate the divine.

The ritual imperative, like its narrative counterpart, is deeply embedded within us and cannot be ignored. Such imperative notwithstanding, rituals often evolve in ways that we never expected and expose aspects of relationships never before understood. Thus, in a real sense, it is not so much that we invent rituals as much as they invent us (Driver, 1991). Acknowledging this fact is an important step toward reckoning with the ritual imperative of our existence.

Human Ritual and Narrative: Distinct but Not Separate

Because both narrative and ritual are significant ways through which human beings make meaning, they are generally recognized to be complimentary. We believe that the linkage between the two, however, is much more than simple complementarity. For human beings, narrative and ritual are symbiotic: they have an intimate and mutually beneficial relationship despite their individual identities. To borrow a phrase David Tracy used at an address at the Catholic Theological Union in the fall of 1996, narrative and ritual are distinct but not separate realities. This idea of distinctions without separations, as we will suggest later, is also appropriate for understanding the relationship between worship and pastoral care. It is difficult, if not impossible, to treat narrative adequately without ritual, even though each is distinct.

Ritual and narrative are not symbiotic for all creatures. As we described earlier, many species ritualize; that is, they engage in patterned, often shared behavior for the purpose of survival, order, and even comfort. Thus moose mark trees with secretion from their antlers in hopes of seducing a mate, baboons groom each other, and your pet dog will circle many times counterclockwise before settling to rest in his favorite spot. There is no evidence, however, that in these various forms of ritualizations any insect, reptile, fish, or mammal is capable of narration or storytelling. It is true that such creatures communicate information: that danger is near or that the mating moment is nigh. However, they do not appear capable of consciously reporting and interpreting some past event, present occurrence, or hoped-for future in order to make their world a more habitable and hospitable place.

While it might be possible to define *ritualization* for all species as patterned, shared behavior for the sake of survival, order, or comfort, our assertion about the fundamental linkage between ritual and narration renders this definition incomplete and inadequate for human beings. Ritual for us is certainly ordered, patterned, and shared behavior, but, more than that, it is an imaginative and interpretive act through which we express and create meaning in our lives. Thus human ritual has a narrative substratum to it that is not present in the ritual actions of other creatures. Our ritualizing patterns are set apart by the way in which narrative becomes an essential aspect of and motivation for ritual. In our rituals, like our stories, we narrate our existence, that is to say, we individually and collectively express and create a vision of life. Furthermore, through ritual and narrative we mediate the many identities and relationships that shape that life.

Theologian Harvey Cox once commented that we are creatures who not only work and think but who sing, dance, pray, tell stories, and celebrate. We are *Homines festivi,* Cox continues, and "no other creatures we know of relives the legends of his forefathers, blows out candles on a birthday cake or dresses up and pretends he is something else" (Cox, 1969, p. 11). Cox might have modified his comments if he had known that other creatures do "pretend" to be someone or something else, such as certain types of crabs who carry a half clamshell over their body or attach a roof of living sponges to their back to avoid being mistaken for lunch. Further modifications might have been made to this statement if Cox had done any research into chimpanzees, where he could have learned that such highly intelligent species are easily taught to do various tricks, including blowing out candles on a birthday cake. What would require no modification, however, is Cox's insight that no other creatures on the planet relive the legends of their forbears; no other creatures tell stories. And for no other creatures is ritualization intimately wed to such storytelling. To be a human being is to ritualize the human narrative and, as Erikson has demonstrated, ritual is actually the way we access and enter the human story.

To stress the symbiotic relationship between ritual and narrative is not to suggest that they are identical. As previously noted, they are certainly distinct, but this distinction does not suggest that they are separate. Rather, ritual and narrative are analogous to our own existence, which is mediated by body and mind, flesh and spirit, touch and imagination. Ritual is embodied expression, and narrative springs from the human imagination. In our patterned behavior we explore and express our hopes and dreams. Rituals shape our stories, and our instinct to perceive life as a narrative urges us to rehearse that narrative through our bodies. There is no dualism or conflict here.

Ritualizing the Story

Three-year-old Timothy had just heard his mother read his favorite bedtime story for the third time. After the third and final reading his mother witnessed a strange phenomenon. The toddler took the book and set it on the ground; then he opened the book, gently put one foot and then the other on the open pages, and looked down in wonderment; then he began to cry. The mother was quite puzzled at this little display until her eight-year-old daughter offered this simple interpretation: "Timmy really likes the book." It was then that the mother understood: Timothy wanted to become part of the book.

o

While our acting out might not be as literal as Timothy's, it is true that each of us in our own way yearns to become part of a larger story. We do not want to be left out of the shaping of important family tales, emerging sports legends, or promising business narratives. Similarly, believers do not want to be left out of the story of salvation. Whether we are conscious or not of this need, it is nonetheless true that our search for meaning is a search for an appropriate narrative for life. In this quest, ritualization becomes indispensable, for it provides time, space, symbols, and bodily enactment for disclosing, entering, and interpreting the many stories that comprise our individual and communal narration and give shape and meaning to our lives. We are a people who not only narrate meaning-laden stories with our lips but who also perform them with our bodies. Human beings are both storytellers and story ritualizers.

Sometimes our story ritualizations are quite simple. The home team plays a long-time rival, and we support the local favorite—that is to say, we participate in the story of their success or failure—by showing up at the game. This simple form of ritualization can escalate as the story underlying the ritual becomes more compelling. As the team's winning record improves, we are encouraged to enter even further into the story. Not only are we unwilling to miss a game, but we now arrive at these events clad in special clothing that displays the team's insignia, or we appear draped in the colors of the home-town favorites. When the team makes the playoffs for the first time in living memory, ritual engagement intensifies and expands. Now it is not enough for some to show up in an official team hat or jersey. Enthusiastic fans escalate their ritual involvement by painting their faces and dyeing their hair in the team colors. The ritual enactment is often exported outside the stadium into the neighborhood or city, where public statues are refitted in official team apparel, and city signs flash the team logo. When the team finally clinches the championship, the city streets erupt in spontaneous celebration. Days later there are official processions with the mandatory litanies of praise and homilies of success, culminating in the exposition and reverencing of the championship trophy.

The many stories in which we wish to participate do not always entail such ritual escalation. Often our engagement is more modest. We attend the three or four employee gatherings that the company annually provides, join the fall walk-a-thon for our favorite charity or, with varying levels of festivity, observe the birthdays of family and friends each year. Whether our ritualization consists of selecting, signing, and mailing a Hallmark card for the appropriate occasion or grudgingly attending the company Christmas party, each of these acts expresses the level of our desire or capacity to participate in the particular stories and broader narrative mediated by the ritual. Ritual engagement is an important gauge of the seriousness with which we regard the story. Ironically, however, our ritual enactment not only expresses our alliance with a particular story or broader narrative, it also creates it. This is a necessary result of the symbiotic relationship between ritual and narrative.

Private, Public, and Official Meaning

Although we participate in a ritual with others, maybe even at the same level of intensity or commitment, rituals, like the narratives that undergird them, are interpretive acts that mean different things to different people. Since rituals and narrative are both communal and individual events, one could address only the communal and individual levels of meaning in our storytelling. Margaret Mary Kelleher, however, provides a useful threefold framework for discerning the web of meanings that permeate the familial, social, and religious stories and rituals in which we engage.

Her approach calls for distinguishing between not only public and private meaning but official meaning as well (Kelleher, 1988).

According to Kelleher, *public meaning* is an interpretation that is shared by a significant number of the ritual participants and is also apparent to those closely observing a ritual. There is common agreement amongst the Lotti family, for example, that making the Easter pies celebrates a distinctive and treasured family identity: Italian, Roman Catholic, extended, and close-knit. This is, of course, not the only public meaning or discernible story line mediated by this ritual. Anyone allowed to observe the intensity of this event and the ongoing evaluation and critique that marks the process might also surmise that the ritual further symbolizes the competitive nature of this family, its love of food, and its passion for excellence.

Official meaning is the significance that the originators of the rite bestow on it, or the intent of the rite according to certain experts or official commentaries. One indisputable official meaning in the making of the *calzone* is the liturgical announcement of the end of the Lenten fast. Ironically, this official meaning does not always coincide with the public meaning of the rite. Many in the extended family, for example, are only nominal Catholics and do not observe Lent. Furthermore, even for the practicing Catholics in the group, the official change in fasting laws means that few, if any of them, have fasted from meat for more than a few days. Thus, the official meaning of this rite, as a preparation and consumption of the first meat to break the Lenten fast, may be little mediated by this ritual.

Finally, *private meaning* is the individual, often idiosyncratic significance that particular participants find in a ritual. Such meaning is seldom shared by many others. For example, one of Grandma Lotti's granddaughters, Catherine, who has been participating in the *calzone* ritual for almost thirty years, thought that her relatives were not caring sufficiently for the appearance of the pies before they were baked. To remedy this situation, Catherine took it upon herself a few years ago to crimp all of the pie crusts before they were baked. She thinks this adds an important aesthetic dimension to the pies. Her family, however, thinks it is a waste of time. They allow Catherine to indulge in this time-consuming activity only if her other work is finished, and it does not hold up the frenetic pace that the family maintains through the process.

When Rituals Reveal and Conceal

Like the narratives and stories that provide the substrata of our ritualization, our rituals are sometimes vehicles for revelation; at other times they are a shared form of secret keeping. Rituals that reveal or that achieve what Elaine Ramshaw (1987) calls "ritual honesty," are often those in which the public, private, and official meanings converge. For example, acquiring and consuming pies is just as important as baking pies for the Lotti clan. Every participant in the process, however, does not receive a *calzone*. The pies are distributed to each family with children, to newly married couples, and (via Federal Express) to aging relatives living around the United States who at one time joined in the baking event but now are no longer able to attend. As mentioned earlier, there are even some grandchildren who get their own pie, marked with their initials and shaped by their particular instructions about the mixture of the ingredients. Acquiring your own pie is an announcement at the public, official, and private level that an individual has come of age and has acquired status and respect as a self-sufficient and contributing member of the family.

Sometimes, however, rituals conceal. Often a clear indication of this concealment is dissonance between the official, public, and private meanings. For example, two years ago Aunt Cecilia died. Since her death, her family and Uncle Tony's family have held separate *calzone*-preparation rituals. This division of the family is defended at the level of official meaning, especially by Uncle Tony's children, as a justifiable decision following Aunt Cecilia's death. Not only was the group getting too big, but the quality control exercised by Aunt Cecilia's family was suspect. Cecilia's husband, Milton, made poor sausage: he dried it in the basement for three weeks instead of hanging it in the attic for six weeks.

Few in the family, however, know Uncle Tony's private motivation for the division. It seems that early in their marriage, Milton had physically abused Cecilia. Tony learned of the incident and threatened Milton within an inch of his life it if ever happened again. It did not, and the incident was never mentioned after that. Following the death of Cecilia, however, Tony was able to put significant distance between himself and Milton without causing a public scandal or an irreparable rift in the family. At the level of public meaning, therefore, the emergence of two separate gatherings symbolizes the increased growth and natural separation between these parts of the clan. The official interpretation of Uncle Tony's side of the family also includes a critique of Uncle Milton's sausage. At the private level, however, this separation is a way that Tony can punish Milton for an action for which Tony has never forgiven him.

One of the dangers of our rituals is that their ability to reveal and conceal cannot always be controlled. Although Tony's children agreed to the division on the *calzone*-making process and can spout many explanations on the official level, they also know that this split was not about sausage. More than one of Tony's children asked him privately, "Pop, what's the real story?" Thus the dangers of our rituals: even when they attempt to conceal, they still reveal. Unfortunately, the ambiguity of the revelation is often misleading and erodes the authentic relationship between ritual and story.

Myth and Parable Through Ritual

In Chapter One we presented John Dominic Crossan's polarities of myth and parable as a useful frame for understanding the different ways in which we fashion stories. As we stated earlier, myth, in Crossan's sense, is a type of storytelling that demonstrates the possibility of mediation, whereas parables challenge that mediation. Like our storytelling, our rituals span the spectrum between the mythic and parabolic. Those rituals that lean toward the mythic end of the continuum create or perpetuate the story that everything is going to be all right. Mythic rituals ignore the contradictions in the story line that provides the horizon for these domestic or national enactments. The inaugural ceremonies that mark the transition from one president of the United States to another, for example, follow the same rules of protocol and etiquette whether the retiring chief executive and the president-elect were members of the same political party and great personal friends or ruthless political rivals who recently concluded a bruising election campaign. The inaugural ritual emphasizes the smooth transition of power and recreates the myth that we are one undivided nation moving in harmony toward a common goal. Inaugurations invoke this vision, even if the preceding campaign for the presidency shattered any semblance of national unity and contributed to the polarization of the electorate. Presidential inaugurations, like so many family weddings and funerals, gloss over and suppress the negative emotions simmering below the ritual veneer. That is the task of the mythic.

Parabolic rituals, on the other hand, embrace the discordant and admit the painful. The ceremonies that marked the opening of the National Holocaust Museum in Washington D.C., for example, could not ignore the historical horror of the holocaust. Nor did they suggest that the systematic hatred and political ambition that gave rise to the holocaust have been eradicated today. Rather, the speeches and prayers, exhibits and ceremonies that marked the opening of the monument recalled past atrocities and acknowledged the prejudice of the present. It was an unusual display of the parabolic.

Most of our official or domestic rituals do not sit at one extreme or the other of the myth-parable continuum but are ordinarily a mixture of the two. Even the mythic exaggeration of a presidential inauguration, for example, can make room for the parable. One celebrated illustration of this occurred during the 1952 inauguration of Dwight Eisenhower. Part of inaugural protocol requires that the incumbent president and first lady invite the president-elect and new first lady into the White House for a cup of coffee before driving together to the swearing-in ceremony. The election of 1951 had generated such bitterness between Eisenhower and Truman, however, that the Eisenhowers refused to participate in the ritual. Instead, the president and president-elect met at the cars in the White House driveway and made the journey together to the swearing-in ceremony in icy silence. Ironically, although this was only a small ritual eruption of the parabolic in an otherwise mythic inauguration, it is one of the singular events from the 1952 inauguration that the history books and video documentaries all recall.

As with narrative, the rituals that punctuate our private and communal existence require both myth and parable. As Robert Cococh suggests, "Ritual can have two sorts of consequences for the society in which it takes place: either it can provide a process whereby people become more attached to the basic way of life and values of society, or to the major subgroups within it of which the participants in ritual are a part; or ritual can lead to people making new demands on the way of life in society, and a desire to see change both in action and in the values society pursues" (Cococh, 1974, p. 174).

The rituals around leaving home illustrate the need for domestic rituals that fuse these two consequences in a balance of mediation and contradiction. The rituals that families develop to help adult children leave home and, in turn, encourage the parents to let them go affirm two contradictory realities: the necessity of separation and the hope for continued connection. Sometimes, however, families orchestrate a child's departure so that very little separation occurs. A son or daughter may physically leave home, but the emotional system of the family remains the same. If, on the other hand, the process of separation is perceived to be difficult or impossible, the departing offspring may decide that a continued connection with the family is not possible if true separation is to be achieved. The parable of procession and myth of return sustain this paradoxical journey. We leave home in order to go home again.

Parable keeps moving us toward the edge, so that we can discover and chart a better tomorrow. Myth, on the other hand, establishes equilibrium and generates sufficient hope so that we can move on and explore that edge. While the mythic enables us to envision the possibility of real peace and reconciliation, the parabolic is sufficiently unsettling for us to recognize their absence and prods us toward a more authentic peace and reconciliation.

Embracing the Myth, Conceding the Parable

Since myth, as Crossan defines it, appears to be more comforting than parable, it is not surprising that human beings have a special penchant for the mythic rather than the parabolic in their rituals. Many domestic gatherings, for example, include preparatory instructions about how everyone is going to get along. Certain topics—brother Jim's missing spouse, Uncle Bob's financial instability, or Grandma's drinking—are banned from the conversation. Seating plans are meticulously prepared so that the domestic equivalent of Eisenhower and Truman do not end up sitting next to each other. It sometimes appears that peace is to be maintained at almost any cost.

Admitting our inclination toward the mythic in narrating and ritualizing our lives does not deny that fact that we also have some penchant for the parabolic. Sometimes this instinct reveals itself in playful ways, such as ritual teasing or ceremonial jokes. During their *calzone*-making marathon, for example, the Lotti family always serves two beverages: coffee and a rough red wine. The latter is a well-admitted ritual swipe at Grandpa Lotti, whose alcoholism is legendary. This exercise in familial honesty is maintained through the symbolic presence of a *rough* red wine. Grandpa was not a connoisseur but a drunk; consequently, a high-brow classico or vintage chianti would not do.

The parabolic invades the recently transformed Lotti ritual in another way. While the division in the family has given rise to two separate pie-baking events, neither family is absent from the consciousness of the other. The ritual display of this presence-in-absence occurs when the first pie emerges from the oven. The tradition at this point is that all activity stops so that the family can gather around the dining room table, offer a blessing, cut the pie, and savor this year's output. This is also a time when other family members are called, greetings exchanged, and promises to Federal Express pies to distant relatives on Easter Monday reaffirmed. In the revised rites, the first telephone call is made to the separated family. At the level of official meaning, this telephone call is to determine if the other part of the family has finished baking their first pie. Thus the telephone call could be considered one more ritualized expression of the Lottis' competitive spirit. At the level of public meaning, however, this telephone call is a veiled act of reconciliation and a symbolic lifeline that one family casts to another. To call is to admit the division and, to a limited degree, lament the schism.

We may always be better at ritualizing the myth than enacting the parable. Maybe that is a compliment to the natural optimism of the human spirit or at least the strength of our survival instincts to grasp at life wherever we can find it. If we are to do more than survive, however, we need to discover the parabolic in our life narration, the many stories that comprise the narration, and the rituals that mediate them both. One way to maintain a parabolic perspective is to insist on ritual honesty. Elaine Ramshaw has suggested that "the power of ritual to communicate meaning is vitiated when ritual is known to lie or contradict clear experience" (Ramshaw, 1987, p. 26). A ritual is dishonest when its statements do not match the real-life experience of the participants, even when these are painful. If the mythic constantly prevails, people may lose their tolerance for the parabolic and be tempted to abandon any rituals that elicit painful memories. The formation of a ritual identity that cannot tolerate such pain is vulnerable to the ordinary misfortunes of life. Similarly, rituals that do not acknowledge the painful or parabolic cannot sustain an honest narrative. The stories we tell will be vital and life-enhancing if the rituals that sustain them are authentic and if there is a true convergence of private, public, and official meaning.

As the Lotti family ritual reminds us, the challenge is not to create parables in the midst of our myths. Often they are already there. We do not discover the parables; they discover and transform us. Allowing them to surface, embracing them, and integrating them into our myths is the real challenge. In so doing we learn how to live with contradiction in order to discover the deeper truths of life.

The Criteria of Ritual

In this chapter we have suggested that human rituals have certain things in common with the rituals of other species and can be defined, at least in part, as ordered, patterned, and shared behavior. What is different for human beings, however, is that our ritualization is an imaginative and interpretive act through which we express and create meaning in our lives. Thus human ritualization is not simply about biological survival but also about psychological and social survival and development. In the next chapter, as we turn to an explicit consideration of religious rituals, we will see how rituals are similarly important for our spiritual survival and development. Human ritualization is distinctive because it has a symbiotic relationship with narration. We are constantly constructing our individual and communal identities and worldviews through the interaction of the tales we tell and through our enactments of those tales. The narrative web actualized in our rituals is both individual and communal, coauthored by each individual and his or her environment. Some narrative contributions from our familial, societal, or cultural coauthors are positive and affirming of each individual author and ritualizer. Others exclude significant voices, ignore human uniqueness, or damage our self-esteem. Whether our rituals tend to reveal or conceal, however, they are potentially dangerous, disclosing what we sometimes never intended to say and creating a vision of life or relationships never imagined.

Because of the power of the familial, societal, or cultural stories and rituals that surround us, we need some reliable criteria for evaluating and critiquing the narratives and stories we ritualize. Maintaining a balance between the mythic and the parabolic is one of those criteria. It makes room for the contradictory and painful in our lives, yet it generates a kind of hope and freedom that allow us to retell the story and reconstitute the ritual in life-affirming ways. Another criterion is the convergence of the private, public, and official meanings of rituals. Such convergence generates respect for the individuals and communities who narrate and ritualize meaning and respect for the traditions and cultures that provide the context for such meaning making.

Ritual-narrative honesty presumes a double embrace of the mythic and the parabolic and the convergence of the private, public, and official meanings. For people of faith, religion provides certain paradigms for such ritual-narrative honesty; for Christians, this paradigm is to be found in Jesus Christ. We next turn to a consideration of religious narrative and ritual, particularly those of Jesus, to discover further how these can contribute to authenticity and honesty as we weave together the human and the divine.

3

CONNECTING DIVINE
AND HUMAN NARRATIVES

*The reciprocity of narrative and ritual enhances the possibility
of weaving human and divine stories into a single fabric.*

○

When the great rabbi Israel Bal Shem Tov saw misfortune threatening
the Jews, it was his custom to go into a certain part of the forest to
meditate. There he would light a fire, say a special prayer, and the miracle would be accomplished and the misfortune averted.

Later, when his disciple, the celebrated Maggid of Mezeritch, had
occasion, for the same reason, to intercede with heaven, he would go
to the same place in the forest and say: "Master of the Universe, listen! I do not know how to light the fire, but I am still able to say the
prayer." Again the miracle would be accomplished.

Still later, Moshe-Leib of Sassov, in order to save his people once
more, would go into the forest and say: "I do not know the prayer, but
I know the place and this must be sufficient." It was sufficient and the
miracle was accomplished.

Then it fell to Israel of Rizhin to overcome misfortune. Sitting in his
armchair, his head in his hands, he spoke to God: "I am unable to light
the fire and I do not know the prayer; I cannot even find the place in
the forest. All I can do is tell the story, and this must be sufficient."
And it was [Wiesel, 1966, Introduction].

○

THIS WELL-KNOWN rabbinical story has often been used to illustrate the
power of narrative. In *The Gift of Story*, Clarissa Pinkola Estes reminds
us that telling a story evokes love, strength, and generosity for the sake of

the world (1993). Elie Wiesel concludes his reconstruction of this story by suggesting that God created people because God loves stories.

It is true that this treasured rabbinical tale is about stories, but it is also about rituals. Telling stories is itself one of those rituals. According to the tale, Rabbi Bal Shem Tov's practice of finding the place, lighting the fire, and saying the prayer is forgotten, and only the story remains. Conversely, in other situations the story may be forgotten, and only the ritual that enacts that story remains. Story that has forgotten the ritual and ritual that has forgotten the story may continue to be significant. The conjunction of both narrative and ritual, however, is exceptionally powerful. And if this is true at the human level, how much more so when the divine and human narratives meet in the stories we tell and the rituals we enact.

The potential for a personally and communally transformative encounter is significantly magnified when the divine and human intersect in our storytelling and ritualizing. We are transformed in part because we begin to understand our particular story as part of a larger, transcendent narrative. God has chosen to coauthor a redemptive story for us and with us in human history, and in so doing has invited us to reshape radically the horizon of all other storytelling and ritual making. It is the transformative possibility of this invitation that has galvanized our interest in integrating worship and pastoral care more fully in order to deepen the connection between God's narrative and our own.

Creating Religious Meaning Through Rituals and Stories

In the two previous chapters, we have suggested that storytelling and ritual making are interpretive tools human beings employ to shape their perception of the world and discover their place in that world. We use stories and rituals to communicate with others the meanings we construct. These are distinct but reciprocal facets of the fundamental human need for meaning and community. While storytelling and ritual making can be appreciated separately for their ability to enable human beings to create and express meaning, we have underscored how these two human capacities have a special attraction for each other, and both evoke and require each other. The magnetic attraction between story and ritual reveals two fundamental truths about these human activities: storytelling is itself a particular kind of ritualization, and human rituals have a narrative core.

While ritual making and storytelling are reciprocally linked, they may not always be mutually life-giving. The story of Chris in Chapter One, for example, illustrates that his personal narrative may be intimately connected with his ritual of buying and carrying a lottery ticket, but those two actions are mutually destructive. This ever-recurring ritual is consoling to Chris, but not liberating. Furthermore, it is incapable of engaging the full potential of Chris's narrative, because it only reinforces the mythic side of that narration. Both ritual and story—and the unhappy man who employs them—are trapped in a mythic cul-de-sac. Our storytelling and ritual making can become life-giving when they point beyond themselves to larger and transcendent narratives: when they open themselves to the all-embracing story of God.

Narrative and ritual play a crucial role in the religions we fashion, which in turn provide access to God's narrative. To suggest that we "fashion" a religion is not intended to deny its divine impetus. It recognizes, however, that religion is a human activity in response to divine initiative. The practice of religion is always shaped by the people, societies, and cultures that engage in religious activities. Consequently, to the extent that human beings are intuitive ritualizers and storytellers, so is the practice of religion filled with and shaped by sacred—some might even say sacramental—narrations and rituals.

Most of the religions of the world commonly report that these sacred narratives and rituals are divinely ordained. So, for example, Jews, Christians, and Muslims each believe that their sacred writings are the result of direct and divine inspiration. These sacred and repeatable narrations, in turn, are foundational for the stories of redemption and salvation that religious practitioners continue to repeat and reinterpret. Furthermore, the scriptures of these three great monotheistic religions describe rituals that are divinely sanctioned, mandated, and, in some cases, even enacted. The Hebrew scriptures, for example, enjoin believers to recite certain prayers each day (Deuteronomy 6:4–9), the Christian Gospels describe the ritual meals of Jesus, which became determinative for Christian worship (Matthew 26:26–29), and the Koran notes the necessity of each adult to make the pilgrimage to Mecca at least once (Surah 3:97). Paradoxically, recalling such divinely endorsed narratives and rituals does not mean that the God revealed and sought through these religions is necessarily confined to or compelled by particular narratives or rituals—for God will not be so confined.

On the other hand, people who wish to encounter the divine are reliant upon such narratives and rituals, although they are not confined by them. Unmeditated experiences with God or direct knowledge about divine mysteries are rare among humankind. Most of us are not mystics, and whatever direct encounters we may have with God often defy expression or interpretation. Rather, our engagement with the holy—similar to our engagement with virtually every other aspect of life—is mediated through word and gesture, body and song, architecture, poetry, and movement.

Narrative and ritual are ancient and privileged human activities that serve well the mediation of divine presence and are regularly reported to be graced with divine sanction. On occasion, they are even noted to be the source of divine pleasure. Thus, Elie Wiesel's musings about a God who loves stories is actually less a comment about God as it is a comment about those who seek God and the indispensable need for narrative and ritual in that search.

While many religious practices that embody the search for God—such as the recitation of the *shema* or a novena to a favorite saint—can be accomplished alone, religions with officially sanctioned worship ordinarily define such worship in communal terms. Thus Judaism requires a quorum of ten adult males (a minyan) for worship; Christian Eucharist is by definition an ecclesial act of the assembly; and the congregational nature of the five required daily prayers of Muslims is symbolized in the public call to prayer from the minaret of the mosque by the muezzin. The implicit presumption of such public rituals is that they not only provide the opportunity to connect our personal stories with the divine narrative, but they do so through communal mediation. Entering into prayer with a community necessitates engagement with the community's faith narrative, which, by definition, is more comprehensive than the faith stories of any individual. The model suggested here, which aims to facilitate easier commerce between the divine and human narratives, requires reckoning both with the public and private dimensions of story and ritual in religious practice and with what Kelleher (1988) identifies as the "official" aspects.

Linking Human and Divine Narratives

God, angered by the inaccurate reporting and editorial guesses about divine nature and heavenly history, hired a human scribe and began to dictate the divine story. For forty days and forty nights God spoke, and for forty days and forty nights the scribe scribed. The last word having been spoken, the exhausted Deity sat down, for God had paced throughout the entire dictation. As the scribe finished recording the last word a quizzical look came over the human's face—a look that quickly changed from questioning to anger. Finally, the human scribe stood up and, with all the outrage of someone who has been plagiarized, shouted "But this is my story!"

○

In an exaggerated way, this story could simply be another manifestation of human self-centeredness or the proprietary instincts that mark us as human beings. We are inclined to translate the divine narrative into very personal categories. In another way, the story illustrates how ordinary people yearn for a union between their story and God's story. Seldom is this longing expressed as crassly as in the words of our fictional scribe, and it is often more implied than admitted. Nonetheless, whether implicitly presumed or explicitly acknowledged, a large majority of people who belong to organized religions and those who seek religious meaning in their lives through other means hope that—if not in this world, at least in the next—they will become part of God's story.

Besides finding our place in the divine narrative, we also want to discover God's presence in the human saga. Whenever we ask, Where is God? we hope to hear some reassurance that God is very near, that God is present in our story. One of the reasons that the stories of the Bible continue to be treasured is because of their timeless ability to narrate God's presence in the most human of events. The scriptures are full of stories about passion and births, political intrigue and sibling rivalry, military heroics and family tensions. We hear these stories as sacred validations or our own potential for encountering God in the very ordinary events of our lives.

When we are willing to admit the possibility of God's presence in ordinary human events, we will be more likely to fashion our human narratives—composed of so many such events—in the light of that presence. Ordinary life is transformed when we recognize that our stories bear the presence of God. When we can acknowledge the possibility of God's presence in our daily living, it is possible for us to weave the divine narrative into the stories we fashion. Such weaving is ultimately transformative and life-giving.

For Christians, the dual impulse of desiring to become part of God's story and simultaneously hoping that God will be present to our own narrative finds convergence in Jesus Christ—the essential mediation of the human and divine narrative. We see God clearly in the person of Jesus. The divine narrative is uniquely and comprehensively summarized in his living, dying, and rising. Jesus incarnates the hope of everyone who believes that it is possible for the human to find complete union with the divine narrative. At the same time, Jesus symbolizes our other hope—that God will be part of the human story line. The Gospels teach not only that Jesus was attentive to the one he called *Abba* but that the Holy One was present in Jesus. In his birth, infancy, hidden adolescence, and the whole public ministry of Jesus, the Spirit of God accompanied and surrounded him. This was never more apparent than in his dying and rising. The divine-human relationship thus finds its ultimate conjunction in the Jesus story, where God meets us in the midst of our humanity and where a fully human narrative is enfleshed at the center of the Godhead.

The future of faith communities depends on their capacity to foster an environment in which human and divine narratives regularly intersect.

More specifically, the future of Christian communities requires that they enable the weaving together of the divine and human in the image of Jesus Christ. Conjoining these narratives is a way of deepening both our relationship with God and our connections with one another. That is why in this book we characterize the divine-human encounter as a meeting of stories. Human beings, we have said in a variety of ways, co-create both themselves and their worlds by the stories they tell. This is also true of the divine stories we tell. As John McDargh has observed, "Our stories of God reflect, at their deepest levels, our most profound experiences of being met or overlooked, of being taken up and decoded or left unread" (McDargh, 1993, p. 239). If it is true that recognition is a dominant force driving human beings, then there is some urgency to acknowledge human stories in the divine narrative or the divine narrative in human stories.

The integration between the divine and human narratives is necessary so that we will have a language to speak about our human struggles that will, at the same time, open us to possibilities beyond the present struggle. The divine narrative tells of God's longing for relationship with ordinary folk. The human narrative records our desires for God and recounts our perennial difficulties in achieving union with the divine. Weaving together human and divine narratives has, as its ultimate goal, the transformation of individual and communal life. At one level, this transformation manifests itself in human action and communal strategies that seek justice and reconciliation. But this focus on transformation also eventuates in greater openness and response to the ongoing activity of God in human life. The question, What must I do? is, therefore, paralleled by the question, What is God doing? In order to maintain an openness to God's activity, we need regularly to interpret the human story in light of the divine narrative.

Charles Gerkin insisted in *Widening the Horizons* (1986) that pastoral practice needs to recover Christian modes of interpretation. His proposal was that we use the narrative framework to connect our stories with the Christian story. We agree, but there is a more fundamental concern. For us, interpretation is at the service of integration. While we hope that ministers and the communities they serve develop critical skills for interpreting how their narrative intersects with the divine, we are more concerned that they intersect at all. To that end, this book is about integrating worship and pastoral care more fully so as to enhance easy commerce between the divine and human narratives. If, however, worship is focused on the divine narrative without attending to human stories, and if pastoral care is immersed in the human struggle without asking what God is doing, then these disconnected religious practices are likely to diminish rather than enhance the divine-human encounter. The rest of this chapter is an examination of how the integration of worship and pastoral care can enhance the linkage between the human and the divine.

Weaving Together the Divine-Human Narratives in Worship

The public worship of organized religions is regarded as a particularly privileged place in which the divine-human relationship is rehearsed and realized. Here, often with all the authority a tradition can muster, believers are promised the possibility of encountering God, of hearing a divine word, experiencing the divine touch, and in some traditions even receiving the divine presence. The potential power and significance of such public rituals is often reflected in the exacting rubrics and ministerial restrictions that are imposed on them. The divine presence is possible in such settings, some will insist, only if rubrics are followed and ministerial restrictions heeded.

Despite all of its potential for facilitating the encounter between the human and divine and thereby enabling believers to engage with God in the active coauthorship of their life stories, public worship often fails. Rather than the awesome or mystical arena in which the human and the divine meet, it is frequently experienced as boring and irrelevant. While there are many complex factors that contribute to this situation, one reason for this failure is a paradox: public worship, especially Christian worship, does not adequately mediate divine presence because it is inattentive to the human story. As a result of this separation, the practice of worship does not facilitate the kind of integration of human and divine narratives that is necessary in order for us to discern what God is doing in our lives and how we need to respond.

Worship in general, and Christian worship in particular, are subgenres of the larger category of human ritual introduced in the previous chapter. Like other human rituals, worship is neither just an exercise in divine data distribution nor a rehearsal of celestial rules. Rather, public worship is a significant, even indispensable way for believers to exercise and acquire faith. It is a way in which believers discover how God is or can be a part of their lives. Worship is also an important medium for discovering the significance that belief in God has for the way one shapes personal relationships or conducts worldly affairs. Worship is a critical exercise in meaning making for believers. An ancient Christian maxim sums it up well: *lex orandi, lex credendi* (roughly, "worship is foundational for belief").

Public worship is sometimes treated as if it were of an entirely different nature than other forms of human ritualization. While a distinctive form of ritualizing, it is not altogether different. A faith-filled public ritualization cannot achieve its purposes apart from the means that humans employ in other ritualized aspects of their lives. Therefore, public worship cannot enable the human-divine encounter without adequate attention to narrative. In particular, sacred rituals must respect and balance human stories—both individual and communal—with the divine narrative without manipulation or deceit.

○

One Monday afternoon a minister was working with the pastoral staff in planning next Sunday's worship. It was agreed that during the sermon there would be an appeal for money to help pay off the church's mortgage. The pastor then said to the organist, "When I finish my sermon, I will ask for all those in the congregation who wish to contribute $500 or more toward the church's mortgage to please stand up. In the meantime, you should provide appropriate music." "What do you mean, 'appropriate music'?" asked the organist. The pastor replied, "Play the 'Star Spangled Banner.'"

○

This pastor is determined to get people to stand up, no matter what it takes. Although most manipulation in religious worship is less callous or bold than that recounted in this story, still it occurs with some regularity. The aim is to effect a particular response or induce a particular course of action through worship. Public worship is in danger of succumbing to deceit whenever it promotes the divine narrative to the detriment or denigration of the individual and collective stories of the gathered community. The implication of this one-sided storytelling is that human narration is unimportant, except as it reiterates or interprets the divine narrative. It is equally problematic, however, if human stories are promoted and emphasized at the expense of telling the stories of God.

It is because of God's graciousness that human beings are called, through community, to coauthor their stories in the light of the divine narrative. Coauthorship, as we mean it here, recognizes God's active participation in shaping the stories we fashion to give meaning to our lives. Coauthorship with God is reflected in the human narrative when the families we establish are informed by hospitality and compassion; when our work in the world seeks to eradicate injustice and engender respect for the other; or when we determine to live a reflective life in which our personal spirituality mirrors the presence of God. However it is imagined or lived out, such enacted coauthorship asserts that through divine invitation, people are bade to join with each other, converging their narrative streams with the Holy One, so that through this human-divine coauthorship a special tale may be woven. The narrative substructure of our worship needs to embrace the human and the divine, the individual and the communal narration to foster this coauthorship.

If, as we contend, public worship is a privileged ritual moment for constructing belief-centered meaning, then the communities who gather for worship must give evidence that divine coauthorship is rehearsed and confirmed in their life together. Local congregations construct their own stories in order to make sense of the Gospel in their particular context. They are, to paraphrase our colleague Robert Schreiter, constructing local stories that will eventuate in local theologies (Schreiter, 1985). Some of those narratives will correspond closely to the official teachings of a church or faith tradition; some will not. In either event, the public narrative of a local congregation shapes the way story and ritual intersect in the lives of those who together pray toward a new story.

One of the critical issues facing congregations of faith is that the practices of a community do not always correspond with what they may teach or proclaim or promote themselves to be. For example, a faith community may understand itself as an open and inclusive place where people are welcomed without conditions. Its practice, however, does not measure up to its ideal. As a result, lonely or alienated individuals who need to find an alternative to their own experience of marginalization find instead that their isolation is intensified in the rituals and stories of a worshiping community. We will return to this theme when we examine the individual-communal dialectic in worship and pastoral care at moments of birth, marriage, and death.

Weaving Together Divine and Human Narratives in Pastoral Practice

The ministry of pastoral care grows out of a profound respect for the particularity of the stories of individuals and communities. From its inception in the early church, a central aim of pastoral care has been to attend to the human story in all its complexity. For many centuries, careful listening in the care of souls became a prelude to the application of the Gospel through admonition, advice, or judgment. The modern practice of pastoral care, in an effort to avoid old moralistic patterns of ministry, attends to the emotional and social world of a person and often relies heavily on psychological language for reinterpreting a person's narrative.

Listening carefully and responding accurately to the story of another is a true ministry. To be understood and accepted by another person is an treasured dimension of human living. It is also the first movement of any kind of care. We listen carefully in order to get another's story straight. We listen attentively to others so that our response connects with their understanding of their story. Too often, even in conversations with people we know and love, because we do not take the time to listen carefully, we are quick to ignore or eager to advise. Empathy is in short supply. It takes time and careful listening to get another's story straight and to communicate that understanding accurately and compassionately. The determination to create safe environments to tell and retell our most intimate stories is the special gift of relationships in which care is the focus.

○

Jerry was a take-charge kind of guy. It's one of the many things that Catherine loved about him from the beginning. Throughout their twenty-three years of marriage Jerry had been Catherine's primary support and the head coach and camp director for their five adoring children. Everyone was devastated when Jerry died suddenly of a heart attack in early May. Catherine and the children were determined to plan the funeral the way he had orchestrated their lives. It was thoughtful, touching, and exceedingly well planned. In the weeks that followed, the family's grieving did not get in the way of the many church and community commitments that Jerry had championed. While visiting Catherine in early November, Pastor Philips suggested that some other family might take responsibility for distributing the fifteen Thanksgiving baskets that Jerry and the youth group at church had prepared every year. Catherine protested, reminding the pastor how very strongly Jerry felt about the Thanksgiving charity. The Pastor then asked, "And Catherine, what are *you* feeling these days without Jerry here?" It did not take long before Catherine's brave face dissolved in tears. "Oh Pastor," she sobbed, "I'm scared, I'm so scared."

○

Good pastoral care attends to the personal and the particular. It does not take its cues from appearances but pays attention to the stories beneath the surface. Persistence in asking Catherine how she was doing after the sudden and tragic death of her husband, despite her brave veneer, was a necessary and appropriate act of pastoral care. While her behavior might have been promoted by family expectations that she be strong or congregational expectations about Jerry's overactivity, the pastor was rightly intent on helping Catherine explore her own story after her husband's death. Moments of pastoral care usually have a very personal focus and are often precipitated by some event or crisis that has touched people in a significant way.

This attentiveness to each individual's story is the strength of pastoral care as practiced in recent decades; it is also its vulnerability. While communal concerns or larger social issues are not necessarily absent from the contemporary practice of pastoral care, they are not in the foreground. The focus has been on the individual and the particular. As a result, the interplay between the individual and the communal or between the personal and the social is often overlooked. When connecting the individual's story with the larger human story or with the stories of faith traditions, the liberating gift of the divine narrative is overlooked also. Whereas conventional practices of public worship tend to focus almost exclusively on the story of God at the expense of human stories, the contemporary impetus in pastoral care has been to attend so carefully to human experience that the divine narrative is often muted or ignored.

A truly Christian approach to caring for others requires an appropriate theology of the church. If our approach to pastoral care is informed only by a personal view of faith without the complementarity of a communal perspective, we are without a credible framework for attending to the nuances of the divine-human relationship, which Christianity teaches is mediated by faith communities. When the divine story is connected to my story, it may be done so outside of any ecclesial context and framed only in personal terms. This limited focus ignores the wider faith story that Christianity presumes to be essential for individual faith. In the Judeo-Christian tradition the stories of faith and stories of salvation are entrusted to the community, exist for the community, and require interpretation by the community. Attempting it any other way almost ensures the distortion and diminishing of these stories of faith.

One reason regularly given for the absence of the communal and, by extension, religious framework in pastoral care is the power of the psychological paradigm, at least in the United States, to name and interpret human experience. A related dynamic in the cleavage between the human and divine story has been the separation of pastoral care from worship and from the ritual life of believers. For many centuries, a principle mode of care was found in the rituals of the Church. As the therapeutic relationship has become the dominant model for such care, however, pastoral care has become more individual than communal and increasingly disconnected from the worship of faith communities.

Several recent changes make it both possible and necessary for us to rethink the task of pastoral care and its relationship to worship. First, our awareness of the moral bankruptcy of individualism has prompted renewed attention to the communal aspects of life and care. When we understand the work of pastoral care as the church's response to the personal, relational, and spiritual needs of persons, then the community unquestionably emerges as both the context and the agent of this care. Communities of faith, when they work well, are also recipients of care from their leaders.

Second, one of the contributions of contemporary hermeneutics to the practice of pastoral care is the recognition that therapeutic neutrality is seldom, if ever, possible. When we listen, we interpret, whether we want to or not. Every response to another's story is interpretation. The contemporary demand for ministers to admit the assumptive worlds we employ to listen to another's story has, in turn, challenged us to discover to what extent the divine narration has a central role in our listening framework. We are all interpreters, that is sure. In the work of pastoral care, we have drawn heavily from psychological theories to make sense of modern human struggle. What is less clear, however, is the extent to which the Christian story is our normative, or at least primary framework for interpretation in pastoral situations. Gerkin has suggested, and we concur, that ordinary human affairs of life gain new coherence because they are "seen as enacting a Christian story" (Gerkin, 1986, p. 47).

Third, narrative is a central ingredient for understanding situations in pastoral care. If we are defined by narrative, then caring for people means listening for stories, not for historical facts or psychological symptoms. People are invited to tell a story in order to find a story or reformulate a more fulfilling life narrative. In our ministry with the dying, as we will suggest later on, it is more beneficial to think in stories than to identify stages. When we listen carefully to people, we will discover that they often live with competing stories but no narrative, no overarching way of weaving their stories together and little understanding of the ordinary, daily connection between the human and divine narratives. The promise of practical theology, as we intend it here, is that telling a story can lead to the discovery of a deeper and more satisfying narrative (Winquist, 1980).

Fourth, and finally, the development of methods for theological reflection have provided a more dynamic means for understanding our stories in the light of God's story. The dialogue between modern experience and the faith tradition is mutually critical. We do not listen to another in order to suggest some remedy from the storehouse of religious wisdom. Rather, the conversation between my stories and the stories of a faith tradition merge into a new narrative that is liberating and empowering.

In the light of these influences, we understand that the primary aim of pastoral care is to assist people in weaving the stories of their lives and God's stories as mediated through the community into a transformative narrative that will confirm their sense of belonging, strengthen them to live responsibly as disciples in the world, and liberate them from confinement. This narrative focus for pastoral care does not eliminate the necessity of empathy. The first task of care is always to accept the givenness of experience. We must know our stories in order to reframe them. Moreover, stories of the mighty acts of God are meaningless unless they connect with what we understand to be real and important about our life. But we live our stories best when we understand them in relation to the larger human story, the stories of our faith traditions, and the story of God. The second task in pastoral care, therefore, moves beyond honoring the present narrative by inviting people to fashion their story in new ways. This is not something they can or must do alone for, as we have noted before, all human stories are coauthored. The task of pastoral care is to help people expand their own narrative in ways that recognize and accept God as an active agent in our personal narrative.

Enhancing the Divine-Human Narrative Through Ritual and Story

The practice of pastoral care in the past has focused more on individual human stories than on the larger stories of God or the faith community. At the same time, and in a related way, it has emphasized the narrative side of the narrative-ritual axis, sometimes to the exclusion of ritualization. While it is true that, as noted in Chapter Two, storytelling is itself a kind of ritualization, we also recognize that storytelling without further ritualization is incomplete. Ritualization is indispensable for entering the story, exercising coauthorship, and realizing a narrative's full potential. Thus, we contend that ritual and narrative are symbiotically related.

From the viewpoint of pastoral care, therefore, it is not only critical to narrate the story web of the human and divine, the individual and communal, but it is also helpful, and in some cases essential, that these stories are ritualized. In the symbolic enactment of such stories, their full power is realized, deep truths are encountered, and sometimes demons are exorcised. The power of ritual is recognized even among secular helping professions as a means to help people function more effectively by establishing dependable patterns of symbolic action.

Ritual has therapeutic value not only because it attributes symbolic meaning to experience. The repetition of ritual also helps create a sense of continuity in our lives by linking the past to the present and the present to the future. In the midst of life's discontinuities, rituals become a dependable source of security and comfort. Rituals provide a way for families to define boundaries and confirm identity. They give tangible shape to our hopes and dreams. Although the power of ritual does not necessarily depend on shared beliefs, rituals do provide a effective mechanism for shaping what people believe by encouraging a particular construction of reality.

Apart from the personally therapeutic value of ritualization, worship and pastoral care bind an individual's story to the story of the larger faith community through a shared ritual vernacular. This ability to express the divine and human story in public ritual is one of the strengths of faith communities. Public ritual is the vernacular most Christian faith communities employ to express and create their stories of faith. Ordinarily, those stories focus on communal narrative and do not always make appropriate space for individual stories of faith. Official worship ritualizes the narrative web from the viewpoint of the larger ecclesial community and divine narration rather than from the perspective of individual stories. Although sermon illustrations may relay personal vignettes, and faith sharing may be a significant dimension of worship for a few religious communities, public worship in most Christian denominations allows little room for personal storytelling or faith sharing.

Employing ritualization in a pastoral care context achieves an important linkage with the larger community. It symbolically reinforces the belief that the ministry of pastoral care is not simply concerned with the isolated health of the individual but also with the individual's integration into the faith community as a component of true health. Employing ritual elements that are often restricted to communal faith gatherings in the personalized context of pastoral care can provide the individual believer with an important entrance back into the community story. Conversely, making a place for ritualization and the communal story in the practice of pastoral care could be the beginning, in some communities, of making a place for the individual stories and rituals of faith in the public arena of corporate worship.

o

Jack was dying of AIDS. He had been asymptomatic for years, but in the fall he caught the flu, and his decline after that was rapid. In the last weeks of his life, he was resigned to dying and even referred to himself as "lucky," since he was at home, surrounded by family and friends. Despite this growing sense of resignation, even calm, Jack seemed distracted and preoccupied, as if he had unfinished business. Although Jack had not belonged to a church since leaving home, he was glad for the visits of his parents' pastor, Bonnie Carter. From the beginning, he felt he could say anything he wanted in her presence. He vented, mourned, cursed, and cried with her. And with her help, though he still didn't consider himself much of a Christian, he rediscovered his belief in God and learned again to pray. He heard biblical stories that helped him rehearse his life in a more positive way than he had before.

What worried him the most, however, was his family and friends. He would not be around to console them after his death. Since he was the source of their grief, he thought that he should also be the source of some comfort for them. He planned his funeral with Pastor Carter's help. They talked about what she might say when she delivered the sermon. And yet, it didn't seem like it was enough.

It was Pastor Carter who suggested that Jack might want to write his family a letter—a letter that could be read at the funeral, before the body was taken from the church—a final word of comfort and love from him. Jack liked that idea and took it one step further. He decided that he wanted to write four letters: one to his parents, one to his older sister, and one to his kid brother. He wanted to write down his feelings for each of them in a form that would continue after he had died but that they would read while he was still alive. Then he would write a fourth letter—one they would not know about—to be read at the funeral.

On the day that Jack died, while his family and friends kept vigil at his bedside, he heard his parents, sister, and brother read their letters from him. Each reading took a while, as they were frequently interrupted by tears. But the readings were not difficult for Jack, and they actually seemed to calm him. He died quietly, forty-five minutes after having heard the last of his letters read to his kid brother. And then, three days later, in the closing moments of the funeral, before the body was taken from the church, Pastor Carter announced that before the community bid its final farewell to Jack, Jack had a final word for them.

The letter was brief—only three short paragraphs—and they were words of gratitude. In his closing lines he wrote, "I am especially grateful that you helped me die well; that in the final days and weeks together you didn't try to hold on to me, or ever make me feel guilty for having AIDS. You loved me enough to let me go when God called. Know that in my gratitude I'll be waiting for you on the other side, so that when it is your time, you too will not die alone—Love, Jack."

○

Jack's letter precipitated a memorable moment in the worship life of that congregation and in the individual lives of those present. They had heard letters read aloud before from biblical writers such as Paul, Peter, James, and John. The letter from Jack, however, was a moment everyone remembered. His personal narration met the community of faith in its struggle to hear God at a time of profound grief. Conversely, the public rituals and shared faith of the worshiping community had touched the imagination and gratitude of a dying man. In Jack's dying and the community's grieving, personal and communal narrative and ritualization merged.

Myth and Parable, Worship and Pastoral Care

Like the other stories or rituals of our lives, the private ritualizations of pastoral care or communal worship of organized religions are susceptible to the tensions of myth and parable. In Chapter Two we suggested that both the mythic and parabolic are important in the narrations and rituals that punctuate our lives, although the parabolic is more difficult to endure. Since narrative and ritual pervade all aspects of our lives—be they so-called secular or explicitly religious—it might be logical to conclude that in all of life's situations the mythic and the parabolic are again of equal importance. Before coming to that conclusion, however, we must take into account the divine coauthor of our faith stories and rituals and discover to what extent God, who is the ultimate source and object of such stories and rituals, favors myth or parable. Since this kind of consideration is unavoidably faith-specific, for us this is a question about Christianity.

On the one hand, it needs to be acknowledged that for Christians, Jesus Christ is the ultimate articulation of the mythic: the incarnation of mediation and reconciliation. In Jesus the Christ, humanity and divinity are reconciled. According to the prologue of the Gospel of John, the Incarnate One is the preexistent Word who lives forever and yet, as reported by secular historians of the day, lived and died in a particular moment in human history. That is why Christians, we believe, should be well practiced at living with paradox. At the center of the Christian story is the conviction that the Eternal Word became a temporal yet eternal being.

Paradoxically, the divine mediation we name Jesus the Christ achieves mythic reconciliation in parabolic mode. It is true that Jesus proclaims eternal life is possible, forgiveness of sins is possible, peace with enemies is possible, and union with God is possible. None of this is can be achieved, however, through easy rituals or special knowledge. Rather, each of these is accomplished by abandoning the comfortable reconciliation we have constructed for ourselves. Eternal life is achieved only through dying. The rich are made poor. The lowly are lifted up. Forgiveness of sins is conceivable only by recognizing that our story is flawed and embracing our own sinfulness. Peace with enemies is accessible only by embracing those we would rather hate. And union with God is possible, but only if we allow God to be God, calling us to a kind of union we never expected, with a deity we never imagined. While our preference might be the domestication of God, the embrace of the mythic, and the assertion of divine reconciliation at any cost, such an instinct must be challenged by the assertion of the parabolic in order to keep the paradox intact.

This paradoxical balance between myth and parable must prevail in our narrations and rituals of faith and in our worship and pastoral care. Worship is often imagined as a pleasant, almost cultural experience, in which dappled sunlight plays against stained glass windows in a high ceiling building with a Gothic spire, where a smiling, grandfatherly figure leads a well-mannered congregation in mellifluous tones through agreeable prayers and congenial hymns. It is a very pleasant image of worship. We like worship to be a time of centering quiet and restorative peacefulness. But it must be much more. Authentic Christian worship is a disturbing event. In worship God is present among us, challenging us to recognize sin, embrace our enemies, transform our lives, and proclaim the kingdom in the world. It is a dangerous, precarious, explosive undertaking. Thus Anne Dillard writes,

> The higher Christian churches . . . come at God with an unwarranted air of professionalism, with authority and pomp, as though they knew what they were doing, as though people in themselves were an appropriate set of creatures to have dealings with God. I often think of the set pieces of liturgy as certain words which people have successfully addressed to God without their getting killed. In the high churches they saunter through the liturgy like Mohawks along a strand of scaffolding who have long since forgotten their danger. If God were to blast such a service to bits the congregation would be, I believe, genuinely shocked [Dillard, 1977, p. 59].

Much of what we have presented thus far revolves around the interplay of a number of discrete pairs of ideas or practices: story/ritual, myth/parable, human/divine, individual/communal, private/public, worship/pastoral care. While each of these elements and each of these juxtaposed pairs are worthy of consideration in and of themselves, what is more important is an awareness and willingness to hold as valuable the paradox of faithful living that these juxtaposed pairs highlight. Often we diminish the dynamic potential of the paradox by opting for one element over another or by compartmentalization.

For example, when the stories we tell are influenced by our need for myth rather than the gospel imperative for parable, we will find ourselves incapable of a language for capturing the whole story, both human and divine.

---

o

Letty and Frank Norbridge lost their baby-sitter and two of their four children in a fire. Nine days after the fire Letty wrote in her journal, "Mrs. Nemerov stopped by today. . . . She is so eager to make us stop hurting. Today she quoted Paul: 'All things work together for good for them that love God.' It astounds me that she can't see that right now that's precisely what I cannot bear to hear. Timmy dead, Donita dead, and Beth Elton dead; and *all things work together for good?* My soul cries out that they do not, they do not, they do not" [Mitchell and Anderson, 1983, p. 123].

---

o

As these searing words from Letty's journal remind us, an authentic faith journey in all its paradoxical pain and wonder does not allow for facile resolution. It requires something more.

Connecting the Human and the Divine

One important aim of ministry is to enable individuals and communities to fashion narratives that weave together divine and human stories into a single fabric. In the work of pastoral care and in our theoretical reflection about that work in recent years, we have listened more attentively to the human story than to the divine narrative. In worship, however, the opposite has usually been true. The human story has been eclipsed by God's story. The effectiveness of pastoral leadership necessitates attentiveness to both realities, particularly at a time when there is growing hunger for spiritual meaning. For that reason alone, pastoral care needs the perspective of worship to avoid becoming stuck in a horizontal view of experience without transcendence. Worship, on the other hand, needs the pastoral care perspective to keep its praise and intercession grounded in the lives of real people.

The task of pastoral care is to create a safe environment for telling and exploring our most intimate stories with trustworthy people who will hear those stories. The natural inclination to honor the human side of narration is the gift of pastoral care for worship. Ritual honesty occurs, as we have noted, when worship is responsive to the human story and struggle. Ritual loses its power when it fails to address all of the human story, including its shadow side. Both worship and pastoral care need to be rescued from symbolic sterility by addressing the full mythic and parabolic range of human and divine narrative at the private and public level in order to create and maintain vital believers and communities of believers.

There are three moments in the human life cycle in which the intersection between ritual and narrative presses regularly for honesty: birth, marriage, and death. These moments, about beginnings, commitments, and endings are the focus of the next section. Each of these moments is surrounded by stories and rituals that help interpret the meaning of the event and promote continuity in the midst of change. Further, each of these occurs in the midst of a process that precedes and follows it.

We examine the reciprocity of ritual and narrative around these significant moments in order to increase our awareness of the power of narrative, to deepen our appreciation of ritual moments and ritual process, and to assist those who minister through liturgy and care to people who are living through these critical transitions. These processes and events have both individual and familial meaning and are designed to support the organism as a whole while allowing for individual development. They identify and recognize the unique gifts of each individual and incorporate individuals within communities of faith. And they will help people claim their uniqueness as a gift from God for service in the world.

PART TWO

MILESTONES IN LIFE MARKED BY STORIES AND RITUALS

4

WELCOMING THE CHILD

Birth rituals, such as baptism, facilitate hospitality and locate the beginning of each individual's life within a web of communal stories.

○

EACH CHILD IS BORN into a web of stories, myths, and legends. Some stories carry specific expectations of behavior, achievement, or occupational destiny. For others, the expectations are more implicit. Nonetheless, each individual narrative begins in the context of a larger family story. Even when individuals are not fully aware of this larger tale, it has power to influence them, shaping the context into which they are born.

○

As the story was told, everyone was present for my birth: but the grandfathers, J. P. and Karl, were somehow the primary actors. They waited in the living room of the house, the glassblower and the carpenter, helpless craftsmen. They shivered, I am told, from the unusual cold of that late spring, until one proposed to the other that they build a fire.

It was the day for the baby to be born. Due in mid-May, the baby had delayed until now. But it was to be so, they said. The day before, Arlene had taken a big dose of castor oil to start the labor process. Now, in the small hours of the morning, she was at work. Today must be the day. It was Martha's fifty-fifth birthday and her son Edwin's thirty-third birthday; so, of course, the baby would be born on his grandmother's and father's birthday. The baby owed it to them. He— for it would be a boy; no girls' names had even been considered— would surely arrive now. And he did—Patrick Karl Melloy. His world—all nine adults—were gathered to tell him who he was to be, to predict, to adore, to demand, to celebrate, to love, and mostly to define. Does it matter that the day was cold, and was already two birthdays? Oh, yes; oh, yes; it matters.

—PATRICK KARL MELLOY

○

Patrick's birth tale is not an account of notable circumstances, except for the coincidences of birthdays. Yet it is a powerful birth story, told later in life for the author's own children, so that he might interpret his life to them. More important than the details of the story—the building of a fire, the castor oil, a cold June day, or even the birthdays—is the intertwining of tales and expectations that shaped the author in his later life.

Sometimes there are extraordinary events that add drama to the beginning of a personal narration. It may be that the trip to the hospital required a police escort, or the birth occurred before the doctor could be located on the golf course. More often than not, however, the events themselves are not as influential in forming us as the stories families spin around those events. It is possible, for example, that the most unique elements of a birth story are total fabrications. Over the years details have been refined, rearranged, and highlighted with all the smudges removed. A temptation in all storytelling is to supply a form or fullness not originally present. This is especially true around key moments in the life cycle, such as birth. Thus stories of Grandma's birth at the old homestead are embroidered with new details about the weather and the hostile environment. What began as a simple story about "birth on the prairie" eventually becomes a very tall tale, in which Grandma was born in a thunderstorm, in the midst of a buffalo stampede, from which Great-Grandpa was taking refuge in a sycamore tree.

Every family story and its accumulated embroiderings—whether they are historically accurate or not, of legendary proportions or not—are nonetheless influential in forming an individual. This is particularly true of birth stories. Thus Patrick, reflecting on his own birth tale, writes,

Does it matter that the day was cold and was already two others' birthday? Oh, yes; oh, yes; it matters. Their lives and their traditions are all gone, and I am left with all of them within me. Am I uniquely myself, or am I distillation of these wanderers, glassblowers, seamstresses, lawyers, teachers, clerks? Through them, as through a glass darkly, I see the history of families, of a city, a nation. I see more than a century's story. Yet it is only a pittance out of the coin of years, and others have seen more and farther.

The stories of our birth are mighty. Even though each individual is an agent in his or her narrative from the beginning, and even though it is possible to reframe the story of our beginnings later in life, stories about our birth shape expectations of ourselves and our world. Discovering new stories about our birth later in life may also fill in a narrative gap that we intuitively recognized but could not explain. For example, if parents divorce when a child is very young, birth stories are sometimes not told because of residual anger toward the absent parent. Learning the stories of our origins later in life, even when it is painful or messy, is almost always better than not knowing these stories at all. What we understand from common wisdom and studies of human development is reconfirmed in the exploration of our own life narrative: it matters how we begin.

The Individual and Familial Consequences of Birth Stories

Creating and relating birth stories are not only consequential for the individual whose birth is narrated in such tales but also for the family that weaves and sustains them. Families tell these and other foundational stories in order to establish and maintain a particular identity or self-understanding. They are like a verbal coat of arms: an interpretive tool by which a family articulates its destiny, explains why people turn out as they do, and predicts how the family will confront the next crisis.

These stories about my two sisters and me have been repeated and retold countless times throughout my life, mainly by my paternal grandmother. At a recent Thanksgiving family gathering, while basking in the joy of all of her great-grandchildren present, Grama once again ritualistically told of our three births.

Rebecca was first. She was born on Ash Wednesday. My mother was three weeks late before she began labor that was to last thirty-six hours. The delivery was very difficult because Rebecca's shoulder came out first. My mother would often say, "They cut me stem to stern" so that Rebecca could come out sideways. She has always had a difficult time fitting into the family and is now nearly estranged from everyone.

I, Margaret, was born three years later. My birth was quick and easy. I was born fifteen minutes after my mother arrived at the hospital. My grandmother will often say I was "pushed out in fifteen minutes and have been on the move ever since." I have been the easy daughter. I was diplomat, rescuer, peacemaker, and quasi co-parent during my father's emotional absence because of alcoholism.

My mother began labor with Janet, it is told, on a hot and humid August day three years after I was born. During labor, Janet kept turning over in utero and would not descend into the birth position. My mother walked and paced the hospital floors, hoping that she would drop into position. As soon as she did, my mother was whisked into delivery, but Janet changed positions again. Both mother and child almost died. According to Grandmother, the ritual interpreter of the stories, Janet "did not want to be born." Since childhood, Janet and my mother have been inseparable. During Janet's honeymoon, she once told me, she cried and cried because she could never go back home. Janet and her husband built a house behind my mother's house in the same clearing in the woods. She has never left my mother.

—MARGARET

○

Rebecca's role as the family outsider, Margaret's role as rescuer with an impatient disposition, and Janet's continuing physical connection with her mother were formed, in part, at birth and then continuously reinforced by the retelling of this family legend. What is significant about this story, however, is not simply that it provides an important interpretation of individual siblings, their personalities or relational strengths and weaknesses. More than that, such a birth legend also rehearses something crucial about the whole family system. Rebecca is not just estranged from the mother but from the rest of the relations as well. Margaret is not only the "easy daughter" but also "easy sister" who becomes surrogate parent. The inseparable bond between Janet and her mother is mutual and at least tolerated if not sustained by the whole of the family system.

If a family repeatedly talks about how accommodating we were at birth, how mother and child almost died, how our birth during hunting season deprived father of his favoring sporting event of the year, or how our birth was the happiest moment of mother's life, the family is shaping both itself and its offspring through these stories. In particular, these tales play a crucial role in the way a family defines the spectrum of individuality and the level of autonomy that the family system encourages or tolerates. Birth stories in particular, therefore, need to be considered from the viewpoint of the individual-communal polarity mentioned in previous chapters.

While the individual-communal polarity is a helpful frame for considering many aspects of our storytelling and ritualizing, it is of particular significance at key moments in the life cycle. At birth, for example, the narrative that a family weaves in story and ritual is particularly powerful in shaping the kind of autonomy that a family will expect or allow of the newborn in later life. Earlier we suggested that in the rituals and stories of English-speaking North Americans, who are our primary resource for this book, there needs to be respect for both individual and communal meaning making. The development of differentiated individuals capable of a healthy interaction with their particular social context depends on maintaining respect for both of these types of meaning making. As we will demonstrate in the next section, this renders such storytelling and ritualizing especially powerful and dangerous.

The Newborn As a Unique Gift

Every newborn child is a new creation, a unique person. Each has a story to tell that will unfold in amazing and often unpredictable ways. If we regard a child in this way, each new life becomes a miracle, a gift to be protected and nourished. The birth of a child is a promise of the future of our family. At the same time, this arrival is a challenge to the human inclination to search for safety in sameness. Thus the paradox of birth: our children are like us but unique, formed by the families into which they are born and yet remarkably different from the beginning. Authentic respect for children requires balancing this similarity and difference from the start. The communities into which children are born have a special responsibility to provide a habitable and hospitable environment in which those unique gifts will grow and flourish.

The ties we have to our families of origin ordinarily last as long as we live. Given the length of time that children are dependent on others for care, it is not surprising that the emotional attachment between children and parents is so intense. One consequence of this lengthy period of dependence is that parents may come to regard their children as a possession rather than a gift. This possessive instinct can reveal itself in the stories and rituals parents construct even before a child is born. This one will become president, and that one a singer; this one will be rich, or that one will write books; this one will be an athlete, while another will be a doctor or teacher.

Sometimes such hopes and dreams are not verbalized but symbolized in the dolls or baseball mitts, clothes or nursery furnishings that accumulate in anticipation of the birth. Other times these expectations are embedded in the names chosen for the newly conceived or recently delivered. The namesake might be sainted Aunt Olive, beloved Grandpa Joe, or Uncle Herbert, who died tragically in a farm accident as a young boy. Each name is a code of hopes and expectations, richly modeled or sadly unfulfilled in the previous generation. Such dreams for our children are almost inevitably mythic. When children are born, we rehearse untold hopes for them in the tales we tell, the toys we buy, and the names we bestow.

Parables of Birth

In the story presented at the opening of this chapter, Patrick entered a world filled with expectations about him. His life began with the expectation that he would share a birthday with his grandmother and his father. Although his family clearly surrounded him with love, they also defined him. Some families believe that defining a child is a way of loving. There is always the danger, however, that the desire to define is a denial of a child's uniqueness. In that sense, birth stories and their ritual enactments are not only mighty; sometimes they are also dangerous. When Patrick asks whether he is uniquely himself or the distillation of all those expectations, the answer is clearly yes. Both are true. His uniqueness—and ours—is, in part, revealed in the ability to respond to the expectations of others rather than avoiding them. If family expectations are overpowering, however, children may never find their own voice, tell their own tale, or assert their rightful coauthorship in narrating their lives. Like wearing hand-me-down clothes, one could end up living another's story. The lack of ownership in what should rightfully be one's own stories may continue for some through adulthood and into old age. In such situations, it is possible that the first time an individual effectively asserts their autonomy is in his or her dying. This is an image we will explore more fully in Chapter Six.

Even when parents acknowledge the parable of birth from the beginning and recognize that their child is a new creation with a distinctive story yet to unfold, it is still difficult to act on that conviction. It is difficult to recognize that our children's stories are different from our own and, thus, to acknowledge that in one of the great paradoxes of our existence, we bring life into the world in order to give it away. Kahlil Gibran reminded parents of this when he wrote, "We can house their bodies but not their souls, because their souls dwell in a place of tomorrow [where] we cannot go, not even in our dreams" (Gibran, 1923, p. 18). They will pursue relationships we will not approve of, engage in studies we will not understand, challenge us with ideas and ideals we may not accept. Sometimes they will simply move away, or die. To love children means to rehearse letting go of them from the inception of their story. It means allowing them to write their own story and coauthor ours in a way that is both mythic and parabolic, that honors their own uniqueness in the midst of generational sameness or continuity.

A Father's Tale of Two Births

When Joshua was born, we had expected that all the doctors and nurses would be attuned to us emotionally. We learned otherwise. Exhausted in our different ways after an unsuccessful night of labor, we found ourselves in a struggle with our obstetrician, who saw no reason why the father needed to be in the operating room for a cesarean. No sooner had we navigated this obstacle than we encountered another roadblock with the director of the recovery room, who decreed that fathers and babies were not allowed in the room with mothers if there were any medical abnormalities. Joshua and I found ourselves banished from the room, while Linda recovered from some minor kidney difficulties.

During that time Joshua and I started to develop a deep connection that continues to thrive. It began in the operating room, right after birth. After talking with Linda, I walked over to the warming table where Joshua was being cleaned. As I approached, I spoke to him and he immediately turned in the direction of my voice, because I believe he had heard it from the womb for weeks. When I could pick him up, we walked the hallways for the better part of three hours. I held him in tired arms as close to my face as I could lift him, telling him how wonderful it was finally to see him.

Jeremy's entry into the world was different. The ultrasounds showing a possible prolapsed cord required that it be so. Linda's c-section took place in the same operating room where Joshua had been born, but the tension of earlier events was gone. After Jeremy was born, I did not have as much time with him as I had with his brother. I was able to rock him for a half-hour in a hard wooden chair and talk with him as I had with his brother, holding him close to my face. I told him how special he was to me because soon after he was conceived I had become seriously ill and had almost died. As I heard myself speak, I realized that his prolapsed cord and my heart condition were a bond between us; we both had survived, and our lives were a gift to each other.

---

o

It is not only in the stories we tell but in the ways that we ritualize those stories that the uniqueness of our children is enacted or ignored. A narrow view of ritual—especially one that takes as its paradigm some traditional or elaborate ceremony—makes it difficult to recognize and appreciate the power of the simple ritualizing, which, for example, characterizes this father's tale of two births. Yet the patterns of talking to a child while still in the womb, carrying a child shortly after birth, holding him close, and calling him a gift are potent forms of ritual making. Improvising upon this pattern for each child does not, of course, jeopardize the ability to value both of them as unique and special. As noted in Chapter Two, human ritual is not simply patterned and shared behavior; it is an imaginative and interpretive act through which we express and create meaning in our lives. The father was able to repeat something of a pattern with each newborn, while providing a particular interpretation that could appreciate each child as unique.

The daily interaction with our children provides many such opportunities. The ritualizing that surrounds bathing, eating, and being put to bed communicates in a subtle but enduring way about the value and uniqueness of our children. Does each child get her or his own story? Are individual preferences respected at table? Is each child metaphorically held close to the face and assured of a special place in the family and in the world? The stories we tell and the rituals that enact such stories communicate powerfully and paradoxically about our offspring and ourselves.

Even when they do not intend it, families often err on the side of creating a narrative that maximizes continuity and sameness at the expense of freedom and individuality. It is our proposal that religious rituals at birth—particularly Christian baptism—have the potential to challenge a family's tendency to diminish individuality. Properly understood and appropriated, rituals such as baptism affirm uniqueness and autonomy while simultaneously promoting our membership in community. They weave the human and divine narrative through the affirmation of the individual, the family, and the faith community. Such rituals contribute to the balance of individuation and incorporation through the paradoxical linkage of myth and parable.

Narrating the Baptism

Baptism embodies the Christian narrative in a paradoxical mix of the mythic and the parabolic. In its announcement that all things can be reconciled in Christ, infant baptism is certainly a mythic ritual. It enacts the embrace of family and church, commits both to the protection and the support of the child, and ultimately promises eternal life.

Without denying these strong mythic overtones, it is yet difficult to imagine a sacramental process that has more parabolic potential than baptism. In many traditions, for example, the child is physically or metaphorically marked with the cross. This is not a perfunctory gesture. As St. Paul reminds us in his letter to the Romans, those who are baptized are immersed in the mystery of Christ's death. Baptism is a parabolic moment, because it does not resolve the mysteries of uncertainty, identity, and death for the life journey ahead. It proclaims loudly that dying comes before rising.

Although baptism is a family event, it is not simply a continuation of a family story. The baptized individual is joined to the Christian community's story and a life of faith that calls for new loyalties. Birth begins a sojourn of uncharted potential and a story with an undetermined conclusion. Bringing the child to baptism is an act filled with promise that the human mystery of a child and the divine mystery of grace will be united in a life of faithfulness that will not end in death. Through this rite of baptism, the human is invited to a special relationship with the divine in the dual promise that the gracious unfolding of a life will be a revelation of God, and that the child's story will be God's story too.

At the same time, bringing a child to be baptized is a sobering acknowledgment by parents that this child is simultaneously theirs and not theirs—their child and a child of God. Akin to the Old Testament story of Hannah (1 Samuel), who knew from the moment of his conception that Samuel was born to be given away, baptism announces that water is thicker than blood. Thus it has power to counter parents' inclination to hold on to children too tightly or mold them too firmly according to family expectations. Baptism is the sacrament that particularizes each individual's story in relation to the story of God and the community of faith.

Although this teaching about baptism is widely known, many parents and godparents still regard baptism as a mythic continuation of family expectations and birth stories. The perspective that baptism is fundamentally a familial act of self-definition is symbolized in the response, "Was I baptized? Of course. The last name is Lotti." Families operating under this assumption often insist upon arranging the baptism as a private affair for relatives only. Ecclesial symbols are overshadowed or sometimes ignored in favor of familial ones. One family we know, for example, decided to forgo a church setting for their child's baptism in favor of the birdbath in their backyard. For other families, ritual validity is achieved only if the baby is clothed in the lace baptismal garb that has been handed down from generation to generation. Insisting that baptism is only and essentially a family affair transforms this dangerous ritual into a tame, domestic event.

Part of the theological significance of baptism hinges on the death-resurrection metaphor, which is so central in the writings of St. Paul. While this is not the only interpretive key for baptism, it is a pivotal one across the Christian traditions. When the World Council of Churches issued *Baptism, Eucharist and Ministry* (1982) as a statement of theological convergence among Christian Churches, it began its discussion of the meaning of baptism under the rubric "Participation in Christ's Death and Resurrection." While this imagery is not always emphasized during the baptismal ritual itself, it is evoked in the funeral rites of many traditions. We know from the beginning that each individual's story ends with death. For the Christian, dying and rising in Christ is a lifelong experience. At the same time, baptism is a reminder for parents of the thousand little deaths they will experience and of the hundred ways that they will need to let go in order for this child to grow and develop. We let our children go even as we love and protect them from the beginning, because they do not belong to us alone; they also belong to God. That is the parabolic beginning of the narrative of every Christian.

Baptism and Pastoral Care

There are four moments surrounding the birth and baptism of a child in which the ministry of care and the rituals of the Christian community intersect. They are (1) the time of expectancy, (2) the moment of birth, (3) the preparation for baptism, and (4) the baptismal ritual itself. In addition, because the event initiates a lifelong process of incorporation into Christ and the Christian community, the significance of baptism may be appropriated later in ways that empower authentic and faithful living. While it is important to attend to each of these four moments, it is also helpful to have an overview of the whole process of baptismal incorporation. This broad perspective enables one to see that baptism is not a single magic moment but a sacramental journey into a relationship with God and a faith community.

The Time of Expectancy

The formation of a habitable and hospitable environment for an infant begins long before the child is born. Pregnant women are careful about what they eat and drink in order to ensure a safe place for their unborn child. Expectant mothers and fathers often remodel rooms, repaint furniture, and reorganize their patterns of living to provide both physical and emotional space for the child. When a child is inserted into a family context that is cluttered with occupational demands and recreational preferences, or when a child is expected to fill a void in the family, the child is almost always victimized. Infant studies show that the most beneficial preparation expectant parents can make is to solidify the marital bond so that they can be emotionally available to the needs and gifts of the newborn.

○

Theresa was nervous about having her first child. She was nineteen. Her husband did not have steady work and did not always give her what he earned. Sometimes they were short of food. When Theresa was hungry all day, she would worry about her baby. She regularly read her Bible and prayed privately for the safety of her child. She also went to her church for help in acquiring food and told the church secretary about her worries. It meant a great deal to her when she was named with several other expectant mothers in the pastor's prayer at church on Sunday morning.

○

The plight of Theresa is not unlike that of many women who have limited economic and social resources for creating a welcoming environment for the child they are carrying. Sometimes the absence of adequate prenatal care is a threat to the well-being of an unborn child. Lobbying elected officials or public agencies for available prenatal care is, therefore, a part of ministry that is informed by the significance of baptism. In other situations, the absence of a welcoming emotional environment may pose a threat to the unborn. Encouraging expectant parents who are preoccupied with their careers to create sufficient emotional space in their lives for welcoming a child is often a delicate but necessary pastoral task.

Parents are sometimes tempted, while preparing for birth, to create expectations of a child that can make it difficult to recognize the unique gifts that each newborn brings to the world. The "Father's Tale of Two Births" narrated earlier demonstrates that our ability to know the gender or monitor the development of unborn life sometimes allows our dreaming about our unborn baby to be more concrete. If the context into which a child is born is cluttered with unrealistic hopes and dreams that develop without such information, however, the birth of a child may be an immediate disappointment. This sometimes happens when parents never admit the possibility that "my son" might actually be a girl, or the perfect athlete might be born with some physical problem. When a child is born developmentally disabled, for example, expectations may be shattered, and the birth of a child can be an experience of loss.

The practice in some traditional cultures of the world not to name a child until it is born is one way to set limits on family expectations for the child. The name of the child, it is presumed, will have some connection with the character of this new life, the nature of birth, or the life into which it was born. Not naming the child before birth is one way to respect the revelation that comes with the birth. While this practice might

not seem appropriate in our culture, if parents are to respect the uniqueness of each child they must keep the context their child is born into as
free of claims and expectations as possible. Even being born on Grandmother's and Father's birthday, as occurred in the opening story, may limit
the freedom for the newborn to actualize as fully as possible his or her
own gifts for the world. Parents and family members will tell stories from
their origins and dream of future possibilities for their children; that cannot be avoided. At the same time, we adults can remind ourselves that the
new gift of life is a stranger in the family wholly other than ourselves.
Despite the mythic overtones of every birth, therefore, we must acknowledge that birth is a parabolic event that has the potential to shatter our
dreams and disrupt our expectations.

As the story of Theresa demonstrates, private and public prayer are
important ritual components in the time of expectancy. Inviting expectant
parents to pray for their child and themselves not only admits the presence of the Holy One in the midst of this nascent family but conveys the
sense that the birth of a child is truly a divine act. Expectant parents, who
are fond of feeling the baby kick while in the womb, are easily invited into
gestures and prayers of blessing for the expected child. These private
prayers need to be complemented by public rituals of prayer and blessing
for the parents and their unborn baby. Community prayers also symbol-
ize that the child will belong to ever-widening communities of responsibility and care. Inviting prayer in one's faith community is a way of
recognizing that bringing new life into the world is not simply a private
family process; it is also a public act of cooperation with the Creator for
the sake of humankind's future. Such public prayer ritually weds the human
and divine stories.

The Birth

The arrival of a child is an occasion for extravagant praise. There is an
appropriate and necessary craziness that surrounds the birth of a child,
because new life is always a wonder. Family members will have different
reactions to the same child. Fathers may be ambiguously glad for the birth
of a competitor for mother's affection; older siblings may have similar feelings of competition; and not all mothers are eager to modify a satisfying
career in order to respond to the needs of the newly born. Because the
birth of a child is an event that occurs in the midst of a process of expectation and welcoming, it is particularly important that our storytelling
and ritualizing pay attention to the possibility that birth is also loss, that
this new life is at the same time an announcement of death.

One dramatic and not-infrequent example of the confluence of birth and death is the intersection of a child's birth with the death of a relative or some other significant event that requires mourning rather than celebration. The child may be overlooked because the grieving is so intense, or the grief may be buried in order to welcome the child. Sometimes, when the grieving is postponed, the child becomes the bearer of grief. Job loss or promotion, physical sickness, general economic insecurity, or family conflict are other factors that can destabilize the context into which a child is born. Sorrow or anxiety is often mixed with joy at the time of birth. When the expectation of new life ends tragically with miscarriage, stillbirth, or premature death, there is acute sorrow.

Although home visitation is less and less common as a pastoral practice (except when people are permanently homebound because of illness or age), a visit in the home when a child is born should be standard practice. Such a visit provides an occasion to weave several stories into one narrative of birth: the expectations of the couple or grandparents; the story of the birth; the significance of the child's names; the recognition of the child's uniqueness; the stories of the faith community into which the child will be baptized; and the divine narrative that has resulted in another new creation. A pastoral visit may also provide the opportunity to respond to particular parental needs that birth can precipitate, such as postpartum depression, or the unexpected emotional strain that birth sometimes exacts on a couple's relationship.

Besides exploring the web of stories surrounding the birth, the visit is an occasion to pray for the child and parents prior to baptism. When a child enters a family through adoption, some ritual welcoming is particularly crucial in order to enhance the process of incorporation even before the baptism. Various traditions have model rituals for blessing a newborn prior to baptism that can be used to create a ritual sanctuary for storytelling. Patterns of public and private prayer that may have begun during the pregnancy need to be continued. It is in the context of such patterns of familial and ecclesial rituals that the pending baptism can be transformed from a magical cleansing rite to a determinative ritual moment in the incorporation of a new life into the family of faith.

Prebaptismal Catechesis

Our emphasis on the potential of infant baptism (or child dedication) to influence the psychological and spiritual well-being of the child is a consequence of a significant shift in baptismal and sacramental theology over the past three decades. Baptism is no longer viewed primarily as the great washing ritual that ultimately removes the stain of inherited sin and saves an infant from permanent death. While the document *Baptism, Eucharist and Ministry* (World Council of Churches, 1982), for example, does employ "cleansing" language, it is used in the context of broader ethical insights about confession and conversion. Furthermore, that document and the rites of many Christian communities emphasize baptism as a critical public ritual in the long process of incorporating a newborn Christian into the family of faith. This shift in perspective is well summarized by John McKenna, who remarks that the key question around infant baptism today should not be, What happens if the infant dies?—a question that occupied many in the past. Rather, the life-implications for baptism prompt us to ask, What happens if the infant lives? (McKenna, 1996, p. 206).

Prebaptismal catechesis has as its goal not simply the preparation of the parents and godparents to perform the mechanics of the rite without embarrassment but the family's initiation into a mode of thinking and believing that is grounded in the church's public prayer. Because infant baptism has significance for both the process of parenting and the salvation of the child, these are the two points of focus in the prebaptismal catechesis. Parents need to be reminded of the meaning of baptism for Christian living. It is an extraordinary thing that God does to initiate us into the realm of graciousness before we are old enough to make an enlightened decision. God has chosen us. In response to that remarkable gift, the promise of parents to raise a child in the faith should not be taken lightly; it is, as Martin Luther observed, "the noblest and most precious work on earth." This image is richly echoed in the Catholic rites for the baptism of children, which acknowledge the family as the domestic church through which every child is introduced to the faith.

The intersection of the stories of the newborn, parents, and the faith community is the rich soil in which baptismal rituals flourish. Some rites, for example, begin by asking the name of the child. Rather than a simple formality, this ritual moment suggests that in the prebaptismal visits and time of instruction, parents have begun to explore the impact of this new child for their family through reflection on the name. Why was this name chosen? Who chose it? What is the story behind the name? Does it have any connection with either parent's birth family? Is the name a clue to unspoken mythic expectations that family might have for the child? Does the child's name link her or him to the wider Christian story?

Other ritual components of the baptism rite can serve as entry points into consideration of the intersection or collision of newborn, familial, and ecclesial stories. The lessons that are read, the promises that parents and godparents make, the blessings that are bestowed, and the use of symbols such as candles or special clothing can be quite powerful. If appropriately prepared, narrated, and ritualized, these various facets of the baptismal ritual invite parents and godparents to discover if there are any shadows cast over this birth, if there are relationships that need healing, if the family's expectations will make it difficult to see the uniqueness of the newborn, or if there are other children or relatives who need blessing. These and similar questions may help families understand the baptismal moment in the context of a larger process of human growth and spiritual development.

The Baptism

While there are many elements from various contemporary baptismal rituals that could claim our attention in this discussion, the most important factor for determining whether the ritual is to be a mythic balm or a parabolic encounter is whether or not the baptism ritual is the first time (or the last time) that the stories and rituals of newborn, family, and faith community intersect. If there has been little interweaving of story and ritual through the previously outlined three stages, infant baptism tends to transpire as an isolated ritual moment, prone to mythic display. An unusually effective minister or particularly receptive couple can provide an exception, however.

Parents and godparents who have not previously begun to weave the stories of newborn, family, and faith community together in word and ritual—even though they may have made the necessary appointments, filled out required forms, or even attended the classes—are usually parents and godparents only capable of monosyllabic responses and gesture-upon-instruction during the baptism. Enhancing the significance of baptism for the family and so for the child underscores the reciprocal connection between worship and pastoral care, between the divine story and the human story. Preparation that engages more than it informs, and catechesis that is more ritual and storytelling than data gathering or instruction is an important antidote to the kind of formalism that pervades so many baptismal rituals.

When baptism is treated as the end of a chapter of a child's story instead of the beginning of one, it is prone to mythic interpretations because it ignores the journey ahead: the pending lifelong struggle for personal identity, for self-worth, for faith, and for meaning in the face of death. Baptism reveals God's invitation to become immersed into a community of faith and to set out on a life journey of ongoing renewal in which the meaning of the baptismal action will continuously unfold. The

Christian life, as Martin Luther insisted, is "nothing else than a daily baptism, once begun and ever continued" (Luther, [1538] 1959, p. 445). Infant baptism is the ritual beginning of a process that ends with death. It is the foundation for all ministry, for every life commitment of a believer, and for embracing the whole of the Christian mystery.

A Pastoral Resource of Unusual Riches

The process of welcoming a child into the world and the baptismal ritual that occurs within that welcoming context are sources of unusual riches for faithful living. Private decisions about the name are transformed into public dialogues between family and ministers about the significance of the name and the faith-filled hopes for the child. The renewal of baptismal vows by family and community is not a rehearsal of empty promises but a mutual commitment to a common struggle to be faithful. Experiences of loss and death, tensions and conflicts, hopes and fears that come with being family weave their way into the prayers, the testimony, and the preaching that punctuate baptism. If, however, baptism is viewed mythically as the once-and-for-all extinguishing of original sin and the definitive bestowal of a Christian identity, then its life-giving possibilities are decidedly diminished.

In some sense, the journey from myth to parable requires us to accept over and over again that baptism is what the New Testament calls *musterion*, a divine secret in the process of being revealed. More clearly than any other stage of human development, infancy underscores that each human being is herself or himself a "mystery" to be honored as a divinely initiated story on the verge of unfolding. Sacraments do not ensure that we will narrate our story according to a prearranged plan. Nor do they solve the mysteries of uncertainty, identity, and death that face us on the way. Sacraments do, however, allow these and every other mystery to be redeemed; they invite us to connect our human development with the divine call; and they promise us that if we are faithful, the unfolding of our lives can be grace-filled revelations of God. Bringing the child to baptism acknowledges the mystery of a life of uncharted potential and permanently links it with the gracious mystery of God. When parents understand their child as mystery, they may more easily love the child and let go of them from birth.

The spirit of Christian hospitality reveals baptism as a symbol of God's providential care. In spite of the reality of evil in the world, baptism is a promise that the child will be held in the care of God and sustained by the witness and prayers of the faith community. The ritual can also be a sobering occasion for parents and congregations, who not only admit in the ritual that the child will be confronted by evil in the future but that sometimes families of origin and families of faith teach evil to their children in the form of prejudice and dishonesty. The baptismal rite reminds the family and faith community, however, that they are not to hand on evil but to be vehicles of God's grace.

Although it is essential that parents nurture and protect their children, baptism is a sign that God's trustworthiness ultimately transcends their own efforts to be dependable. For that reason, baptism is more than a hospitable ritual of welcoming; it is a divine act by which a child is claimed by God. "It is, in fact, the celebration of our helplessness, our dependence on God. Like birth, baptism precedes all will, all choosing, all thinking" (Hamilton, 1990, p. 7). Baptism is thus the beginning of a life of discipleship that demands ultimate loyalty. Our emphasis on baptism as an individuating ritual is therefore not an end in itself, but a vehicle for discipleship and mission.

In baptism, at the beginning of life, God is ritually acknowledged as an active coauthor. When we recall our baptism later in life, we need not be timid or afraid, because we do not write our narrative alone. God is in partnership with us from our baptism, and nothing can sever that bond. When we wonder as adults whether we are loved, we know that we belong to God. But we also belong to the world. We are baptized into solidarity with the world in Christ at the level of deepest danger. In that sense, baptism is always a precarious political act. Because we have been baptized, we are linked to the sufferings of the world for which Christ died. Because we have been baptized, our hospitality always has room for the weak and the vulnerable.

The human story begins in the pangs of childbirth and continues in paradox. The life journey of a Christian begins with water and continues in paradox. A paradox is seeming contradiction. It is two things together that should not both be true but nonetheless are. Baptism initiates a process of human renewal that Martin Luther characterized as daily dying and daily rising. This is the fundamental paradox of Christian living revealed in Jesus Christ: if you want to be first, you have to be last; if you want to live, you have to die; and if you want to hold on to anything—including your children—it can only be done with an open hand. Baptism is a dangerous ritual because it invites us to discover death as the way to life. When we are signed with a cross in baptism, we begin a journey that is marked by contradiction and swallowed up in paradox.

Baptism is not just an invitation to death. It is also a pastoral source of promise and certainty in the midst of cynicism and despair. In that sense, it is both parable and myth. This may be the most important meaning of baptism for unfolding the story of an individual's life. The human ills of fear, doubt, anxiety, melancholy, depression, and despair that come to us in the dark moments of life drive us back to baptism and the graciousness of God embodied in a community of faith. The worst malady of the soul is to despair without hope for any remedy and without a future. As the sacrament of certainty, baptism is an unusually potent antidote to this malady and a rich resource for pastoral care. Thus it need be imaginatively employed in our storytelling and ritualizing so that in those dark moments of life, we are able to reclaim our baptism and there discover empowerment for reentering the rich story web of the human and the divine, the personal and the communal that it symbolizes. It is our promissory note. Although everyone's dark night is different, all darkness is in part a dread of abandonment. Whenever we are in despair, we are sustained by the promise of baptism that God will not abandon us, even when God seems absent.

PREPARING FOR MARRIAGE

*Because the process of becoming married is a wedding
of stories, telling and ritualizing the family narrative
is part of the preparation for marriage.*

○

MARRIAGE IS A WEDDING OF STORIES. Whether two people fall in love
and decide to marry, decide to marry and then fall in love, or become married and never fall in love, they embark on a weaving process. They spin
a narrative out of values and patterns borrowed from their families of origin, and their new ways of being together are fashioned from their particular history. The work of becoming married requires molding these
separate stories into a new and distinct tale. This process is punctuated
by numerous private and public rituals that both separate a couple from
others for the sake of forging a new bond and, at the same time, provide
them a special place within a community that celebrates their love and
promotes fidelity.

There are two parts to this chapter, much as there are two aspects of
wedding preparation. These two aspects presume that the process of
becoming married continues after the wedding. While it is useful to invite
couples to explore their relationship prior to the wedding, the process of
becoming married needs continued attention in the first years of marriage.
The first focus of a couple before the wedding is to identify and understand the legacy each brings from his or her home of origin. That legacy is
most often carried by stories that in turn determine the roles, rules, and
rituals for interpersonal relationships. The second focus is on planning for
the wedding as preparation for marriage. This chapter will explore the
interaction of narrative and ritual around these two phenomena.

Because wedding rituals have lost some of their spiritual power to counter the claims of family narratives and challenge the personal agendas of individuals marrying, they are often dangerous only by default. Although the church continues to regard marriage as divinely instituted, many pastoral ministers admit privately that they hate weddings. In this culture, however, weddings are very important, even though the rate of divorce suggests that staying married is very difficult. People will spend huge sums of money to stage the perfect wedding. Couples who marry in the church are often caught between this cultural expectation and the theological imperative about marriage as divinely instituted. Our intent is to address this conundrum in the hopes of contributing to its pastoral resolution.

In order to increase the possibility of fashioning what Ronald Grimes (1995) has called "a wedding that weds" (p. 84), we will examine the stories and rituals of wedding preparation by means of four polarities: (1) myth and parable; (2) individual and communal; (3) public and private; and (4) moment and process. We attend particularly to the paradox of public and private in this chapter. Story and ritual are not magic. A picture-perfect wedding will not make a perfect marriage; nor will strengthening the storytelling and ritual making around preparing for a marriage counter all the social forces that make it difficult to become or stay married today. We believe, however, that religious practice can contribute to strengthening the process of marital bonding by revitalizing becoming-married rituals in relation to personal and familial narratives. The work of weaving together narrative and ritual for the sake of stronger Christian marriages not only links worship and pastoral care; it recognizes the interaction of human and divine stories in forming families.

The Power of Family Narratives

Despite efforts to form new marital bonds without undue influence from our home of origin, couples regularly struggle with loyalty to their family story as they seek to develop their own ways to be married. Telling stories of our first families is a way of recognizing continuity of identity across generations and of celebrating our membership in particular human communities that have both a history and a future. Because they locate us within a particular community, family stories are both more necessary and more powerful than we think. The first step in preparing for marriage is to identify the family narratives that have formed us, even if we have rejected them, and explore the ongoing power of those narratives in shaping our life. It helps to know where we have come from when we are determining where we want to go. That is what we mean when we suggest that marriage is a wedding of stories. When the family narrative cannot be freely told, the ritual power of the wedding is diminished.

○

Wendy and Jim were both graduate students when they decided to marry. Although Jim was more practical and Wendy more theoretical in their approach to things, they seemed to have much in common—until they began telling family stories. Wendy was from an old Southern family—the "first family" in the town and pillars of the Episcopal Church. Legends were more available than direct rules, but it was clear that nothing should be done to embarrass Wendy's family. For example, when she decided to leave Alabama and head "north" to Missouri for graduate school, Wendy discovered that she had exceeded the acceptable limits of difference. Since she had never questioned or challenged her family's values, Wendy did not expect the rejection she received from her grandfather, symbolized by his comment that women did not need so much education. Furthermore, Grandfather was afraid Wendy would marry outside their circle. In ways that startled Jim, Wendy spoke about her family with anger and shame as being elitist and stuffy. She enjoyed being with Jim's parents because, in contrast, they seemed to her down-to-earth and real.

Jim's father and mother immigrated from Germany just before World War II. Jim's father could not get work at his trade as a tool and die maker, so he bought a small farm. The farm provided for a stable context and a livelihood, but Jim does not remember having much fun as a child. There was little play time and many chores. Although his parents had been raised Lutheran, there was no more time for church than for play after acquiring the farm. Jim had gone to school in Missouri because it was what he could afford. Although he loved his parents, Jim wanted to leave behind his home family and a life of mere survival. Until they began sharing stories, he thought that it would be much more fun to belong to Wendy's family.

○

Wendy and Jim discovered through storytelling that each wanted to marry into a family that the other was hoping to leave behind. Because Wendy and Jim both wanted to move beyond their origins, they had never spoken together seriously about their families; hence the surprise. Had they not been invited to tell family stories as part of the marriage preparation process, Jim and Wendy's surprise could have turned to serious disappointment, if they each later discovered that the other's family, which each wanted to join, was not what they thought it was. Their determination to leave behind the families they had come from also prompted them to overlook the power of the narratives that had formed them.

The experience of Wendy and Jim is only one variation on a wedding of stories. Most people expect that they can balance equally the influence of their families of origin when they are married. Sometimes newly married couples will go to great lengths to meet this expectation—such as driving through the night in order to celebrate Christmas Eve with one family and Christmas Day with another. When there has been divorce in a family of origin, parceling attention to several competing family groups becomes even more complex. Sometimes becoming married resembles a "corporate takeover," as one family's traditions dominate the new family being formed. Other couples decide to reject the models of family living learned in their origins. This is particularly true if there has been persistent conflict or violence or abuse. When couples are determined not to imitate the story of their parents' marriage or perpetuate inhospitable patterns of family living, they sometimes overlook the power of the narratives that formed them.

Because each family narrative has interpretative authority, creating a new narrative is seldom without struggle. Even when not intended, our families influence the development of the new marital narrative. Sometimes we do not discover this familial influence until there is a clash of values in a marriage. Because of their emotional claim on us, the legacy of roles, rules, and rituals we carry from our families of origin has a significant impact on becoming married, even when we are not aware of it. Through telling their family stories at a formative stage in their relationship, Jim and Wendy had the time and capacity to shape their own narrative without having to reject totally their origins.

As a wedding of stories, marriage not only builds on the narratives from families of origins; it draws on the couple's own story, which began when first they met. Furthermore, since people often marry later today, each partner may also have tales from living alone or from previous relationships to add to the web of stories. For those who have been married before, the account of the first marriage needs to be included in the new family story being written. Because of the grief and pain they often generate, stories of a previous marriage are both difficult and necessary to recall. Telling these stories before a second marriage is also a critical act of self-revelation that builds trust in the new relationship.

Marriage is not only a wedding of stories and legends. It is a decision to write the rest of one's life story with a new coauthor, permanent editor, and resident critic. The decision to make this permanent commitment to another as husband or wife requires a willingness to compromise personal preferences for the sake of a common story. It also means letting go of beloved memories from our homes of origin or cherished habits from living alone so that something unimagined can grow. Because people are changed by events, the passage of time, and significant relationships, becoming married is an act of promising to one another to move together toward a yet unknown future. Knowing the stories that bring us together in marriage will not determine what is yet to come.

If God is understood to be an active partner in forming the marriage covenant, the couple will weave the divine narrative into their new family story so that it might become a tale of transcending love and enduring joy. Although each couple will incorporate their faith tradition into the newly unfolding narrative differently, there is one biblical motif about God's activity in human history that is particularly beneficial for the process of becoming married. While the prophets frequently admonished Israel to remember what God had done for them in the past, Isaiah offers a contrast to this insistence on remembering that makes a splendid wedding text. "Do not remember the former things, or consider the things of old. I am about to do a new thing; now it springs forth, do you not see it?" (Isa. 43:18–19). This text is a wonderful antidote to the temptation to cling to the past, harbor treasures, or dutifully replicate family traditions. When a wedding of stories embraces God's story, we are empowered to remember the past in freedom. We recall the past without being bound by it, which allows us to preserve what we will—not what we must—in order to imagine the new thing God is doing.

Claiming Autonomy, Finding Community

Storytelling about our families of origin is one of the most significant elements of marital preparation. The primary purpose of family storytelling is to enhance appreciation of our origins, facilitate our separation from those origins, and enable couples to discover the potential marriage patterns that they wish to keep or discard. Such storytelling also diminishes our inclination to hide family skeletons while increasing our awareness of the power families have to make it harder or easier to become married. If there are family secrets or resistance to storytelling, it is necessary for the bride or groom to recover their family stories in order to understand the hidden legacy each brings to marriage. Often the untold stories are the ones with the most power. When a family is closed, hidden, or at least reluctant to be known, simply telling family stories as part of wedding preparation is an act of autonomy in the process of separating from home because it violates a family rule.

We have found that a genogram is a most useful method for enhancing the process of storytelling. Like a family tree, a genogram seeks to identify at least two or three generations of membership in the families from which we come. Unlike a family tree, however, a genogram communicates that stories and patterns of interacting are more important than the dates or places of birth. We do not invite people to tell family stories using a genogram to evaluate compatibility or locate trouble. Rather, prospective marriage partners need to tell the whole story of their first families in order to begin freely a family that combines myth and parable.

A genogram has many advantages for pastoral work with couples preparing for a wedding. A genogram does not presume literacy. A genogram is portable—a magic marker and a large art tablet will do. A genogram also diminishes defensiveness by shifting the focus away from a relationship that may be in a formative stage. Couples determined to marry are reluctant to look too carefully at their relationship, lest they or someone discover hidden flaws or reasons they should not marry. They are less inhibited in telling stories about their original families. Moreover, a genogram is a public document. Because no one knows all the family stories, we will need to ask our parents or grandparents or aunts questions, some of which we may never have dared ask before. When couples travel up and down the generations in search of stories, the wedding is more likely to be a multigenerational event and a communal act.

Pastoral work with couples preparing for marriage should help clarify each individual's relationship to his or her family of origin. Moreover, pastoral care should encourage the process of separating emotionally from one's family of origin. It should also enable the couple to see clearly the most important features of their relationship. Pastoral ministers facilitate these very important processes with one eye on the human story and the other on the divine narrative. The aim is to help the couple become more conscious and intentional about what they will keep and what they will modify or discard from the legacies—including the place of the divine narrative—each brings from the first families.

Pastoral ministers are distinguished from other counselors or therapists in their use of the genogram because, besides asking the couple to tell the stories of relationships, myths, and alliances, pastoral ministers are interested in uncovering signs of the divine narrative. There are obvious questions about religious practice in the family. Who read them Bible stories as a child? Who were the saints and who were the religious enthusiasts in the family? Other questions will elicit more implicit religious values or practices in the family. Which charities were supported? How were difficult decisions made? In what ways did the family welcome strangers? Was forgiveness or reconciliation as evident as conflict? How did your family show hospitality to people outside the family? Nevertheless, the questions we ask are not as important as helping the couple discover signs of the divine narrative, however hidden they may seem, in their families of origin. Further information regarding the use of genograms in marriage preparation may be found in *Becoming Married* (Anderson and Fite, 1993).

Leaving and Cleaving, Individuality and Community

Being separate together is one of the fundamental contradictions of married life. It is reflected in the paradox that celebrates autonomy in community and promotes community for the sake of autonomy. We explored this individual-communal polarity in the previous chapter, when we observed how birth stories balance the expectations of a family with the celebration of the unique gift each child brings. Baptism, we suggested, fosters autonomy in the midst of community by reminding parents that their children are not their children because they belong to God. When parents take seriously this understanding of baptism, children are free to leave with a blessing, find their place in the world, and marry, if they choose. Enhancing the process of leaving home in order to become married is the second dimension of marriage preparation supporting the transition from one family to another.

While the ways of leaving home and the images of marriage have changed through the centuries, what is necessary to become married has not. One must leave home; that is, one must achieve enough separation from one's home of origin to commit oneself to another in a covenant of marriage. The admonition from Genesis 2:24, reiterated by Jesus, that an individual must leave father and mother in order to "cleave" to a spouse is both theologically true and psychologically necessary. One must separate from one's parents and home of origin in order to be free to become emotionally committed to another person in marriage. We must leave before we can cleave.

The biblical admonition that leaving comes before cleaving continues the individual-communal paradox. Leaving home is prelude to becoming married. Separation from father and mother is what makes marital togetherness possible. If we understand leaving home as a metaphor for emotional separation from our families of origin, we need to be separate in order to be together. Being married presupposes the capacity to be autonomous persons, and leaving home is an avenue to autonomy. We also know that it is easier to be alone if we can count on the residual support of being together in community. Being at home in a family is necessary in order to leave it. In that sense, community and autonomy, the communal and the individual have a reciprocal relationship.

The desire of original families to repeat previous family patterns or honor traditions that maintain continuity with the past is in tension with the need for daughters and sons to leave home in order to marry and the couple's task to form something new for the future of their marriage. A noted family therapist once observed that there is really no such thing as marriage; families simply elect scapegoats to reproduce themselves. Although the statement is obviously an exaggeration, it does point to a truth: families often insist that their children maintain continuity with the past by reproducing old patterns and traditions in the new relationship that, ironically, undermine the autonomy that is necessary for becoming married. Planning a wedding is an important symbolic rehearsal of autonomy for husbands and wives in relation to their homes of origin.

○

Ellen was thirty-four when she married Brendan. She had lived away from her parents since she was eighteen, owned her own home, been the chief surgical nurse of a large regional hospital, and had developed tastes quite different from her mother. Ellen and Brendan decided to have cheesecake at their wedding made by one of Ellen's friends who owned a bakery. Her mother was livid. She could not imagine a wedding without a wedding cake. In response, Ellen told her mother, "This is my wedding. You already had your own." "No, I didn't," her mother said. "That was *my* mother's wedding." Ellen's mother did not speak to her for weeks before the wedding, but Ellen held firm on the matter of the cheesecake. On the day of the wedding, a large wedding cake appeared at the reception so that, as Ellen's mother put it, the children could have some cake. Now that she has two grandsons, Ellen's mother tells the cheesecake story whenever they reminisce about the wedding.

○

The struggle between Ellen and her mother is neither surprising nor uncommon. The question, Whose wedding is it? frequently disrupts planning for the event. Decisions about where the wedding will be, the guest list, the type of wedding cake, and the number of bridesmaids are sometimes occasions for tension between parents and children. No matter what the size or complexity of the families from which we come, their stories continue to have power in our lives, long after we have physically left home. For that reason, planning a wedding becomes an important rehearsal of autonomy.

There are many variations on the theme of leaving and cleaving in the ways couples marry today. Some children have no home to leave or, because of divorce and remarriage, several homes to leave. Others have no positive image of emotional intimacy, because their homes of origin are marked with instability or excessive violence and abuse. Couples who live together before marriage often insist that they have left home already. Cleaving, however, does not ensure leaving. When people have been married before, there is a temptation to overlook one's family of origin and focus on the previous family. In all of these instances, it remains necessary to explore the relationship with one's home of origin as part of marriage preparation. It is the foundational experience of being in community from which all subsequent human relationships evolve.

Making the Private Public

The decision to marry is ordinarily made in private. There are, of course, exceptions such as Jack, who hung a sign on a bridge over the freeway that Clarissa traveled every day asking her to marry him; or the suitor who rented a plane to fly a banner proposing marriage to an unsuspecting sunbather on the beach. Then there are circumstances in which people not only decide to marry privately, they marry in secret and continue as secretly married. Becoming married involves transforming a private promise into public reality. The public-private dimension of wedding preparation also enhances the rite of passage from being single and belonging to one's home of origin to being married and committed to a spouse and a process of bonding. The movement from private promise to public wedding ceremony introduces another framework for examining the relation between narrative and ritual: the public-private polarity.

The rituals surrounding birth, marriage, and death are not just private or simply public. They move in and out between public and private realities. Although the promise of baptism may be a private source of sustenance during times of trial, it is also a public event that inaugurates an individual into a faith community. Dying rituals, as we explain in the next chapter, create communities that sustain the one who is dying on the journey to death. When death occurs, the funeral not only mobilizes public support for private grief; it is public recognition that a community has lost one of its members. A wedding is a public declaration that two people make to each other, in the company of family and friends and in the presence of God, that they intend to become married. What makes the wedding ritual different from baptisms and funerals, however, is that it is a public event that celebrates a private promise. Sometimes the ways in which couples make public their private commitment continues the leaving-home process.

In a short story by John Hersey, Mrs. Bronson's thirty-eight-year-old son Gordon announced his intention to marry Beverly Zimmer by proposing a toast at the Thanksgiving dinner "to the two women I love the most in this world":

> Beverly spilled her wine. When that crisis had been averted by a generous dose of salt, Gordon's mother turned to Beverly and said, "Tell me more about my Gordon." "Well," Beverly said, "he's sort of muh-muh . . . m-my Gordon right now." "Ah," Mrs. Bronson said. "You stake a claim. Do you believe his intentions are honorable, as they used to say?" "Better ask him," Beverly said, without a trace of stammer. Gordon felt a stab of anger. His mother had humiliated him in front of Beverly and the family. Careful to control his voice, he said, "Beverly and I are going to be married." "And you chose to tell me this on Thanksgiving dinner?" Gordon's mother said. "I thought you'd be happy for me, Mother," Gordon said [Hersey, 1981, pp. 88–92].

For people such as Gordon who are still separating emotionally from their homes of origin, making public the private decision to marry often elicits previously unresolved fears and unrecognized parental claims. In such circumstances, the public announcement of engagement may first of all be an uncomfortable moment in the process of leaving home. Sometimes an offspring's fear of parental disapproval or rejection of their chosen partner elicits a private reactive decision about whom or when to marry. If the person we marry is significantly linked to leaving home, too much is at stake in the success or failure of the marriage.

Typically, the movement toward greater public participation as a couple unfolds without difficulty. There are several ritual moments or actions previous to the wedding that facilitate the transition from private decision to public reality. Deciding whom, when, and how to tell of the intent to marry is often chronologically the first major decision a couple must make as they move toward planning the wedding and fashioning a new narrative. Telling family and friends, announcing an engagement in the newspaper, wearing an engagement ring, publishing the marriage banns, engagement dinners, wedding showers, stag parties, rehearsal dinners, or receptions are all ritual moments in which the intent to marry is made public. The ritual gatherings preceding a wedding enable family, friends, and the couple to practice recognizing their new public status and form a new narrative. They also indicate how a couple is likely to embody the public-private polarity. It is important that these rituals reinforce the public side of marriage and the formation of a new family story that turns both outward and inward.

It is inevitable, however, that the move from private declarations of love to a public commitment to become married is linked to the process of leaving home. Both are significant acts of autonomy. When couples make public their freely chosen, private decision to marry, they are seeking support and a new role in the larger family story rather than critical examination. This support is more likely to come when parents have previously rehearsed and even embraced the parabolic aspects of parenting and have come to know over the years that their children are not their own. If, however, parents have mythic presumptions about children as heralds of familial continuity—presumptions often concretized in clear expectations about the kind of person their offspring should marry—this delicate pre-wedding dance may become a fierce struggle for independence.

Pastoral ministers can provide an important perspective in this process. The perspective arises from a minister's advocacy for the parabolic in weaving together the human and divine stories. In this advocacy, ministers support leaving for the sake of cleaving, separateness between the marital couple for the sake of being together, and the autonomy of the engaged couple for the sake of the community. The theological resource for interpreting this process is the Christian teaching on free will and grace. God has created people and set them free. God does not coerce us into returning the divine love showered on us. Rather, we are to love as we will. It is actually this freedom that makes the human response to God even more of a gracious gift. That same gift is evident in the love that draws people together in marriage. Understanding love as a gift will also help parents to love their children freely.

A wedding is an emotionally charged moment. Even those who have lived apart from their homes of origin or lived together as a couple are surprised by the intensity of the emotions surrounding the wedding. The situation is further complicated today by individual careers, separate furnishings, and personal pension plans that must be merged in a responsible and just way. It is like maneuvering between two boats in choppy waters. Few of us are sure-footed at such times. We need more rituals for becoming married that acknowledge the reality of contradiction and chaos in this time. In that sense, we need weddings—and the stories and rituals that prepare for such weddings—that are more parabolic than mythic.

Mythic and Parabolic Weddings

Planning the wedding is the second task for couples that simultaneously prepares them for marriage. If the wedding is to reflect their vision of marriage, then couples must be the principal actors in the planning process. The connection between weddings and marriage, which we regard as fundamental, has eroded recently because of the pressures of the "wedding industry" and the abdication of many churches to the wedding culture. Even when couples want to plan a wedding ritual that expresses their Christian faith, reflects the values in their relationship, and anticipates the kind of family they would like to become, their intent is challenged by many forces inside their families, church, and culture.

Judging from what is included in the pages of bridal magazines, weddings are not about marriage. Rather, they are about being beautiful, making a good video, fulfilling dreams, making an unforgettable impression "in deceptively rich satin," being queen (and king) for a day, fulfilling mother's dreams for the wedding she did not have, and maintaining or establishing the social status of the family. This desire to have a perfect wedding day is understandable, but it is dangerous. For a wedding to be picture perfect, it must be cut off from the very human stories that make it possible and necessary. The tendency to cover over flaws or blemishes with a fairy-tale wedding is a dangerous symbolic invitation to ignore those flaws not only in the ritual preparation but perhaps in the marriage itself. Even when we know that the person we are marrying is not without flaws, there is the longing for a perfect wedding. There may also be a hidden agenda of magical thinking—if the wedding can be a magic moment of perfection, then the hope is that perhaps the marriage will be perfect also.

Mythic Weddings and Bella Figura

In the city where we live, a major department store ran a two-page newspaper advertisement announcing the Annual Bridal Registry Fair. They made the following offer: "Let [the store] offer you our expert advice on planning your wedding. Our fabulous guest speakers can provide you with ideas for a picture-perfect wedding and the bridal consultants and our 'Life-Style Questionnaire' can help you define your living and entertaining style." Bridal magazines are filled with pictures of chic gowns, bridesmaid dresses, dazzling accessories, plans for the perfect reception, a thirty-minute workout for a better bridal body, twenty-five stress busters for the bride, and an occasional brief insert for grooms. Promoting picture-perfect weddings is big business.

o

From as early as she could remember, Priscilla dreamed of her wedding day. She had kept a notebook of ideas from bridal magazines she read and insisted on attending all the weddings to which her parents were invited. When Mark asked her to marry him, he agreed to be part of her dream of a perfect wedding. Both Mark and Priscilla lived at home until they were married. Neither had attended college. Mark drove a delivery truck, and Priscilla worked in a cookie store. For more than a year they planned all the details of that day. They would each have six attendants. Because Mark came from a large family, they would also have four flower girls and two ring bearers. For months before the wedding, Priscilla's mother spent her weekends sewing dresses for the attendants and the flower girls. She lined flower baskets with white linen and made silk pillows for the ring bearers.

The priest who had baptized Mark agreed to return and preside at the wedding. In order to keep the focus on the wedding itself, the couple decided not to have a Eucharist, even though Priscilla had just become a Roman Catholic. Friends of Mark and Priscilla performed three popular songs that had been significant in their courtship. Priscilla's father rented an antique car with a rumble seat to drive them from the wedding to the reception and dinner dance. Priscilla and Mark wanted the wedding to be a perfect celebration of their love that would begin a very special marriage. And, except for the baby that cried during the second solo and the botched video, Mark and Priscilla indeed had a perfect wedding day.

o

Even when the appearance is perfect, however, the reality is not. Mark and Priscilla now know that all too well. Since their marriage eight years ago, they have had two sons, two hunting dogs, a heavily mortgaged house, two jobs far from home at different shifts, loans on the mortgage, a bankruptcy, and a divorce. The children were cared for, but the marriage was not. Those who know Priscilla and Mark agree that they did not expect marriage to be work. They had no time to work on the marriage because they were too busy working to make money in order to continue the myth of a perfect wedding in their marriage. It is tempting, in this case, to make a connection between a magical, picture-perfect wedding and magical thinking about marriage that led to a divorce. They are certainly part of a cultural confusion about marriage that invites disillusionment by promoting perfect weddings.

A student of ours, Audrey Brosnan, has used the Italian phrase *bella figura* to describe this disjuncture between what appears to be the case and how things really are. The ritual may look good or give a good appearance, but the internal circumstances are far from perfect. Mythic images of marriage invite us to dream and invest in the future. Even though the divorce rate continues to be high, people do not plan a wedding and a marriage with the expectation that the latter will end in divorce. In that sense, we need mythic weddings. So we still marry, despite the obstacles, because of the mythic promise of marriage: all contradictions can be resolved or endured if only people love one another.

Sometimes, Brosnan has observed, *bella figura* is unavoidable. Things are not what they appear: the most cordial of wedding rituals occurs before the parents of the groom have accepted their new daughter-in-law; a father's funeral takes place before an estranged daughter can make peace with the dead parent; a child is baptized even though the parents are getting divorced. We go on making the ritual and telling the story without ever knowing for certain whether reconciliation will happen, injustice will be resolved, or the juncture between the outside and the inside will be bridged. We do the best we can to endure difficult circumstances and act imperfectly in the confidence that God will complete what we cannot.

Parabolic Marriage, Parabolic Weddings

Marriage is not just mythic; it is also a parabolic reality. To suggest that it is both implies that marriage, like every parable, embraces the ultimate contradiction: death. Though we think of marriage in terms of new life, this new life is not possible without innumerable losses. Choosing to marry one person sets limits on the freedom to love and touch and explore unknown paths. Letting go of familiar and trusted patterns from one's family of origin is itself loss. Marriage means the end of the romantic ideal that "only love will be spoken here" and the beginning of a willingness to fight fair. It means changing from "Daddy's little girl" or "Mommy's special boy" to an interdependent daughter or son. It means shifting the primary alliance from parent to spouse without severing the parental bond. Finally, it means learning to live with contradiction.

○

Although it was not especially apparent to everyone else, it was clear to their families: Ron and Sheila should not marry. True, they appeared compatible. Yet both sets of parents agreed that the marriage would not work. Sheila's family was definitely upper crust—a crust resulting more from hard work and determination than from breeding. Her father was a self-made man, and her mother a successful attorney. Ron's elderly father was a retired journalist from small-town Minnesota. His mother's life work was raising six children in spite of economic decline. Ron and Sheila acknowledged their familiar differences and their dissimilar career goals early in their relationship. Sheila did want to try her hand at business, and Ron had accepted a job at the county delinquent center. The wonder was that they allowed the preparation process and the marriage rites to acknowledge these differences.

It began with planning the rehearsal dinner. Ron talked his folks out of borrowing money for an upscale soiree and convinced his mother to make her county-famous lasagna for the lot of them. The pastor offered his house for the dinner, and the invitation was eagerly accepted as neutral ground. The wedding itself was a great deal like the rehearsal dinner. Without tuxedos or lace, Sheila and Ron greeted each guest at the church entrance. Their decision to welcome people as they came was the result of a conversation with the pastor about the opening greeting in the wedding ceremony and the importance of hospitality in their lives. There were plenty of flowers, but only for people, not for pews. There was no communion service: Ron's family was Lutheran, and Sheila's family wasn't much for church. The pastor said a few words. Ron's brother played classical guitar. Sheila and Ron each took a reading, spoke their vows with unnerving calm, and led their families in very touching bidding prayers. The sign of peace that everyone shared is remembered as the ritual high point of the service, even though there are no pictures to jog the memory. It was probably a moment, however, that would not have transferred well to Kodachrome.

o

Ron and Sheila's wedding was a parabolic rendition of the contradictory expectations from their origins. It set a tone for their life together that made it easier to deal with three disappointments in the first five years of marriage: a miscarriage, the failure of Sheila's business, and the sudden death of Ron's father from a heart attack. Obviously, their marriage did not endure because their wedding had been parabolic, any more than Mark and Priscilla's marriage failed because their wedding had been mythic. Even so, if the wedding is an invitation to a process filled with contradiction, there should be some indication in the ritual moment of the journey ahead.

In baptism we are initiated into the Jesus story and sealed with the mark of the cross. The marriage of Christians is a special entry into the death of Jesus that lies at the heart of the narrative taken up in his name. The death of Jesus is the ultimate parable that defines our faith and every invitation to new life. No wedding garment, seven-tiered cake, string quartet, or familial toast can ultimately distract those believers who say "I do" from the challenge of this parable. A Christian wedding is a parabolic event that celebrates the beginning of a marriage in the midst of many endings. For that reason, a wedding that is faithful to baptismal life in the mystery of the cross will ritualize both the sadness and joy that characterizes marriage.

Planning Weddings That Wed

From the Christian perspective, the wedding ceremony is ordinarily the only religious ritual in this transitional process from private promise to public reality. The rite of betrothal was once an important ritual moment for making public the intent to marry. This ancient ritual developed in part to prevent engagements from being secret. Until the Middle Ages, as Kenneth Stevenson (1987) has observed, the betrothal was a rite of separation that initiated a time of engagement. It was a public recognition of separation from one's home of origin that included a blessing by parents that was quite distinct from the celebration of marriage, which was a ritual of reincorporation into a new family. Since the Middle Ages, the previously separate events of betrothal and marital incorporation have been collapsed into the modern marriage ritual. It is not surprising, therefore, that the wedding ceremony, as a fusion of two separate rites, is expected to carry more emotional weight than it can endure.

While some religious traditions do have rituals for blessing the newly engaged, or publishing the banns of marriage, these rituals are often underused, ignored, or perfunctory at best. The wedding becomes the only public liturgy in which to weave together the stories of the couple with God's story for the sake of forming a new family narrative. The wedding is *the* liturgical moment in which two people declare publicly their intent to marry, receive the promise of a believing community to support them in that process, and accept the divine promise that their union will be a blessing. In the absence of a *marriage catechumenate,* which recognizes Christian marriage as a process rather than a single ritual moment, the wedding ceremony often stands as an isolated, sometimes mythic event unrelated to that which precedes or follows it.

Given this problem, what can be done to strengthen the wedding ritual as an effective rite of passage to marriage? First, the ritual needs to have enough *complexity* to enhance the transition from private to public and enough *honesty* to help couples move toward an authentic public declaration of their intent to be married. In addition to the public-private paradox, each of the other polarities we have explored in our stories and our rituals illuminates a dimension of the complexity of preparing for marriage today.

Second, the movement between private and public realities of marriage depends on authentic ritualizing and equally honest storytelling. We need to know the family stories in order to understand their claim and utilize their contributions. We also need to find ways of weaving the divine story into the ordinary making-public rituals that precede and follow the wedding. For example, announcing an engagement may be the occasion for parental blessing; receptions make it possible for the couple to practice hospitality; rehearsal dinners become an opportunity for reconciling alienated family members.

Third, linking narrative and ritual in the process of becoming married shifts the focus of pastoral pre-marriage preparation. We believe that preparing the wedding for the sake of the marriage is both a significant theological task and a extraordinary pastoral opportunity. Few aspects of pastoral ministry connect worship and pastoral care, God's story and the human story in the way that pre-wedding preparation does.

Finally, we will enhance the process of becoming married for the sake of strengthening marriage if we understand the wedding as a moment in a sacramental process, a communal act, and a proleptic reality. The wedding couple stand together before God in the midst of a community looking toward a uncertain future that beckons.

The Wedding As a Moment in a Sacramental Process

The wedding prayers for marriages in the Christian tradition invoke the presence of God and the promise of grace for two people who begin a marital journey together in faith. "Faithful Lord, source of love, pour down your grace on [name] and [name], that they may fulfill the vows they have made this day and reflect your steadfast love in their lifelong faithfulness to each other" (*Lutheran Book of Worship*, 1978, p. 204). Although most Christian traditions do not regard marriage as a sacrament, few would challenge the notion that marriage needs the grace of God to be a sign of God's love. God's covenant with humankind is like marriage, and human love is like God's covenant. It is a promise not to be broken. The wedding ritual is sacramental because it is a moment in a process that is itself sacramental. Couples need to understand that in the wedding they marry each other as they embark on the process of becoming married, which is itself sacramental. James and Evelyn Whitehead have developed this idea of sacramentality in their book *Marrying Well* in the following way: "The sacrament of marriage cannot be understood in terms of a single ritual which magically transforms us from two into one forever. The sacramental celebration of marriage in the rites and ceremonies of the Christian Church must be a celebration of a process already well under way and of a process which has still some considerable way to go" (Whitehead and Whitehead, 1983, p. 124).

In one sense, the sacramental nature of the marriage process continues the experience of baptism and the determination to live each day with the freedom to let go as a sign of faithfulness. "It is in marriage that couples are called to be Christ for one another, to minister to one another and ultimately where Christ bids them to 'come and die' for the life of their partner" (Trokan, 1996, p. 151). The danger of baptism becomes the dynamic of marriage when women and men learn the delicate rhythm of holding and letting so, of being close and being distant, of sacrificing desires and requesting for needs. The promise to be together for each other in marriage is not at the expense of a commitment to be in the world for the sake of others. We need our mythic dreams of unity in marriage to sustain us through the parabolic realities of becoming and being married. Understanding marriage in the light of baptism, however, helps us understand that living with the contradiction and paradox of marriage is simply another variation on the theme of Christian living.

The Wedding As a Communal Act

We understand the wedding to be a communal act in three ways. First of all, it is something that families do. Even when they have very little to do with the negotiating process, families are joined together at least in story in the wedding ritual. This corporate dimension of family stories needs to be reflected in the communal character of the wedding. If we understand the process of becoming married as a wedding of stories, then we must ask how those separate family stories participate in forming the new narrative.

Second, the wedding is something that a bride and groom do in the midst of a sustaining community. The ritual is the action of the couple and the assembly, even though the only thing that the gathered people have in common is a connection to the marrying couple.

Third, the wedding is a communal act because it presumes and requires the commitment of a community of the baptized to support the couple on their marriage journey. The African proverb "It takes a village to raise a child" is understood as common wisdom about the needs of children; but it also takes a village to make a marriage. If a couple does have an ongoing relationship with a believing community, that sustaining "village" is a continuing resource in the first years of marriage. Without extended families and mediating communities and villages, couples are forced to find sustenance from the vague emptiness at the center of human life. Studies indicate that people who marry where they are known by a community of family and friends are more likely to stay married than people who do not have such support. We need to work toward diminishing the gap between the private, personal family and the impersonal, public sphere by fostering mediating communities and villages that will sustain marriage in its private and public expressions.

The emphasis on the wedding as a communal act has implications for the rituals we plan and the stories we tell throughout the process of becoming married. Ideally, people becoming married are free to draw on the resources of family. Emotional separation from the homes of origin should not lead to disconnection between parents and children. We leave home so we can go home again. If children have left, and parents have let their children go, children and parents are able to honor the needs of each other in ways that make the wedding a communal act. Negotiations between the marrying couple and their parents need not be warfare. The wishes of parents should not dictate the wedding ritual, but neither should they be ignored altogether. Negotiations with parents in planning the wedding become part of the ritual process and indicate the values of the forming couple. If liturgy is the people's work, then intention and negotiation increase participation and understanding of the whole people in the wedding without taking primary responsibility away from the couple.

The community that gathers at the invitation of the marrying couple is there to celebrate and bless. Typically, there is much more opportunity for the community to do the former than the latter. Except for occasional applause at the conclusion of the vows, there is little official ritual opportunity for a community to say its blessing, to surround the couple with its joy, and to overwhelm the couple with words and symbols of God's blessing. It is important for the communities that surround a couple on their wedding day to speak their blessing and welcome the couple into the public arena, where people work together for a common good (Anderson and Fite, 1993).

Although we have emphasized the communal dimensions of the wedding, we recognize that marriage is always both a private and a public reality. We emphasize the public nature of marriage, however, for two reasons. First, drawing attention to the public nature of marriage is a way of countering the individualization and privatization of marriage and family living that is increasingly common in this society. Second, it is a way of clarifying the practice of living together before marriage that has confused this public/private dialectic. Even when it is generally known, living together remains a private commitment between two people that can be changed without any public accountability. The public dimension of the wedding ritual changes things in surprising ways for people who have previously lived together privately. What they thought would be the same about their relationship cannot ever be the same, because it is now and forever a public reality.

The Wedding As a Proleptic Reality

Becoming married is a gradual process that includes both leaving and cleaving. The wedding occurs in the midst of these twin processes, in which storytelling and ritual are woven together to assist couples in forming a marital bond that mirrors the myth and parable of Christian living. As with baptisms and funerals, the wedding ritual informs and is informed by the process in which it occurs. In the next chapter, we explore further the value of this polarity between moment and process for understanding the relationship between narrative and ritual at the time of death. While innumerable initiatory rites are available during the journey toward conversion, and the rituals for the sick, dying, and grieving offer a rich context for the narrative process, Christian marriage is essentially a single ritual act: the wedding.

The wedding is a ritual that bridges past stories from families of origin and from courtship with a future story that the couple will write together. It not only recapitulates the past; it anticipates the future. We need to know where we have come from. For that reason, discovering the legacies we bring from our families of origin to the process of forming a new family is a necessary dimension of wedding preparation. We also need to know where we are going. The Danish philosopher Søren Kierkegaard once observed that we understand our lives looking backward, but we live our lives looking forward. In the sense that the wedding looks to the future, it is a *proleptic event* that seeks through ritual to anticipate and embody the future toward which the couple intends to travel. From the Christian perspective, this anticipation of the future in order to transform the present is based on God's promise and belief in God's faithfulness.

Understanding the wedding as a proleptic moment shifts the focus of the couple from the past and the story of their origins and their relationship to each other to the future of their life together. This change of focus diminishes anxiety about becoming married by suggesting that the future is not stuck with the precedents of the past. A wedding is a hopeful moment in a complicated process when it can anticipate future possibilities in the present. One of the purposes of telling family stories as preparation for marriage is to acknowledge their power to shape our future. Understanding the wedding as a proleptic moment exposes the power of the future to pull us forward alongside the claims of the past. To be alive is to have a future. We die whenever we lose the future to the claims of the past, even if those claims are wonderful and cherished traditions from our families of origin.

If the wedding is a proleptic moment in the way we have been describing it, then it is important to invite couples to imagine a future that will draw them forward. As part of planning the wedding, individuals and couples anticipating a life together might be invited to bring a story, song, film plot, saying, or poem from any source that conveys something about their hope for the family they are beginning to form. The aim of this exercise is to develop an image that anticipates the kind of family they would like to become. Developing an image that anticipates the kind of family the marrying couple would like to become is a way of linking the stories from families of origin and the couple's own story with the Christian story.

Wedding the Human and the Divine

When Dan and Carmel met the minister to plan the wedding service, Dan's image of marriage revolved around the camper he already owned. He liked to camp and fish and hunt and hoped that Carmel would go along. It was clear that Dan enjoyed her company even if she didn't particularly like to do what he did. Carmel had never been camping but was willing to try in order to please Dan whom she loved very much. Because Carmel was fearful of the future and because they were both quite shy, the conversations took time to unfold.

Carmel's family story was littered with abandonment and divorce. She worried all the time that she would "run out of love." She was fearful of having children because she did not have enough love. When asked if she had a favorite Bible story, she could only remember about Jesus feeding five thousand people and having leftovers. She had little experience of leftovers. In planning their wedding, the pastor suggested they make the story of Jesus feeding the five thousand [Matt. 14:13–21] the focal point of lessons and prayers. Although she remained fearful, Carmel was able to entertain the possibility that maybe her life with Dan would be one of God's miracles with more than enough left over.

o

Carmel's fearfulness about not having enough love was diminished some-what by the Gospel story of loaves and leftovers and God's promise that there will be more than enough. Even though the images people start with may be vague and unformed, they are part of their past and shape their future life together. The pastoral task is to take these stories, from what-ever source, and link them with the divine narrative, with stories from the Christian tradition, in order that the couple might envision their new future in God. We begin with the human story, making overt the covert images or hidden expectations and unspoken values each couple brings to becoming married. It is a delicate and wonderful pastoral task to take seriously where people begin while directing them toward an image that reflects a new life together in God.

The marriage ritual is a nonthreatening place for a couple to begin to explore the relationship between the Jesus story and their life together, because it focuses on an objective liturgy and not on the couple's faith. It provides a useful framework for reflection on the future of their marriage. Since the marriage rite consists of a series of prayers, readings, and bless-ings interspersed with musical interludes and symbolic gestures, the task of planning the ritual could simply focus on selecting and arranging these various elements. If, however, our aim is to foster "weddings that wed," preparing for the ritual is more like theological reflection than logistical planning. As they consider various parts of the wedding ceremony, the couple is invited to search for the Jesus story in their own narratives of faith in order to enhance their practice of living with contradictions.

Marriage is a wedding of stories. For that reason, storytelling is a cen-tral part of the process of becoming married. Preparation for marriage not only invites couples to tell stories from their families of origins and the story of their courtship; it invites couples into the Christian story. They are encouraged to tell stories from both their relationship and their faith perspective in order to fashion symbols and identify stories from the Christian tradition that reflect and then challenge their vision of being a family of faith. Whatever image of family living from the divine narrative is chosen, however, we need to keep the balance between myth and para-ble. Because the reality of marriage is both mythic and parabolic, the rit-uals that frame the process of becoming married must keep alive that paradox. Yet nowhere is the paradox of myth and parable more difficult or more necessary to establish and maintain than in planning a wedding as preparation for marriage.

6

ENCOUNTERING DEATH

The great mystery of death and the grief and sorrow that attend it require rituals of storytelling and remembering.

○

After the death of her second husband, Mrs. Pratt moved in with her only daughter, Alice, and Alice's family. They had a complicated relationship, Alice and her mother. Mrs. Pratt was demanding, and Alice was stubborn. About two years after she moved in with her daughter, Mrs. Pratt was diagnosed with an inoperable brain tumor. Alice and her mother seldom talked about the illness or her impending death. Moreover, Alice resisted any suggestion to discontinue extraordinary measures to keep her mother alive.

During the last six weeks of her life, Mrs. Pratt was in and out of a coma. On an occasion when her mother was not particularly alert, Alice asked her pastor to perform the service of commendation for the dying. Although Alice was with her mother when she died, they never said good-bye. The conspiracy of silence that governed her mother's dying made it difficult for Alice to begin her own grieving. When Alice finally tried to remember her mother, she did not know enough of her mother's story to make a meaningful memory. The silence and secrecy of her mother's dying had disrupted the natural flow of narrative from mother to daughter.

○

THIS STORY HIGHLIGHTS several themes that connect story and ritual for both dying and grieving persons. Without anyone to hear her story, Mrs. Pratt was isolated for the last chapter of her story. She could not give her final and perhaps best gift, the narrative of her life, because no one was listening; nor did she have any assurance she would be remembered after her death. Without people to listen to her story, it was difficult for Mrs. Pratt to bring closure to her life. Even the ritual moment, which might have enabled Mrs. Pratt to remember her story in a faith context, contributed to a final abandonment. And without hearing her mother's story, it was harder for Alice after her mother's death to invoke the kind of memory that could resolve her own grieving.

Dying and grieving are related but different processes with distinct purposes. The one who is dying has a single focus: letting go of valued objects and loved relationships to get ready to die. The friends and family of the dying have a double task: helping someone they love live as fully as possible until death, while grieving together their common losses. When death occurs, those who grieve need to let go of what has been lost in order to live again. Dying is enhanced when the dying person has someone to hear her or his story. The process of grieving is easier when the survivors participated in the dying person's final narrative chapter. Either way, however, either in dying or grieving, narrative is crucial.

Autobiography and Biography

The narrative form differs between the dying and those who grieve. A dying person's story is more like autobiography, while the griever's tale resembles biography. In autobiography, the author or narrator is also the subject. The narratives we fashion throughout our lives have an autobiographical character. We tell our personal stories from the inside out to make sense of our world. What matters is that each of us has the freedom and authority to tell our story our way, even though we are never the only author. The autobiographical form is particularly important for those who are dying because it validates their freedom to conclude their own story. Unfortunately, some individuals are not free to claim authorship of their own story, even when death is near. Those who are dying need to know that it is never too late to claim authorship of their own story.

Stories told by the dying are privileged acts of self-interpretation. They may simply communicate the experience of dying, or they may be the final rendition of a personal narrative—the story we hope will continue to be told after we have died. In either case, they are stories told in the first person by people who have a particular awareness of their mortality. Telling our story is not only a gift to those we love; it is an immortalizing act, narrating the way we want to be remembered. In order to contribute to the way we are remembered, we need to tell our story. Telling our story is also a final intentional act. Even when physical constraints restrict our personal freedom, when medical procedures isolate us from the community, or when survivors are tempted to close our story prematurely, we can still fashion a life narrative.

Biography reverses this pattern. It is an attempt to get inside the life of another by observation and reflection. After a death occurs, the work of grievers is to fashion a biography. They begin to tell the story of a life from the outside in. Like a biographer, those who mourn seek to locate a life in its context and explore its wider significance. The story we tell about ourselves is only one perspective on a life. Others will discover dimensions of our lives we cannot see. A good biography does not ignore autobiographical accounts, but it is not bound by them. If a dying individual's review of life is honest, complete, and accessible, it is, however, easier to construct an authentic memory that facilitates mourning.

The reciprocity between autobiography and biography is at the center of Frederick Buechner's novel, *Godric*, about an earthy twelfth-century hermit saint by the same name. Godric contends with Reginald, his appointed biographer, to tell the truth about his life and is forever correcting Reginald's "impulse to blessedness" where there is none. At one point in his struggle to ensure that Reginald tells an honest tale, Godric makes this observation about his biographer: "Thus like a child that fashions poppets out of muck, [this] monk makes saints of flesh and blood" (Buechner, 1981, p. 88). Making saints of flesh and blood is a griever's temptation. After the eulogy for her elderly father, one of our friends whispered to her sister: "Check the casket and see if it's dad. It sounds like somebody else." Hearing the dying person's own version of his or her life story is a corrective against people such as Reginald who want to make saints in their grief.

The aim of this chapter is to explore the significance of storytelling and ritualizing for those who are dying and those who grieve. Rituals not only create a hospitable context for those who are dying and grieving; they enhance telling the kind of story that becomes a life-affirming memory. Storytelling, for the sake of making a memory, is not only the central work of grieving; it is the way each of us closes the story of a life. We are indebted to Larry Churchill for suggesting that stories are both logically prior to and pastorally more appropriate than the category of "stages" for attending to the dying process. "It is morally incumbent upon those who care for the dying to reduce their reliance upon stages and instead listen to stories" (Churchill, 1979, p. 39). Stories come before stages because it is how we remember.

For both the dying and the grieving, remembering our stories evokes a mixture of emotions. We are alternately embarrassed, sad, and delighted by what we remember. Feelings of shame or fear of disclosure sometimes keep the dying from recounting a life. Those who grieve are often put off by the sadness of remembering. As a result, they resist doing their most important work: making a memory of stories. This grieving work is made easier and deepened if the stories the dying tell at the end of a life are available to the survivors for their grieving work.

After her brother John died from AIDS, Susan Ford Wiltshire wrote the narrative of his life, titled *Seasons of Grief and Grace* (1994). It is John's story, told through the eyes of a sister who was his best friend. John's voice is heard through the letters he wrote to friends and family or the introductions he prepared for the speakers at his memorial. Wiltshire is correct when she observes that "the stories of those we love keep getting written, even after the loved one has died" (p. 181). Death is not the end of the story. Autobiography turns to biography in the work of grieving. Moreover, if we tell a story, we might get one in return.

Memories are the place of consolation. It is also where we can get stuck in our grief when we resist recalling the whole story. In order to find healing in our grieving, we need to remember where the wounds hurt most. The possibility of transforming painful memories into occasions for consolation is increased when they are understood in the light of the Jesus narrative. The embrace of death by Jesus as the completion of his life became one of the stories his disciples remembered in their grieving. For Jesus and for us, the end of life is a new beginning in the memory of God and in the memory of those we loved and who loved us.

This experience of transformation also depends on respecting the paradoxical connection between myth and parable in our narratives at the time of death. Without such a paradox, the temptation for those who mourn is to create a false or superficial story. Keeping a balance between myth and parable in the stories of grief is also enhanced by appropriating the autobiography of the deceased as part of the biography we write through the process of grieving.

Not Just the End of the Story

Story and ritual for both the dying and the grieving are potentially inauthentic when the reality of death is ignored. Care of the dying and the work of grieving remain unfulfilled if death is denied. Margaret Mead once acknowledged that, though she knew societies where birth, puberty, or marriage were treated casually, she knew of no society for whom death is not a critical event (Mead, 1973). Whether we regard death as enemy or friend, as obliteration or transition, as a fact of being human or the consequence of sin, it is still an end. Death is personally critical because it is the ultimate expression of human finitude. It is also a significant social reality because it severs emotional bonds, disrupts human community, and creates moments of discontinuity that destabilize families and other human systems. Mead is correct: death is a terrible personal reality and a significant social event. Our response to death is one mark of maturity. And yet when the subject is death, words die. We are mute before a life ending that is equally unavoidable and mysterious. And because we are mute, it is a struggle to tell our story at the end.

Death, whenever or however it occurs, is both a problem and a mystery. Whether persons have any agency about the moment of death is one of death's mysteries. We often experience death like a thief in the night, a car suddenly crossing into our lane, or a stray bullet from gang warfare: something that comes from outside us suddenly to snatch life away. In common speech, we may say that "death took" Aunt Helen, as if death had independent agency to invade or destroy. Death is like a thief, according to theologian Karl Rahner (1961), but death is also something we do. It is therefore as important to say that an individual died as it is to say that death "took" someone. Like the stories we tell about our birth, stories of dying reflect that it is a human act. Dying is something I do. The following story illustrates the mystery of human agency at the time of dying.

o

It was Christmas day. I had gone to see an older woman from the church who was in a nursing home. She had once been a vital, lively person, but on this day, she lay still in her bed, with her eyes closed, covered with a blanket to her chin. I had brought some food, but she did not want to eat. I felt hopeless as I sat beside her in silence. Because she was also very hard of hearing, I shouted in her ear to ask if she wanted to receive the Lord's Supper. "Yes," she said. I was not sure how to shout the service with five other old and dying persons in her room. Quite by impulse, I gave her the service to read. She put on her glasses and read the entire service, not just silently for herself but very loudly so everyone could hear. Her bed was her pulpit. The other women joined in. Her old face, which moments before had seemed dead, was radiant. After communion, she ate some soup, and I took my leave, saying I would see her in a day or so. "I doubt it," she said. "It's time for me to go home." That night she went to sleep and never woke up.

o

Karl Rahner articulates his paradoxical view of death in this way: "This simultaneity of fulfillment and emptiness, of actively achieved and passively suffered end, of full self-possession and of being completely dispossessed of self, may, for the moment, be taken as a correct description of the phenomenon we call death" (Rahner, 1961, p. 40). Respecting this paradoxical mystery is an essential part of story and ritual both for those who are dying and for the communities that survive them.

Death is a mystery to be experienced, but it is also a problem to be solved. Those who believe that more life is better life usually understand death as a problem. The definition of death is also a problem. After a person has been comatose or kept alive artificially for some time, there is frequently common acceptance among family and friends that an individual's story has ended. However, accepting the reality that a person is irreversibly dying is a more difficult decision to make. Even though it is a difficult decision to make, determining that an individual is irreversibly dying is necessary because it has consequences for care, for ritual making, and storytelling. Aggressive treatment is no longer called for because it will not change the outcome. Care, not cure, is the focus. The ritual focus shifts from healing to preparation for death. It is also time to tell the last stories, give the final blessings, or seek the reconciliation that has been avoided.

Care of the dying depends in part on making this difficult determination that an individual is *irreversibly dying*. A person is understood to be dying irreversibly when he or she is not likely to recover or continue living for any length of time, when a serious or even life-threatening illness has progressed beyond repair. If it cannot be determined that an individual is irreversibly ill and moving toward death, confusion or denial may lead to false hopes, insistence on restorative treatment, prolonged hospitalization, the search for a life-saving cure, dependent behavior, and a deterioration of relationships between family and medical caregivers.

If the reality of impending death is denied, the care of dying people is diminished. Only at the point when the inevitability of death is acknowledged do continuity of care and greater independence within the limits of declining resources become the priorities. It is beneficial, therefore, if everyone involved can acknowledge that an individual is irreversibly dying. It is equally important for the sake of care if everyone agrees that the irreversibly dying person is still a living person until death occurs.

How one dies and the complications surrounding a death significantly influence the course of grieving. If death is regarded as a blessing at the end of a lingering, painful illness or at the conclusion of a long life, the grieving is often less intense than if death occurs suddenly and without warning in the midst of life. When death is unexpected, the initial grief is intense and the work of making a memory protracted because they must occur without the benefit of a dying individual's closing reflections. When dying happens over time, there is at least the opportunity for the dying one to fashion a personal closure to her or his story. While the complexity of a death undoubtedly does affect grieving and our ministry with grievers, the focus of this chapter is on narrative and ritual before and after death.

The processes of dying and grieving are generously punctuated by rituals. These rituals recite the divine narrative and mediate the promise of God's presence in the midst of death and grief. We also know that remembering and telling stories about the deceased is an essential part of healing our sorrow. It is easier, we believe, for the surviving family and friends to make a memory when grievers have heard the stories of the deceased in his or her own words. The benefit of storytelling for the one who is dying is also real. Storytelling and the rituals that enhance it help the one who is dying to endure suffering and sustain faith by weaving together the human and divine narratives into a single web. For that reason, it is important that opportunities for human storytelling to be structured into the patterns of care for the dying.

Storytelling for the Irreversibly Dying

Beyond the anguish of pain and our anxiety about death as an experience of the unknown, there are three common fears that dying people experience: the fear of incompleteness; the dread of abandonment or isolation; and the terror of letting go and losing control. Each of these fears challenges the narratives we have woven to make sense of our experience in the world. When we are dying, our personal, sometimes private belief system becomes the primary lens through which we interpret our experience. If we believe God causes all deaths to occur, we will look for a reason why our particular death benefits God. As an example, a man who owned a bowling alley who was irreversibly dying with malignant melanoma declared his death to be God's doing because "maybe He needs me up there to run the bowling alley to make thunder." This dying man used his understanding of God's need for a bowler to make sense of his experience. Although we may not agree with his interpretation, he is not alone in weaving the human and the divine at the moment of dying in order to make sense of something unexpected and disorderly and to diminish the terror lurking in the shadows of our lives.

The Fear of Incompleteness

It has been said that dying persons fear incompleteness more than death. Behind the bargaining stage in Kübler-Ross's (1969) schema of dying is the desire for more time to do one more thing, attend one more wedding, finish one more task. Ted Rosenthal, whose dying was captured on film and expressed in a collection of poetry titled *How Could I Not Be Among You?* made this observation: "I don't think people are afraid of death. What they are afraid of is the incompleteness of their life" (Rosenthal, 1973, p. 45). If the dying person fears incompleteness, then the awareness that there may not be enough time to finish the story becomes a crisis. We bargain for more time on the assumption that we will be ready to die if only we have an extension to complete our life story.

o

Francisca knew she was dying. When she spoke of her six-year struggle with cancer, she would sigh and say, "*Lo que Dios quiere* (whatever God wants), but I'm not ready. I still have work to do." When, however, Francisca was told she had less than a month to live, she mobilized her failing energies for one last trip to Mexico. Before she died, Francisca was determined to be reconciled with a daughter she had dismissed years ago. When that reconciliation was accomplished, she died in peace as her family prayed the liturgy around her. The reconciliation was short-lived, however. Planning her funeral erupted into a feud between insiders and outsiders in the family and disrupted the peace Francisca had worked to achieve before her death.

o

Most of us are not as fortunate as Francisca. Death is an unwelcome intruder that disrupts our plans and dissolves our dreams unexpectedly in the midst of things. Dying is not usually the perfect ending to a finely woven tale but the unwelcome rupture of the middle of the story.

When we insist on a mythic narrative at the end of life, we either deny the impending reality of death or overlook the incompleteness of a life. Leading dying persons into parabolic thinking, however, enables them to tell their story in all its finitude. The story may be unfinished, but we die just the same. Sometimes what we complete before death is disregarded or undermined, as in Francisca's story, by those who mourn. In any event, narrating the parable is an act of dying before we are finished with the story, of concluding the story we are telling before the story ends at death. Thus the parable teller becomes the parable.

When we see in review that the whole of one's life has been meaningless or a huge deception, the pain of the illness is magnified by the phoniness or incompleteness of our life. In Leo Tolstoy's insightful novel about dying, *The Death of Ivan Illich,* the central character, Ivan, comes to the end of his life and wonders if it has been all wrong.

> "But if that is the case," he asked himself, "and I am taking leave of life with the awareness that I squandered all I was given and have no possibility of rectifying matters—then what?"
>
> He began to review his whole life in an entirely different manner. . . . In them [his family] he saw himself, all he had lived by, saw clearly that all this was not the real thing but a dreadful, enormous deception that shut out both life and death. This awareness intensified his physical sufferings, magnified them tenfold [Tolstoy, (1886) 1981, p. 128].

Most of us are aware, as Ivan Illich was, that telling our story will not eliminate the fear of incompleteness. Even so, rounding off our story before we die enables us to see it as a whole and move with integrity toward the end of the journey. For that reason alone, it is important that dying persons be encouraged to rehearse the past. Even when there are things we have done that we wish to hide, or remembrances of things past that we are ashamed of, or old wounds that still hurt, or damaged relationships unreconciled, it is never too late until death occurs to redeem our story. Although he loathed his life and was ashamed of its shallowness, when Ivan Illich received a kiss from his son, he felt that "though his life had not been what it should have been, this could still be rectified" (p. 155).

The framework of our personal narrative becomes clearer in the final editing because we see the dominant threads of a life better in retrospect. The patterns in human life, like grammar, organize chaos, structure diversity, and order differences. There is, of course, always room for improvisation and spontaneity, even in the rehearsal of a life. When we observe the provident presence of God in our lives, improvisation finds meaning in the conviction that all things, even untimely death, work together for a larger good than we could have imagined beforehand. Our life story, even when we see it as an incomplete whole, is the gift we give to those who survive us. We are empowered to give that gift by the promise that God does not judge our lives by finite completeness. Our story matters, even if it is incomplete, because after our death it still belongs to the stories of God.

The Dread of Abandonment

There is nothing more crushing for a dying person than to be isolated or abandoned. As a result, many societies of the world take elaborate measures to ensure that no one dies alone. Someone is always present to attend to their needs and hear their last words. In this society, however, the dread of abandonment is regularly reinforced by the way in which dying persons are isolated from families and friends by technology and by emotional withdrawal. Telling our stories to one another is essential to diminish barriers, overcome fears, and establish bonds. When our story is kept secret or our living is defined by secrets, we impoverish those we love and isolate ourselves.

The metaphor of autobiography is particularly appropriate for the dying experience because it emphasizes the way telling and hearing stories challenges the isolation that often accompanies the journey toward death. Mrs. Pratt, whose story was told at the beginning of this chapter, was abandoned because her daughter did not want to hear her story. Sometimes, however, the opposite is the case: dying persons are reluctant to tell stories that family members are eager to hear. Telling our stories when people important to us are listening diminishes isolation and modifies the inevitable loneliness of dying. The full account of a life may, in fact, be the dying person's most gracious legacy to those who survive. For that reason alone, family and friends of the dying need to be attentive to storytelling at the end.

○

Americo was a homebound man living alone in West Virginia. The day before I tried to visit him at home, he had been taken to the hospital. When I finally met him in intensive care, he was a frightened old man hooked up to many machines and monitors. He asked for communion. When we said the Lord's Prayer, I was struck with his voice, uncertain, longing, and prayerful. He told me about his wife, who was dead, and his sons. For some reason, I asked Americo if his wife was his first girlfriend. His face lit up immediately, and he told me about a girlfriend he had to leave behind in Italy when he first came to America. With affection undiminished by years, Americo talked about all the things they used to do together as youths in Italy. When the conversation ended, I promised to visit again the next day. It was then I learned that Americo had died a few hours after my visit. In the visit, I did not know what Americo knew: that he was getting ready to die. His sons were so happy that their father had communion before he died. I never told them about the girlfriend.

○

America's loneliness was diminished in the telling of his story. His own dread of abandonment reminded him of another abandonment story from his life. It was almost as if Americo was free to die once his narrative was complete. His sons, however, did not hear the last story their father told. They were happy to know that he had received communion. They did not ask about his last words, and the pastor did not tell.

The pastor's action reminds us how important it is to ask the dying if their stories can be told. When stories of the dying are not told to family and friends, the grievers' remembrance is impoverished. Because of the young pastor's visit, the sons will tell a story about Americo's death rather than a story from his life. Dying stories are indeed an important part of a family's legacy that is handed on to succeeding generations, but they are seldom enough to convey the sense of a person. Americo's grandchildren would not know all they could about their grandfather because they did not hear his last story.

The Terror of Losing Control

The dying person has a singular task: to get ready to die. For some people, that task will include sorting out relationships with those who will survive, making sure that things are properly distributed or cared for, saying good-bye to family and friends and favorite activities. The dying one recalls his or her life in order to prepare to let it go. We also give away things that we value to people we love in order to get ready to die. That kind of activity reinforces bonds of affection, increases a sense of continuity with the future, and is a constructive alternative that counters the terror of losing control.

Those who hold on to people and things embody their fear of death and magnify the pain of letting go by holding on more tightly to what they have. Dying is unavoidably an experience of the loss of control. Letting go of valued objects or old hostilities and saying good-bye to the persons we love or wished we loved is a painful experience of discontinuity. Some people hold on to everything they can, either because the pain of letting go is so great or because the worth of their lives has been defined by what they possess. In the process of reviewing our life to let it go, we may also make amends for old hurts, identify and let go of regrets, acknowledge unresolved relationships, and tie up loose ends from the journey.

Caregivers, family, and friends may help the dying person rehearse his or her life, so that the formulation of the story corresponds to the community's version of the narrative, but the dying one must tell the story.

The one who is dying may, however, choose to narrate a life without much reference to honesty or authenticity. While that fabrication will make it more difficult for survivors to deal with their grief, the privilege of self-interpretation holds. The narrative of a life is inside the narrator. Those who care for and watch with the dying need to respect the dying person's story without judgment or correction. That is the dying person's privilege of self-interpretation.

○

The relationship between Deborah and her father had been stormy since her adolescence. Even after she was an adult with a family of her own, Deborah seemed to be trapped in a contest with her father in which she was always the loser. From her childhood, Deborah's father had been able to deflect her anger at him back to her and make it her fault. During his long process of dying, Deborah tried to speak with her father to resolve this anger before he died. Her mother always interfered to protect a dying father from his daughter's rage. When he died without the reconciliation taking place, Deborah's husband promised to slip a letter to her father under his pillow in the casket. It said "Dear Dad, I am sorry I have disappointed you. I will try to do better after you are dead. Love, Deborah."

○

Deborah's story is all too common. Even if those who are dying can let go, family may not. Our best efforts at telling the story and even our most ingenious ritualizing may fail to bring healing to a relationship or closure to parental claims. This time the story is inside the griever. Deborah's grief for her father will be complicated by her inability to find release from his claim on her life, even from his casket.

Pastoral ministry with the dying and the family and friends who watch with them is a delicate balance between supporting people in their desire to die as they have lived, even when that isolates them from the love of friends and family, and advocating for a transforming experience of community at the end of life. Although we believe that it is beneficial for the mourners to have heard the story of the deceased "in their own voice" before death, it is too burdensome for some who are dying to insist that they speak honestly for the sake of the survivors. Moreover, we are not saved by a good death. We will need to be respectful of a desire to die privately while advocating with dying persons or their families for a ritual framework in which people can tell their story for the sake of closure.

Ritualizing the Dying Story

Rituals for the sick and for the dying in most Christian traditions follow the same distinction we have already outlined between being seriously ill and irreversibly dying. We expect people who are sick to desire health, obtain competent help to regain health, and cooperate with treatment prescribed for the sake of healing. The prayers we pray and the rituals we enact with the seriously sick seek healing and promote the restoration to health. The Christian church has traditionally responded to sick persons through ritual actions that promise the special help of God's grace to diminish isolation, strengthen a flagging spirit, and support those whose faith has weakened. For Protestants, the rituals for healing are often informal, as caregivers surround the sick one with biblical stories of God's promised care and the prayers of God's people.

In Roman Catholic practice, those whose health is impaired by sickness or old age receive the sacrament of the Anointing of the Sick. Its aim is to support those who struggle against illness and continue the healing work of Christ through the ritual act of anointing. In order to diminish the isolation of the sick and foster the community's care, "the sacrament of the sick should be celebrated with the members of the family and other representatives of the Christian Community whenever this is possible" (United States Catholic Conference, 1983, paragraph 99). Even when the rituals of care for the sick are more informal and spontaneous the same elements are evident: the promise of divine presence mediated through symbolic actions and the presence of caring persons that seeks to sustain people in their suffering.

When it is determined that an individual is irreversibly dying, there is a special ritual in the Roman Catholic tradition called Viaticum. It is food for the dying person's journey through death toward God. Because it presumes that an individual is now irreversibly dying, Viaticum makes a new moment of honest reflection possible for everyone, including the one who is dying. It is ritual transition into a time when there is new urgency for remembering and for gentle reconciling care. Within the covenant of baptism, the dying person is invited to remember at the close of a life how the faith journey began.

There is also a communal emphasis consistent with the public character of the church's rituals. Viaticum should be celebrated when possible "while the dying person is still able to take part and respond" (United States Catholic Conference, 1983, paragraph 179). In other Christian traditions, prayers for the "commendation of the dying" seek to effect similar goals at the point of death.

One of the distinctive features of Viaticum is the renewal of baptismal vows by the dying person. This is an important component of any religious ritual for the dying, because it connects us with our spiritual beginning. The covenant of baptism, which we have already said was a dangerous beginning ritual for the spiritual journey, is now a safe context for rehearsing the whole narrative. Our baptism is a significant thread whenever we weave together the human and the divine in the moments of dying. When the dying person is able, and the surrounding community is willing, honest conversation about life and death can occur as the story draws to a close.

There has often been a separation between the divine and human in the stories we invite the dying to tell that is both unfortunate and artificial. Sometimes spontaneous prayers with a dying patient bridge this gap. Prayer to God often becomes a form of indirect speech in which stories are told, confessions made, and final words of instruction or blessing are given. These are moments of intimacy without exposure in which patients such as Americo tell yet untold stories of the past. Ordinarily, however, Christian rituals for the seriously ill or dying have not invited the rehearsal of a life or been the occasion in which we stitch together the stories of our lives. Our ministry with dying persons should foster the natural connection between storytelling and ritualizing at the time of death. We need to infuse traditional Christian rites for the dying with human stories at the same time we discover the religious dimension of ordinary dying rituals.

The Litany of "Lasts"

Once it has been acknowledged that a person is irreversibly dying, the dying individual and families or friends begin to make a special moment of the last time something happens. The last dinner out, the last lovemaking, the last time a person can leave the bedroom or the bed, the last meal with food to chew, and so on. While it may seen to some a morbid focus, each "last" provides a time for recollection and an invitation to mourn. Marking the litany of "lasts" is also another way of continuing to be an agent in giving up one's life.

○

Sam loved the lake house. He and Shirley bought the land with a shack on it when they were newly married. Over the years, the lake property was a prized getaway. In early years, they would camp there. When the children were born, Sam bought a trailer that housed Shirley and the kids while he slept in the tent. On their fifteenth wedding anniversary, they broke ground for the modest A-frame that became "the house." It would be where they would live when Sam retired. Two years before his retirement, Sam was diagnosed with lung cancer. They went to "the house" as often as they could. It was where they made love for the last time, where he went fishing for the last time, where Sam said good-bye to his grandchildren, and where they had his last Fourth of July picnic for friends and relatives. He was able to convince his doctor to let him out of the hospital for one last visit on Labor Day weekend. Sunday night, he remained out on his lawn chair long past dark, while Shirley cleaned up the kitchen. When she came to take him to bed, Sam was dead.

○

Not every life ends as peacefully as Sam's. We do not all get to end our lives just the way we want to, as Sam did. Sometimes the last days are more ambiguous, as the dying person seeks to control the future through the gifts that are given or promises extracted. Unmarried adult children who promise a dying parent to care for the surviving parent or a wife who promises a dying husband never to marry again fundamentally alter their future in response to the dying of a loved one. The litany of "lasts" is often a highly charged emotional time for the dying one and for family and friends. This may mean that it is important to accept the last gifts without accepting the claims that go with them.

In the process of bringing closure to a life, the dying person needs to say many good-byes. What we thought was the final good-bye is seldom the last because the moment of death remains a mystery. Sometimes the farewell cannot be said until after the person has died. Because dying takes place inside the soul of a person, dying people may distance themselves before saying good-bye, sometimes with no intention to do so or no control over the process. Freedom to ritualize the litany of "lasts" at least provides a structural framework that keeps the dying person connected to those who wait with them until they die. It also provides a context for mourning. In a book on *Letting Go: Morrie's Reflections on Living While Dying*, Morrie Schwartz makes the following observations that link the litany of "lasts" with the grief of letting go: "Grieving never ends with one outpouring. Let yourself feel the depth of your tears, your sense of loss, the pain, the emptiness that you feel because of it. Don't be afraid to come back to it as many times as you need to. . . . After going through this kind of mourning, it's so much easier to face the day, so much easier to do the things I have to do with my family and friends, to be loving and ready for whatever comes" (Schwartz, 1996, pp. 31, 33).

The paradox of the individual and communal that begins in the birth of a story continues to the end of life. Although we are not the only author of our life story, it is ours to tell. It is crucial that we honor the freedom to tell our own story until it is no longer possible. Death by illness or old age gradually robs us of our independent, self-sufficient, functioning center. This unity of the whole self is what death, by definition, asks us to surrender. The experience of baptism, of daily dying and rising again, of losing life in order to find it, is lifelong preparation for dying. Practicing the art of the baptismal life does not diminish the darkness of dying nor eliminate the unspeakable terror of death. But daily baptism does teach one thing in preparation for dying: we will find life by letting go.

A Biography Colored by Grief

Autobiography ends and biography begins when someone dies. The task of those who grieve the death of someone they love is to tell the story as fully and as honestly as possible in order to make a memory. We piece a life together from bits and fragments, strong memories of the recent past, faint recollections of the distant past, stories that fashion a biographical narrative of someone we loved. Grieving is therefore delicate work, honoring the dying story, gathering up a life in order to weave a narrative durable enough to be a memory, respecting secrets, recognizing that different family members will have different responses to the same death. Grieving is more than collecting memories; it is an interpretive process colored by loss.

The first stories told by grievers do not provide a definitive interpretation of the life of the deceased. They are rather scattered recollections of the deceased that eventually will be revised again and again through the process of forming a narrative. Sometimes it is difficult to get past the present moment because images of the cause of death or the process of dying are so intense. When the death is unexpected, our remembering is also clouded by the shock of grief. Family members who mourn may need to move past recent years of dementia or Alzheimer's disease to have a more accurate remembrance of a person they knew long ago, as the following story suggests.

o

Bernice died recently at age ninety-two after over fifteen years of dementia. She had been well taken care of during that time, but she did not seem to know her sons whenever they visited her. She had attended her own daughter's funeral, but no one knew whether her tears were for her daughter. After her death, her surviving children opened a letter written before the onset of her dementia giving instructions about her funeral and burial in the clear, straightforward manner they remembered about their mother. They heard her familiar voice again. The letter triggered a wonderful process of remembering the mother they once knew that might not have happened had not her own voice appeared at her death. The letter was a voice they had not heard for fifteen years and had almost forgotten.

○

Making a memory is easier if those who mourn have heard the dying person's own version of her or his life. Certainly we will amplify the dying person's autobiographical account by locating its context or adding overlooked details or modifying misunderstandings or by introducing a different interpretation altogether. Still others will correct misinformation or give a more accurate reading of a person's significance because of their perspective. But we have, as a place to begin, the story the deceased person wanted to tell. When the authentic voice of the person we mourn has been silenced for a long time, as Bernice's was, the work of making a memory is more difficult and usually takes longer.

Grieving Work: Remembering and Hoping

When death occurs, one kind of relationship with the deceased ends and another begins. Effecting the transition from relating to a living presence to building an enduring memory is the work of grieving. We continue to love someone whose life has ended by means of the stories we remember and tell. And with each retelling of the stories we discover new and unexpected rewards. The stories we treasure will both delight us and bring us to tears. They may inspire us to bold action or lead us to examine ourselves deeply; they may remind us of the fragility and wonder of life itself; they may prompt a new sense of gratitude for the people we continue to love. Forming the narration of a beloved person's life is never a static thing. We tell the story of someone we love who has died over and over again in order to grasp its full meaning.

Storytelling for the sake of making a memory is the central work of grieving. We make a memory by remembering—we set out to create something like a scrapbook of memories. The language of biography expands the process of remembering to include dimensions or perspectives on a life story that had not been known previously. If, however, we resist remembering because it brings emotional pain, then the process of grieving is aborted, the memory is not formed, grieving is prolonged, and it takes longer for the survivor to resume his or her ordinary activities and commitments.

Remembering is reciprocally connected to hoping in grieving work. If we cannot remember the past, it is difficult to anticipate a future without the one we have loved. When the future seems bleak and empty, we do not want to think about the past. That is how grievers come to be stuck in the present. The kind of hoping that makes remembering possible is most likely to be found in relationships of care, from people who are willing to hear our pain and carry our sorrow. It is the presence of this mutuality that makes both remembering and hoping possible, that transforms individuals who dread abandonment and the terror of isolation into communities of memory and hope.

Every person who has survived significant loss has a story to tell about how that loss profoundly changed his or her experience of the world or how the loss will limit the next chapters of the survivor's own autobiography. So the cycle continues. Not only is each person bereft when death occurs; the world is different after significant loss. Our own life story changes when an individual is missing from our life. Because significant loss disrupts our way of being in the world, Canadian philosopher Thomas Attig has suggested that we must learn the different ways a death disrupts the flow of each survivor's life story. Each mourner has a story to tell about "how the loss has changed profoundly his or her experience of the world and has limited what is possible in the next chapters of each biography" (Attig, 1996, p. 7).

Grieving, according to Attig, is a matter of relearning how to be in the world. "Through such relearning we find and make ways of living with our emotions and struggle to reestablish self-confidence, self-esteem, and identity in a biography colored by loss" (Attig, 1996, p. 14). Our search for answers to questions about a death of a life invites us to ask more questions about daily life patterns not of our own choosing. Storytelling in grieving is an exercise of making meaning when nothing makes sense.

There are two dimensions to grieving, both of which are about story. One dimension is the gathering and interpreting of stories, making a cherished memory of a life that has been lost. But the death of someone we love also disrupts the flow of each survivor's life story. For that reason, the second dimension of grieving is relearning how to be in the world, to reshape our lives and reinterpret our stories taking into account the loss that has occurred. When our narrative is significantly intertwined with the narrative of the one who has died, the process of grieving requires careful sorting in order to determine where memory ends and living begins. Grieving is an intermediate stage between life as it was before a death occurred and life as it can be again in spite of the death. Paradoxically, we often need encouragement to grieve while at the same time receiving the assurance that our grieving will end.

The Funeral Moment and the Grief Process

In the previous chapter we explored the wedding as a moment in the process of becoming married. People are married at the wedding, and they are in the process of becoming married before and after the wedding. The same is true of baptism. We are never more Christian than at our baptism, and yet the whole Christian life is an unfolding of the meaning of that ritual moment. The paradox of moment and process is one of the lenses through which we examine ritual in relation to narrative and worship in relation to pastoral care.

The dialectic between moment and process is most clearly demonstrated by the relationship between the funeral liturgy and the process of mourning. The process of mourning begins at death (or before) and continues long after the funeral liturgy has ended, and yet the form and content of that grieving is embodied in the ritual moments surrounding death. Every ritual moment in the funeral process should therefore be evaluated in the light of its effect on the process of grieving; yet the funeral liturgy cannot carry the weight of grieving. It may, at most, help grievers move out of numbness and into active mourning. Moreover, remembering the life that has ended not only brings the person into clearer focus; it sharpens awareness of the finality of loss and the pain that comes with it and intensifies the need to plan for a new future. The funeral ritual, however, only begins the grieving process.

What Rituals Do

Storytelling is an essential part of individual and communal grieving. So are the rituals that form the context for rehearsing a life. A ritual in grief needs to be a safe place bounded by time and space to recall painful memories and express intense emotions. As Walsh and McGoldrick (1991) state, such a ritual provides a "special time out of time; that is, an encapsulated time frame that offers an opportunity for experiencing the overwhelming emotions that death evokes, while also containing such expression" (p. 56). Grief rituals need to be big enough to hold differing realities simultaneously and express conflicting thoughts and emotions in response to the death of a loved person. They need to be communal enough to transform the isolation of grievers. The presence of a faith community absorbs grief and transforms it into hope within a framework of ongoing trust in the promises of God.

The process of grieving is an alternation between remembering and hoping, between making a memory and planning a new future. Christian funeral liturgies themselves embody this paradigm by weaving the Jesus story and Christian stories of hope with the human story of one who has died and the community that mourns. On the one hand, we are encouraged to go through the pain of remembering someone who has died because of the Christian promise that no one and nothing is separated from the love of God. On the other hand, hoping for a new future depends on emotional liberation from the claims of a past that included one who has died. We cannot plan a new future after someone we love dies without first making a memory. It is, however, the promise that God is always making things new that empowers us to go through the pain of remembering and makes a memory possible. This paradox links together grieving process and liturgical moment, narrative and ritual, pastoral care and worship for the sake of a beloved memory of the past and a new future in God, whose love sustains us.

There are three moments in Western Christian funeral rituals: (1) the wake or vigil, in which the story of the deceased is remembered in the context of the Christian story; (2) the funeral liturgy or memorial, in which the Christian story is proclaimed in relation to a particular death, and (3) an explicit committal liturgy of final farewells that marks the close of the story. This final commendation includes a profession of faith in God's fidelity to each individual whose life was sealed in baptism into the death and resurrection of Jesus Christ. Although the ritual form at each moment varies, the process is similar among the variety of Christian traditions and practices. The ritual process is a rite of passage from the moment of death itself through the final disposition of the remains within the baptismal promise. It is a time to give thanks to God for the gift of a life that has been returned to God.

The Aim of Funeral Rituals

While the pattern has remained the same, the aim of funeral rituals has changed slightly in recent years. The process of mourning is significantly shaped by the views of death and afterlife of the religious tradition in which it occurs. In cultures in which the dead are active and influential among the living, the ritual process is used to send the dead off in such a way that they remain positively disposed toward the living. Cultures or religious traditions that are agnostic about the future of the deceased or leave it in God's hands are more likely to focus on the grief and suffering of the survivors. When the aim of the funeral was to ensure the dead person's life with God, ritual actions entreating God's mercy for the deceased dominated. Today it is more often said that funerals are for the living. This declaration reflects a heightened sensitivity to the needs of the living to mourn their loss even as they are consoled by the constancy of life in God.

If the ministry of consolation is the aim of the funeral ritual process, then we also need to ask what it is that consoles. In common usage, consolation has often meant the alleviation of misery or distress of mind. When consolation is understood as comfort or cheer or making up for a loss, there is a danger that the focus on consolation might take the grief away too soon. Premature comfort, however, is finally not an enduring consolation but only a temporary reprieve. As Henri J. M. Nouwen reminds us in *A Letter of Consolation* (1982), written to his father after his mother's death, consolation is to be found "in the firm conviction that reality can be faced and entered with an open mind and an open heart, and in the sincere belief that consolation and comfort are to be found where our wounds hurt most" (pp. 16–17). If Nouwen is correct, and we believe he is, then the funeral ritual process, if it is to bring consolation to those who mourn, should provide language of lament to deepen the awareness of pain and create supportive contexts for expressing "where our wounds hurt most."

Moments in the Funeral Ritual Process

As we mentioned earlier, there are three moments in the funeral ritual process, each of which needs to reflect a balance between storytelling and ritual, between the human need to tell stories in order to make a memory and stories of faith that remind us of the enduring promises of God. The first of these is the wake or vigil, which focuses on telling the story of the individual who has died as fully and honestly as possible. One aim of this ritual moment is to create a hospitable environment for telling stories. In the safe space provided by the presence of the believing community and our awareness of God's presence, we begin the painful process of going where our wounds hurt most. This remembering in the presence of the body helps to make our memory concrete and specific, near where our pain is greatest.

The funeral or memorial liturgy is the second critical moment in the ritual process around death. It is a time to remember the particular story of an individual in relation to the Christian story. The practice of including Eucharist at part of this gathering is a sign that the community that remembers the one who has died also remembers Jesus. Funeral liturgies have not always given enough attention to the need for mourning because the focus has been on proclaiming the promises of God or the seriousness of life in the face of death.

Planning for this second moment in the ritual process requires weaving the human and the divine stories. It is easier just to eulogize a person who has died or simply to remember the stories of God than to fashion a narrative that weaves the individual and the divine into a seamless whole. Planning for a funeral is a time for remembering our baptism and the promise of God's enduring care at death and in grief. Above all, it is a time of increased awareness of where our wounds hurt most.

The committal or final commendation of the deceased is the third and last moment in the funeral ritual process. At that moment, we stand at the edge of the story. There is a finality to this moment that is not possible at other times in the process. There is also a mystery to this moment as we stand at the edge of a story. The act of committal is a stark and powerful expression of separation. When this ritual is carried out in the midst of a community of faith, the committal helps the mourners face the end of one relationship with the deceased and begin a new one based on prayerful remembrance and gratitude and the hope for ultimate reunion within the final promises of God.

○

I was particularly touched by the variety of people who came to the funeral home to pay their last respects to my father. They told stories of his befriending them at some point of need in their life. Several young pastors were grateful that he had mentored them after his retirement from pastoral ministry. I used to be embarrassed about the way he talked to grocery clerks in the checkout line, but they were there to honor the friendliness of my father. I wish now we would have had a ritual of some kind at the funeral home in order to offer thanks for the life of my father and for the stories about his presence in peoples' lives.

My father's funeral began with an intonation of Psalm 130. Even though he had lived fully into his eighty-third year, my father's death was a loss for which lament was the first response. The liturgy that followed included scripture, prayer, and a remembrance from the family. Although the family would have wished for Eucharist as part of the service, it was not the practice of the congregation. The service concluded by singing "Lift Every Voice and Sing." The last line of the last stanza reads, "Shadowed beneath thy hand may we forever stand, true to our God, true to our native land."

We had set the funeral early enough in the day so that my father's elderly friends could come and be home before dark. I was looking forward to hearing stories about his last years from his friends. The trip to the cemetery immediately following the service was lengthened because it had begun to snow. It was the moment in the ritual process when my active grieving began. The sound of dirt on the casket had a ring of finality. When we lowered the casket, we gave my father a final benediction and closed the story.

By the time the family returned to church and the fellowship hall that had been named for my father some years before, the people had gone. I was disappointed and angry. I would not hear their stories because I would never see these people again. When I thought about it, I realized it was unrealistic to expect my father's elderly friends to wait around while we went to the cemetery so they could tell me stories. And then I was angry because the ritual process, in this case controlled by the funeral director, did not serve to further the grieving process.

—HERBERT

○

Herbert's story illustrates how important it is that the funeral ritual process serve the work of mourning. Storytelling around the time of viewing or vigil begins the remembering process within a supportive ritual framework. The remembrance may be woven into the homily or it may be told by the family separately. What is most important is that we continue remembering in the ritual context in which the divine narrative is also remembered.

The time at which mourners experience a sense of finality regarding the death will vary. For some, it is necessary to see the body to bring closure. For others, the experience of final closure occurs at the committal. Still others will not experience closure of a life until there is a personal moment, such as a week alone in the house or a holiday celebration or a significant anniversary, when the absence becomes real.

Pastoral ministers and families face serious difficulties as they plan rituals that will simultaneously close the story and facilitate grieving. The ordinary flow of the three critical moments at death presupposes that the people have the freedom and flexibility to participate in the ritual process. Because of work limitations, people often chose either to be present for the vigil or to attend the funeral. Because cemeteries are seldom next to the church, and because the growing number of cremations alters the patterns of committal, more and more often the committal is attached at the end of the funeral liturgy. The loss of the potluck meal, once a fixture in a community's storytelling in grief, creates another significant vacuum in the ritual process. And since the neighborhood store no longer provides a context for tales to be told, we need to be more intentional about planning occasions in which to reminisce.

We need to rethink the funeral ritual process in response to the radical changes in patterns of living that affect and sometimes hinder the possibilities of grieving. In order to develop greater ritual flexibility to accommodate the growing complexity of community living, it may be beneficial to suggest an alternate order in which the vigil and committal occur before the memorial liturgy. The pastoral advantage of this sequence is that the ritual of closing the story at the committal, usually limited to close family and friends, could occur relatively quickly, before the celebration within the faith community. This approach presumes that a body need not be present as a sign of closure for a memorial to be an effective ritual moment that enhances grieving. If the vigil and the committal bring the story of an individual's life to a close for those who mourn, then there is greater flexibility for a memorial service or several memorial services that will publicly mourn a loss and celebrate a life in relation to stories of faith.

Beyond the Funeral Ritual Process

Funeral liturgies cannot carry the entire weight of mourning. Storytelling needs to continue long after the funeral process for the sake of making a memory. The funeral process validates grieving, begins the telling of stories, connects the lost life with the larger Christian story, encourages family and friends to listen, fosters consolation, and provides safe space and communal support for the painful work of finding where our wounds hurt most. It cannot guarantee, however, that we will keep remembering long enough to make a memory. For some, the grieving process ends with the funeral ritual. For others, however, it is just the beginning. The alternation between remembering and hoping continues as it began and is enhanced by informal and formal rituals that foster telling the story.

There are a number of informal moments that occur in the early months and years after a death occurs in which the death of a loved person is acknowledged, and stories are told in remembrance of one who has died. Holidays and anniversaries and birthdays are often painful but crucial times of remembrance when an individual narrative may unfold in some new way or when stories are kept hidden because the pain of remembering is too great, or else no one is listening. The final disposal of an urn with the ashes of the deceased is another painful moment on the journey of grief when care is needed from pastoral ministers, friends, and family to keep telling the story.

○

The family asked their pastoral minister to be with them when they placed the ashes in the vault and to provide a simple service. After brief scripture reading and prayers, the husband asked if he could put the urn in the vault. He was not prepared for the weight of the ashes. "All the months I carried her up and down the stairs, she never weighed this much," the husband said. "Could I see the ashes?" he asked. The box was opened and everyone one present put a hand in the ashes, and then they put her in the vault.

○

Religious communities and pastoral ministers will need to be alert to changing needs and flexible to new possibilities to ritualize closing the story. Sometimes, it will occur at the graveside, long after the death, when true stories are told to friends or ministers who are present. "Our son did not die from cancer; he fooled around a lot, and AIDS finally caught up with him." "Our daughter didn't die of a heart attack; she poisoned herself." The Protestant practice of remembering those who have died most frequently occurs when flowers are placed on the altar near the anniversary of a death. The name may be printed in the bulletin, but it is seldom spoken. In the Roman Catholic tradition, saying a memorial Mass on the anniversary of the death of a loved person is an opportunity for storytelling in the interest of enhancing the grieving process. Sometimes, however, as the following story suggests, even a memorial liturgy, planned to remember a particular death, may be used to discourage rather than encourage the unfolding of the narrative.

○

John had died two years before of Hodgkin's disease at the age of sixteen. Although the family had known of John's illness for several years, there had been considerable denial of its life-threatening nature until John was hospitalized three weeks before he died. John had always been the happy one in the family, even to the day he died. Two years later, John's mother, Eloise, continued to be angry about his death. She insisted on keeping his picture on the refrigerator door. His father, George, had buried his grief in a number of work projects and gave the appearance of happiness to everyone. Three weeks before the second anniversary of John's death, his younger brother, Timothy, refused to go to school. Neither the school counselor nor Timothy's parents would acknowledge that his problems had anything to do with John's death. When Eloise called the pastor to arrange a memorial Mass, she insisted that the ritual be "nice" so that nobody would "come apart."

○

This story is a parabolic ending to a chapter that has sought to develop the interdependence of ritual and narrative in fostering storytelling for the sake of grieving that liberates. Sometimes our best pastoral liturgical efforts fall on deaf ears. John's family continued to perpetuate a myth that he was not really gone. Therefore John was neither present nor part of the family's collective memory. This myth seemed to be working for everyone but Timothy. He could not create a memory of his brother when everyone else in the family insisted on holding on to their grief.

Whereas in other situations a memorial liturgy might focus on the Jesus story as the hopeful context in which to remember the deceased, John's family had not finished telling his story and their stories with him in order to create an enduring narrative. With careful preparation and with the recognition it still might be resisted, the pastor would do well to deny the request of Eloise for something "nice" in order to help them discover where their wounds hurt most. Enabling the bereaved to tell their tale for the sake of making a memory begins to reveal the parabolic truth that things will never be the way they were. To believe otherwise is to create a mythic resolution at death. Baptism is the ritual that begins the Christian in contradiction. It initiates us into a process of dying and rising that is marked by the death of Jesus. The end of a life and the grief that follows is parabolic. So life is parabolic all the way, from the beginning to the end.

You can mess up at a wedding, a pastoral friend of ours has observed. People will laugh about how silly the pastoral minister was at the wedding, but it will probably not significantly affect the success or lack of success in the marriage. But, our pastoral friend went on, you should do everything in your power not to mess up at a funeral. The words we say and how we say them, the scripture passages we read, the way the building looks, our presence and bearing, which brings comfort and acceptance in the midst of chaos, and the hospitality we provide family and friends—all these things help people at tragic moments of loss when they must reconstruct their reality without someone they loved.

PART THREE

TRANSFORMING STORIES AND RITUALS

7

CREATING NEW RITUALS

For the many stories without rituals—leaving home,
divorce, adoption, stillbirth, withdrawing life support—
creating new rituals serves to acknowledge their significance
as periods of transition, growth, or loss.

○

IN AN ESSAY titled "Mythic and Ritual Resources for the Current Crisis in American Praxis," Lutheran theologian Philip Hefner (1993) states that one source of our current cultural crisis is the existence of novel conditions. These new situations, illuminated by new knowledge, have challenged our assumptions about the way things are and created a cultural crisis of behavior. Such new situations and novel conditions also confront the many gaps in our ritual repertoire. The existence of such a ritual gap can exacerbate the crisis brought on by a new situation, for while there is an important new narrative to relate, there is no ritual framework for doing so.

○

In April 1985, one of my older sisters unexpectedly left our house in Colorado to visit a friend in Vermont. When she telephoned from somewhere along the way, I was the only person at home. She promised to be back for my high school graduation the next year. Several days later, she called again, this time from a Greyhound bus terminal in Kansas City. In a trembling voice Dianne told my mother that she wanted to come home. My mother told her to take the next bus back to Colorado. It was the last time we ever heard from Dianne. She never came home. My parents eventually hired a private investigator to find her. All that was found were her purse, a journal, and a suitcase. She has been missing for over ten years.

○

Dianne's mysterious departure is a pointed example of a crisis for which there is little ritual response or relief. True, it may not be a situation peculiar to modernity. In other epochs of human history, accidents, abductions, and wars have left family members and friends wondering about the fate of their beloved. It may be, however, that contemporary advances in information technologies place the absence of information about a loved one in high relief. Furthermore, peoples of other times and places were often narratively and ritually more resourceful in the face of such loss, consigning the fate of the unknown to evil forces or "God's will" and invoking appropriate curses and blessings to acknowledge and address this perception. Our contemporary reliance on forensic science, computer tracking, and other sophisticated tools might provide more data but does not necessarily contribute to the storytelling and ritual making necessary for those who wonder and mourn.

Every poster with the picture of a missing child is a story of loss without evidence or without confirmation that the loss is permanent. Families around the globe mourn for a grown son or daughter abducted off the street or snatched from their home in the middle of the night. The unresolved fate of these offspring is a continual source of anguish that does not quickly fade. In our own country, twenty-five years after the Vietnam War, forty-five years after the Korean War, and over fifty years after World War II, we are still attempting to resolve literally thousands of cases of the Missing in Action. The occasional recovery of remains of one of these MIAs is an opportunity to bring a personal story to its necessary conclusion and to ritualize at long last this narrative ending. In the absence of such story closures and ritual endings, we are consigned to mourning without evidence of loss. Sometimes we simply resort to denial or secret keeping.

o

In the beginning everybody in my immediate family tried to pretend not be affected by the loss of Dianne. We did not talk about her disappearance or even mention her name without a great deal of hesitation. Whenever her name came up in conversations there was an awkwardness in the room. It was especially difficult for Dianne's twin. Eventually we stopped telling stories, and we talked together as a family less and less. Once, when friends of my parents asked how Dianne was doing, they said that she was living in Oregon. When people ask me about my family, I say that I have two brothers, one sister, and a sister who died but we don't know when, where, or how.

o

As the story from Dianne's younger brother illustrates, the experience of loss without evidence can produce conflicted emotions and thwarted storytelling. Dianne's twin will not believe that she is dead, for understandable reasons. Neither will her parents, but for different reasons. The family cannot draw the story to a close. Furthermore, the family seems incapable of narrating either the ambiguity of Dianne's current fate or her past history. They silently conspire together to keep the secret. It is only the younger brother's persistence that begins to reveal something of the complexity of Dianne's story.

o

Recently I learned from other members of my family that the story of Dianne's life was more complicated than I thought. I remembered her as my cool sister. I only recently learned that she had an abortion the year after finishing high school. She struggled with low self-esteem, broken relationships with men, and alcohol dependency. She and my parents had many bitter arguments. Some in the family know these things about her but not everyone. We talk a little more about her now, but we have never publicly ritualized her loss, and we rehearse her story only reluctantly. It is clear that we are not at the same place as a family with our grief. Dianne's twin sister will not accept that she is dead. Because Dianne is missing without a trace, we are not sure if she is dead or alive. We don't know if we should look for closure or hope she will return.

o

As we noted in the preceding chapter, the aim of grieving is to accept the reality of loss in order to make a memory of the lost person that can be cherished. When people such as Dianne's family cannot accept that a loss has occurred, or when it is uncertain whether the loss is final, opportunities to ritualize the loss are limited.

On a much larger scale a similar dynamic is being played out across South Africa in this post-apartheid era. During the struggle against apartheid, especially in its escalation after 1976, many South Africans disappeared or died under mysterious circumstances. After the enactment of majority black rule in 1994, a "Truth and Reconciliation Commission" was established under the leadership of Archbishop Desmond Tutu. The purpose of the commission is to investigate apartheid-era political crimes. The commission was also given the unusual power to grant amnesty to those who confess—regardless of whether they display any remorse or regret. There are some who challenge the wisdom of such amnesty. For example, the family of slain black leader Steven Biko, who died in 1977, does not want pardon for the five policemen who admitted responsibility for killing Biko twenty years after the event. Archbishop Tutu holds, however, that amnesty is necessary so that the whole story may be told. He believes that reconciliation is only possible if all the stories of death and oppression can come to light in their full parabolic range. This is not an easy task, but the end of national secret keeping—like the end of secret keeping in Dianne's family—is essential so that life-giving storytelling and ritualizing may begin.

Throughout this book we have stressed the human need for narrative and ritual so that the world can be rendered a habitable and hospitable place. Narrative and ritual are essential media through which human beings create environments conducive to their psychological, social, and spiritual survival and development. In Chapters Four through Six we brought this insight to bear on three key moments in the human life cycle: birth, marriage, and death. Each of these, we discovered, are rich with narrative and ritual possibilities. What happens, however, when there is no established ritual or acknowledged liturgical response to a powerful story of crisis, transition, or loss? This is our concern in the current chapter, which will explore human situations, such as Dianne's disappearance, in need of ritualization.

Sometimes rituals are absent because, as noted earlier, we are in the presence of novel situations. Modern technology has created genuinely new knowledge leading to new situations—such as in vitro fertilization or artificial life supports—that require radical innovations in both story and ritual. Most situations in need of new patterns of ritualization, however, are a muddle between beginning and ending, between living and dying, between continuity and discontinuity. It is in the hope of bringing some clarity to this human and pastoral confusion that we consider stories without rituals. Before turning to specific situations in need of ritualization, however, it seems first useful to address what some may consider a contradiction in terms: the ability to create new rituals.

Creating New Rituals

In order to address effectively the issue of stories without rituals it is necessary to dismantle one commonly held presumption about rituals: that tradition and repetition are essential for any authentic definition of ritual. This perspective asserts that a true ritual has a very long history, requires periodic reiteration, and has a certain invariability about it. There are many anthropologists who define ritual in these terms. Many pastoral ministers also feel comfortable with such a vision of ritual. Often this is because worship or liturgy, which provides the pastoral paradigm for all ritual, is frequently defined as traditional, repetitive, and composed of certain core and invariable elements. Worship events devoid of these elements are sometimes disavowed as true rituals and demoted to the category of spiritual "happenings."

Recently there has been a spate of research and writing that has effectively challenged the traditional-repetitive-invariable definition of ritual. One of the more lucid ritual theorists to question this perspective is Ronald Grimes, who has been instrumental in establishing ritual studies as a recognized and independent field of inquiry. Through his observation, teaching, and writing, Grimes has disputed the ritual maxim "It has always been done this way." Although some would deny what Grimes calls the "inventability of ritual" (Grimes, 1993, p. 7), he reminds us that there has been an explosion of ritual invention over the past three decades. Some of these newly invented rituals—for women reclaiming their identity as women (Walker, 1990), for survivors of abuse (Keene, 1991), or for communities struggling to remember the Holocaust (Littell and Gutman, 1996)—have found their way into print and may establish new traditions or achieve a level of repeatability. Other such rituals, however, occur only once. Grimes uses the term *ritualizing* only when referring to emerging or newly constructed rituals (Grimes, 1982, p. 56). While we acknowledge Grimes's insight on constructing rituals, we have not adopted his restricted definition. In this book, we use *ritualizing* and *ritual participation* synonymously.

What may be more startling is not that rituals can be invented but Grimes's insistence that even our most treasured rites are not simply inherited and repeated; rather, they are always in the process of being created (Grimes, 1993). In fact, they need to be re-created. Each succeeding generation with its new stories and fresh challenges must weave together recent tales with those of one's ancestors. Furthermore, believers of each age must reckon with the ritual newness that is born of the intersection of the ever-changing human narrative as it encounters the divine narrative.

Our intention in writing Chapters Four through Six was to encourage and challenge believers to renew and revitalize traditional rituals. Seeing the parabolic and mythic in paradox, or balancing the human and the divine, is, in Grimes's language, an act of ritual re-creation and transformation. It is often also a first step for pastoral ministers on the way toward creating new rituals. If, however, a minister is uncomfortable with renewing traditional rituals through, for example, stronger integration of the human story or the parabolic into worship, then it is unlikely that such a minister will be either comfortable or competent in creating new rituals.

While there are few ironclad rules for the creation of new rituals, there are some useful principles that should be kept in mind during this process:

o *Respect the chronological priority of the human story in the shaping of the ritual.* Let the story of crisis or loss, change or transition—the whole story—be heard. Give the storytelling time without rushing in too quickly with mythic resolutions or divine tales; otherwise the ritual could inappropriately suggest that facile divine answers arrive with equal speed.

o *Allow a significant role for nonverbal symbols in this ritualizing.* There is a time when words inevitably fail and symbolic gesture becomes necessary. Be prepared for such times with simple yet rich ritual action.

o *Resist the compulsion to explain such action.* Honor its ambiguity, which may find great resonance in the participants, who themselves, may be experiencing a baffling array of feelings and thoughts.

o *Attend to the particularity of the moment.* While ritual patterns can be employed across a variety of situations, it is also important that such patterns be specifically tuned and improvised so that the real crisis, transition, or event be appropriately acknowledged.

o *Beware of overcomplicating the ritual.* More is not always better; sometimes less is more. A single act of blessing, laying of flowers, burning of a document, or handing over a gift may be far more effective than piling a number of ritual gestures together.

Previously we noted that most situations in need of new patterns of ritualization are a muddle between beginning and ending, between living and dying. While there is no single way to categorize these situations, some are clearly related to key moments in the life cycles. We first consider examples of unexpected moments of birth, marriage, and death in need of ritualization. Next we turn to other life transitions that need to be ritualized. Our hope is that this sampling will not only map out some of this unfamiliar terrain and provide some helpful ritual responses but, more important, encourage pastoral ministers to be bold and imaginative when confronting the enormous diversity of unritualized stories that exist in people's lives.

Unexpected Moments in the Life Cycle

Virtually all human societies have ways of acknowledging the significant milestones of birth, marriage, and death, and most religious traditions provide rituals for offering blessing and solace for individuals, families, and communities as they live through these major transitions. Often these ordinary transitions have extraordinary dimensions that press for new levels of narrative and ritual honesty. The child to be baptized may be developmentally disabled; a bride or groom at the beginning of their marriage preparation may be told that their own parents are divorcing shortly after the wedding; or, in the midst of planning the funeral for a beloved grandfather there is a public charge that the deceased sexually abused his granddaughter.

In these and similar situations, it is essential that the storytelling and ritualizing be sufficiently re-created in order to allow honesty at a narrative and ritual level. By attending to the mythic and parabolic, the individual and communal, the human and the divine, and the other juxtaposed pairs we have explored, we believe it is possible to shape many of the standard religious rituals for these events into grace-filled and transformative worship. What is often more challenging is responding in story and ritual to unexpected moments in the life cycle for which there are few ritual response patterns. It is to these situations that we now turn.

Miscarriage and Stillbirth

Few experiences evoke more anguish than the end of a life before it begins. It is a frequently overlooked and underritualized experience of loss. For the mother, there is loss of a life that she has been privileged to share for a few months or more, but that life never became independent. Here is the ending of a story even before it begins. Saying good-bye to a child who has died through miscarriage, ectopic pregnancy, stillbirth, or newborn death is both difficult and necessary. Parents have lost part of themselves. They have also lost a dream. And all of this occurs before they are able to welcome the child. They mourn a secret loss in silence, sometimes in shame and frequently alone. And to the extent that the grief is secret, it also is prolonged.

---

o

It was ten years after the tragedy occurred that Patricia began to heal the grief. She had experienced a miscarriage in the fourteenth week of her pregnancy. It would have been her fourth child and her second boy. Patricia has very little memory of the night she was taken to the hospital with severe pain and bleeding. The child had been buried in a nameless grave without any ritual and without Patricia. As a result, the loss was unresolved for her.

Until she had the miscarriage, Patricia was the caretaker of her family. Even after the loss, her family continued to depend upon her. Patricia was always willing to do for others, sometimes to her own neglect.

When she showed signs of depression, her parents reminded her that she had three very healthy children. When she stopped responding sexually to her husband, he got angry. When Patricia began to withdraw from her children, she knew she was in trouble. She entered counseling in order to overcome a pervasive sadness that would not leave her.

○

Patricia's story is a poignant illustration of the lingering impact of unresolved grief and unritualized loss. It is also a reminder that family members seldom mourn in unison. Grief is personal and unpredictable; so is the timetable for mourning. In Patricia's case, even a decade after her loss the residual grief would not abate but had actually increased. It was a grief that required ritual acknowledgment.

○

At the suggestion of her counselor, Patricia sought to recover an experience she could not fully remember. She visited the hospital and the room in which the miscarriage took place. She gathered toys, a blanket, and other items she had bought or had been given ten years earlier in anticipation of the birth. Patricia and her immediate family took them to the family plot at the cemetery and buried them underneath a flower bed. She made a grave marker with the name Scott David on it. From that time on, she counted Scott David as one of her four children.

The conclusion of Patricia's remembering was a Eucharistic liturgy attended by family and friends in which Scott David was prayed for publicly and by name. She had wanted a funeral. A memorial Eucharist was her pastor's compromise. It was a helpful ritual, but it did not fulfill Patricia's need to bring closure to the unborn life and death of Scott David [Anderson, 1995, pp. 76–78].

○

The burial of toys and other mementos that Patricia associated with Scott David was a beginning step toward resolving her grief. It was a ritual announcement that a loss had occurred and that not only a child had died but that her dreams for that child had died also. It is discouraging to note, however, that her minister was less resourceful than her counselor in helping her to ritualize this grief. Her church does not have an official liturgy for helping her to bring closure to Scott David's story. Instead of improvising one, her pastor offered a "compromise." In fact, it was only a compromise for Patricia, not one for her church.

Here was a missed opportunity for crafting a ritual never employed before, and maybe never used again, but one that could have allowed the stories of Scott David, Patricia, the family, the faith community, and God to bond and heal. The ritual could have been an adapted rite of committal at the graveside to accompany the symbolic burial. It could have been constructed of songs or texts from the burial rite of children and interwoven with images and symbols from the baptismal or child dedication rite, which would have reminded the community that although Scott David was never baptized, his faith was a birthright from a believing family, and in his death he had received full initiation in the divine presence.

The standardized liturgies of our various traditions are not ceremonial cookie cutters that need to force every human situation into their mold. Rather, they are resources and models of ritual wisdom that should inspire rather than constrain those who employ them. Sometimes it is very clear that the official rites of the church should not be employed. Baptism, for example, is ordinarily not the appropriate ritual to use at the time of stillbirth. It is understandable that parents may want a stillborn child to be baptized. It is the only ritual most people associate with birth. In the face of stillbirth they need to do something to counter their feelings of powerlessness and grief. A ritual response other than baptism may be devised, however, that helps parents to affirm their relationship to the dead child, to connect the child's short-lived story with the divine narrative, and to enable the process of separation and grieving to begin. JoAnn Post, a former student of ours, demonstrated how this can be simply and effectively achieved. In a letter she wrote,

○

A young couple from one of our rural congregations came into town to deliver their baby. It had been a perfectly healthy pregnancy. The couple was happily married. When [the mother-to-be] went into labor and came to the hospital to be checked, they discovered that the baby had died in utero. Apparently it had died only hours before she went into labor. When I first met the couple they could not speak. When I asked them to think of holding their child after it was delivered they both began to sob. I promised them I would return after the baby was delivered to pray over it and name it.

When the nurses called the next morning, the labor was very difficult. It took another twelve hours before the child was born. It was as if the mother did not want the child out of her womb. At least when the child was unborn, it was still with her. The husband was in and out of the hospital all the time because he could not stay at her side very long. Finally the child was born. I pray I never see such a thing again. The infant was white as snow, lifeless and limp, but warm from his mother's body. The father left the room, crying as though his heart was broken.

When the nurses brought the little boy for the mother to see, she extended her arms instinctively to hold the child. She told him how she loved him, what a gift he was to them, and how they had longed to meet him. Then the father held him a little and cried some more. They named the child Joseph Alan. I read Isaiah 43 and sang "Children of the Heavenly Father." Then we prayed. There settled a quiet calm, knowing that Joseph Alan was at peace. I hope that I shall never be in the presence of such pain again.

○

The story of Joseph Alan poignantly illustrates a ritual response that had power to heal the grief for a child lost through stillbirth. It is an unusually honest illustration of the way story and ritual embraced a searing anguish. Painful, compassionate, and genuine, this unusual intersection of worship and pastoral care required improvisation. In a quite disarming way, this tale reminds us that true care and worship are not found in a book. Ritual books are not to be discarded, but we should also not hide behind them. Such books are not the end of our ritualizing but the beginning. Attentive to the wisdom the books embody, ministers need to explore ways to ritualize the story in all of its pain and complexity. Such is the beginning of true worship and authentic care.

Divorce

The breakdown and breakup of a marriage is never easy. It is frequently fraught with bitterness and sadness. For some, going through a divorce is a relief; for others it is a matter of shame; for still others, it is a situation of deep hurt and rejection. Until the end of a relationship has been acknowledged, it is not possible either for reconciliation to occur or for healthy new relationships to develop. Coming to terms with the end of a marriage and the reality of loss calls for the same kind of honest storytelling and remembering that characterizes other kinds of grieving.

Churches have an understandable dilemma when it comes to narrating and ritualizing divorce as an act of pastoral care. On the one hand, there is the desire to attend to people's real experiences and pain. Ignoring the reality of divorce is not, however, a remedy for marital breakdown, nor will it make the anguish of those involved in a divorce disappear. On the other hand, it is difficult for churches and their ministers to shape a narrative and ritual response to divorce if the primary emphasis is upholding the sacredness of marriage through the same means of storytelling and ritualizing. This is especially true for those religious traditions that do not officially acknowledge divorce and remarriage for their members.

Sometimes churches and their ministers have much to learn from so-called "secular" counselors and therapists who are exploring how ritualization can help to acknowledge and resolve at least some of the difficulties that divorce presents.

○

Karen and David kept finding their reasonable attempts to divorce overpowered by the extreme anger that kept them tied to each other. I asked them to write detailed accounts of all the memories that currently fueled their anger and stood in the way of their moving on. It took about a month before they finally agreed that their troubled marriage was encapsulated in these individual written memories. Already they were calmer with each other.

Together they burned the pages one by one, mingled the ashes, and put them in a jar. I asked them to take the jar of ashes and an envelope containing my instructions and drive north to an old log chapel on a ridge in a virgin white pine forest. At the old chapel they were to sit quietly for a time and then decide whether or not they were truly ready to let their marriage go. Deciding that they were ready, they picked a spot outside the chapel, took off their wedding rings, dug a hole, and quietly placed the ashes and their rings in an unmarked grave. Both Karen and David drove home with a sense of lightness which they said they hadn't felt since the beginning of their marriage. They went on to complete the divorce and peacefully finalize a visitation agreement for their two children [Price, 1989, p. 45].

○

In some respects, this symbolic enactment might be considered an *antiritual,* or a reversal of the ritual gestures employed at the ceremony that publicly marked the beginning of the marriage. Instead of putting rings on, they are taken off; signing and enshrining a marriage license is replaced with burning and burying the ashes of written memories; a familiar church filled with family and friends is traded for an isolated chapel in the woods, where the only witnesses are the divorcing couple. For Karen and David and others in their situation, antiritual may be the most appropriate ritual response because it symbolically announces reversal, contradiction, and the deconstruction of meaning. Yet for Karen and David and others in their situation, this may be exactly what is required. If ritual is a symbolic activity that helps individuals construct the world as a habitable and hospitable place, antiritual is a sometimes necessary step for deconstructing a world that is no longer habitable and hospitable so that another may be constructed. Antiritual is a symbolic way to pull down the empty shell of a relationship and clear the terrain, in the hopes that something new can be built on the same spot.

Ritual making at the time of divorce can be an unusual experience of antiritual. It is a moment for acknowledging thwarted dreams, for admitting ignored grace, and confessing whatever ways in which love had been withdrawn, withheld, or discounted. One resource that religious traditions can contribute to the process of divorce is their ritual wisdom for reconciliation. In the breadth of the Christian tradition, there have been many forms of reconciliation. Some of these have been individual, others have been communal; some have emphasized the need for penance, others have stressed the graciousness of a forgiving God. What may be most important to remember from the breadth of this tradition, however, is that rituals of reconciliation are neither to be punitive nor degrading. They are not simply or even primarily announcements of human sinfulness but of God's faithful mercy. People at the end of a marriage that has been publicly blessed as an image of covenantal love need to acknowledge their failure in realizing the promise of that covenant in their marriage. They also need to forgive each other and themselves, as God forgives. In this process of scrutiny and blessing, confessing and absolving, a rite of reconciliation might serve as the most appropriate antiritual to a failed marriage.

When the Mind Dies Before the Body

Alzheimer's disease is one of the tragedies of aging that modern medicine has named without yet curing. What previous generations might have considered simple forgetfulness or the onset of senility can now be diagnosed with considerable accuracy as a debilitating condition that may eventually deprive an individual of memory and of the relationships that are sustained by it. The diagnosis of Alzheimer's disease begins a long good-bye. One of the difficulties of this long good-bye is that people grieve from the beginning a loved one who "disappears before yours eyes." As one husband put it, "You don't get to say good-bye once; you say good-bye a lot of times. It is torture." Husbands and wives, children, and lovers of Alzheimer's patients tell the same story. How does one recognize and live with the end of a mutual relationship as it is transformed into a one-sided relationship?

Sometimes the unwillingness or inability to engage in appropriate story-telling and ritualizing after a diagnosis of Alzheimer's or other such debil-itating disease can impair the grieving process that inevitably ensues. Furthermore, as illustrated in the cases of Dianne and Patricia recounted earlier in this chapter, diminished storytelling and the absence of ritual at such moments can lead to unhealthy secret keeping and contribute to the development of unbearable guilt.

○

Although Philip was the youngest of seven children, the twelve-year gap between himself and his next youngest sibling made him feel like an only child. This feeling was intensified by the fact that his other six siblings were about eighteen months apart. While he was very close to his parents and adored by his brothers and sisters, who doted on him, Philip left home at a very early age to attend a military academy.

While Philip was away at high school, his mother began to mani-fest symptoms that would later lead to a diagnosis of Alzheimer's dis-ease. Each home visit was both a joy and a trial for Philip. By the time he graduated from high school, Philip's mother was institutionalized. She never recognized him after his freshman year in college. Although she did not die for several years, Philip felt that he had already lost his mother. Sometimes he wondered if going away to school had made it worse for her.

This gnawing guilt was unbearable at his mother's funeral, until one of his mother's best friends said to him, "You know, you were always your mother's favorite." Philip said that he thought his mother loved all her children equally, for that is what she faithfully repeated to all of them. "Oh no," the neighbor responded. "I remember before you were born, the doctor advised her not to have another child. But she insisted, saying that she wanted one more, just for herself." Philip's guilt dissolved. It was an unexpected gift; one that could have been better only if he had heard it from his mother.

○

Philip's tale is a poignant illustration of the pain that arises from living with the "presence of absence" that comes with Alzheimer's. It also points to the importance of ritualizing a good-bye. Ignoring or denying that the loss of mind and memory is inexorable and inevitable makes leave-taking even more difficult; sometimes, it makes saying good-bye unbearable and impossible. Happily, Philip heard a liberating narrative at a crucial moment in his grieving that allowed him to say good-bye to his mother with significantly diminished guilt. One can only imagine how his wish to have heard this tale from his own mother might have eased or dissolved the decade of remorse that preceded her funeral.

It is a delicate process to determine the appropriate moment and then to craft a way to bid farewell. Precipitous farewells could be the occasion for melancholy rather than closure and healing. Equally as difficult as identifying the moment is crafting the manner in which to begin the leave-taking. Two married friends, when they finally acknowledged their need to bid farewell to their relationship as they knew it, employed a line from Shakespeare's Julius Caesar as the structure for their first good-bye. In it, Brutus says to Cassius,

> Whether we shall meet again, I know not.
> Therefore, our everlasting farewell take.
> For ever and for ever, farewell, Cassius.
> If we do meet again, why, we shall smile;
> if not, why then this parting was well made.
> [Act V, Scene 1]

Christians might find comparable inspiration in biblical texts, such as the great seasonal hymn from Ecclesiastes that recalls that there is a time for everything (3:1–8). St. Paul, at the end of his First Letter to the Corinthians, also provides textual inspiration for such good-byes:

> If it is at all possible
> I should like to remain with you for some time
> even to spend the winter with you
> that you may provide me
> with what I need for the rest of my journey.
> I do not want to see you just in passing.
> I hope to spend some time with you,
> if the Lord permits [1 Cor. 16:6–7].

Beyond texts, another Christian resource for ritualizing such leave-taking is the practice of pilgrimage. Pilgrimage serves many purposes across religious traditions. One of these purposes is the making of a memory. Christians, for example, retrace the movement of Christ across Palestine and through Jerusalem as a way of remembering his life on earth and, more important, for confirming in pilgrimage the meaning of his life, death, and resurrection. In a similar way, revisiting places that were important in a relationship can both solidify those memories and revitalize their meaning. Such a memory-making pilgrimage can be literal or virtual. Sometimes scrapbooks or photo albums are the best way to make such a journey, to bid farewell to important places and moments in life, and to recall the trials or reconfirm the graces that were experienced in those sites. For believers, this could include a literal or figurative return to a church that was the setting for a wedding, a baptism, or a significant religious experience. Returning to a ritual site might also help recall the texts and symbols from the worship enacted there, such as the exchange of wedding vows or the rededication to baptismal promises. However constructed, a pilgrimage of memory may be both appropriate and fortifying for the unknown journey that lies ahead for victims of Alzheimer's and their families.

When the Body Lingers While the Spirit Leaves

We noted at the beginning of this chapter that modern technology has created genuinely new situations that require radical innovations in story and ritual. The withdrawal of life support systems is one such situation. At earlier times in human life, when living might have been simpler, and dying certainly had fewer options, it was important to support the dying lest their suffering at the end turn them from God. In our time, often the suffering for the family and friends of a comatose patient is aggravated more by technology than by disease. We have the technical capacity to delay death and sometimes to hold it off for a very long time. Although the action of withdrawing life support systems is simple, the decision to do so is ethically and emotionally complex.

There is technically a difference between withdrawing life support systems from those who are unconscious and dying and turning off mechanical ventilators for those who are already brain dead. The difference may not be clear or important for the families of the patient; emotionally they may register as the same. It is valuable, however, for caregivers and ministers to be attentive to such differences, as they contribute mightily to an ability to shape authentic and honest ritualizing at these distinct moments.

As with some of the other stories without rituals we consider in this chapter, the decision to withdraw life support systems or turn off a ventilator is a moment in a larger process. Furthermore, the decision to take such an action is separate from the action itself and even the ritualizing of that action. Similarly, divorce and ritualizing the end of a marriage, or acknowledging the onset of Alzheimer's disease and saying farewell, are moments in a larger process. As noted in earlier chapters, effective ministry requires the integration of moment and process while maintaining their paradoxical connection. The process of withdrawing life support or turning off a ventilator can be very long and taxing. It is important that the process not be rushed, however, so that the final decision and ritualization be ultimately a moment of peace.

Thomas Shannon and Charles Faso have produced an unusual resource for addressing some of these questions in their wonderful book *Let Them Go Free* (1987). In the introduction to this brief book they address some of the important issues that need to be processed in deciding to withdraw life support systems from a love one, such as trying to discern the patient's wishes or trying to resolve disagreements among family members on how to proceed. They certainly suggest that the discussion of these issues is a treasured moment for storytelling about the patient. At the conclusion of the book, they provide a sample "Family Prayer Service" consisting of prayers, scriptural texts, and ritual gestures to accompany the withdrawal of therapy or a life support system. A poignant moment in the rite allows for disconnecting the life support systems while a prayer of commendation is offered. The authors of the book recognize, however, that some may be unable or unwilling to bear such a moment. Thus they offer the option to say the prayers of commendation then allow the family to leave before disconnecting the life supports.

As important as the ritual outline in *Let Them Go Free* is the ritual acknowledgment that such a book brings to this difficult moment of transition. Increasingly, pastoral ministers of various stripes are confronted with new and challenging situations that beg for a ritual response, although there are few official models. The complexity of these situations suggests that time-honored practices such as a long pastoral prayer or the recitation of the rosary may be insufficient. Something more is required, so that the ending of a story may be adequately told, symbolized, and even celebrated. Furthermore, the particularity of the situation would seem to demand a parallel particularity in the ritualizing.

Margaret Smith and Frank O'Loughlin (1991) have respected this principle of particularity in an Australian version of Shannon and Faso's work. Instead of a single prayer service, they provide three: one for withdrawing life support systems when a person is unconscious and dying; a second for the withdrawal of ventilators when a person is brain dead; and a third for the withdrawal of ventilators when a person is brain dead and there is a donation of the organs of the deceased. Their attentiveness to the ritual need for symbols beyond words is especially apparent in their third ritual, which suggests that a representative of the hospital staff be present to receive the body from the family and friends. After recalling the baptism of the deceased—which may including sprinkling the body with baptismal water—the service includes a ritual dialogue in which a family member or friends entrusts the body of the deceased into the care of the hospital representatives, who acknowledge and receive this gift in death.

Difficult as such moments may be, they call for careful and deliberate ritualization. The resources of a religious tradition as well as the imagination of pastoral ministers are certainly taxed at such times. What is required of pastoral ministers is imagination and the courage to improvise. For that reason, ingenuity is required of pastoral ministers in difficult times if the authentic stories of individuals and families are to be heard and honored and then woven respectfully into the divine narrative.

Other Life Transitions

It is not only unexpected or tragic moments in the life cycle that present themselves as stories without rituals. There are also other important transitional events—some of them quite festive—that punctuate the lives of individuals and families that also need ritualization so that they might be properly woven into the personal and communal narrative. It is certainly not possible to examine all of these here, nor even list them as they are so numerous. Rather, in the final section of this chapter, we will hint at the wide spectrum of important life events that call for ritualization by highlighting a significant few. It is hoped that this sampling will not only encourage pastoral ministers but also ignite their imagination so that they may respond respectfully and resourcefully to the many life variations manifest among the people of God.

Adoption

There is an ancient maxim that notes that Christians are "made, not born." With increasing frequency, the same could be said of many families in this country. While most are still defined by marriage and the birth of one or more children, a growing number of families are defined by marriage and adoption, by domestic partnership and adoption, or even simply by adoption. Since many legislative changes and revised adoption policies allow for single adults to adopt, it is now possible for adoption to be the primary or even only means for constituting a family. For this reason alone it is valuable to ritualize the significance of the event.

Whether the act of adoption constitutes a new family or reconstitutes an existing one, it is an announcement of change. If the child being adopted is no longer an infant, the change can be difficult, even traumatic. Ritualizing the entrance of an adopted child into the family can contribute to the acceptance and integration of that child into the family. The lack of such ritualization, however, could be symptomatic if not symbolic of the marginal role of the adopted child in the family system.

○

> Adam was twelve, Betsy was eleven, Charlie was eight, and Alan was seven. Charlie had been adopted a year or so earlier. . . . Adam seemed to welcome Charlie into the family as an ally—"us brothers have to stick together!" Betsy and Alan on the other hand experienced Charlie as a competitor for parental attention, and had a hard time with the transitions. Charlie's concerns were typical of many adopted children: Would his new parents love him as much as their "real" children? Would he be treated fairly? Would his brothers and sister tease him about being different? Would he be abandoned by this family also? His anxieties sometimes expressed themselves in violent temper tantrums [Close, 1993, p. 382].

○

In the face of Charlie's very obvious unhappiness, the parents consulted a family therapist. In the family gatherings that followed, the therapist spoke extensively about abandonment, control, and adoption. The therapist concluded that some ritualization would be beneficial to Charlie and his new family. In an act of ritual reversal, she asked Charlie if he would like to adopt his parents. It was hoped that this antiritual might give Charlie a sense of power in a situation in which he seemed to have little control. Charlie not only agreed but thought this was a great idea (Close, 1993, p. 382).

Unlike some of the other situations we have presented in this chapter, there are official or semiofficial rituals in various Christian denominations that address the adoption of a child. In the official Roman Catholic *Book of Blessings,* for example, there is a ritual entitled "Order for the Blessing of Parents and an Adopted Child." The service includes introductory words, a scripture reading, a psalm, a brief dialogue with the parents and child, intercessory prayers, a blessing, and a conclusion. As is sometimes typical of official rituals, however, this blessing ceremony is word-heavy. Furthermore, it provides little opportunity for the parents and child to be central actors in the ritual and has no provision for acknowledging any other family members.

Charlie's therapist, in consultation with a colleague, provided a richer model for such a ceremony. It began with a few words on the meaning of adoption and a prayer. This was followed by a relatively long and inclusive exchange of family vows, which began when the therapist asked

Charlie, "Do you, Charlie, take Holly and Mark to be your true and loving parents, and do you commit yourself to being their true and loving son, to share with them your hopes and your sorrows, to forgive them for their mistakes, to appreciate them for their love, to learn from them and enjoy them even beyond the years of your growing up?" To which Charlie responded, "I do" (Close, 1993, p. 383). This was followed by a story about families and an exchange of gifts, which became the most touching moment in the rite.

o

At the exchange of gifts . . . Adam gave Betsy a poster he had been given by their grandfather, and which Betsy had always envied; he gave Charlie an autographed baseball he had prized for years; he gave Alan a baseball cap that had been given to him by their uncle. Betsy gave Adam a malachite egg that grandfather had sent her from Africa; she gave Charlie a stuffed bear that she had slept with for years—up to the previous night; she gave Alan her favorite book of nursery stories. Charlie gave Adam, Betsy and Alan three framed pictures that had been taken of him and them four years earlier when he had been visiting their family—pictures he had kept on his dresser all these years. . . . Father, whose hobby was wood carving, gave each child a goblet carved from a different rare wood. Mother had written a letter to each child. She moved over and sat next to each child in turn to read the letter to him or her—thus affirming the uniqueness and individuality of each child [Close, 1993, pp. 385–386].

o

Specific, symbolic, and simple, this is not so much an adoption ceremony as it is the ritual transformation and reconstitution of a family. It is a well-crafted interplay of the individual and the communal, of each member of the family with Charlie, but also all family members with each other. The human and the divine narratives are also well woven here but without overshadowing the fragile story of an eight-year-old finding his way in a new web of relationships. Would that all of our ritual shaping was so thoughtful and respectful.

Leaving Home

Leaving home is a long and sometimes complicated process. It is the way we travel toward becoming a separate and distinct individual. In order for this to happen, each of us much sever, or at least alter, the emotional umbilical cord that has kept us close to our parents or homes of origin.

Frequently, that emotional separation is accompanied by physically leaving the home where we lived with our parents. Moving out of the house does not necessarily signal the end of the process, however, which may continue long after our parents are dead and we are middle-aged. As we stressed in Chapter Four, each of us is a unique gift of God from birth, yet we become autonomous through an extended process of affirming our uniqueness and individuality. Leaving home for college, to join the military, or to get an apartment on our own is often one of the more dramatic moments in this process.

The process of leaving home is often highly charged because there are so many variable and sometimes conflicting emotions. Some children are eager to go; others are afraid. Some parents cannot wait for their children to leave; others do not know how they will get along without a child; still others are fearful that once children leave they will never come home again. When the fear or sadness is particularly strong, parents will tuck a load of guilt into an offspring's luggage in the hopes of keeping them close. All parents, it is said, want their children to grow up, but not too big; to go away, but not too far.

The moment when children leave home is sometimes an awkward one, because parents often feel pressured to impart a morsel of wisdom that, according to tradition, will be remembered by the child forever. Unfortunately, what we planned to say does not always come out as we intended. Good-byes are too long or too short. Though everyone means well, the ritual insecurity of the moment keeps everyone just uncomfortable enough to be off their stride. In the awkwardness of the good-bye parents sometimes resort to well-worn maxims. One of our students recalls that his father's final words upon leaving home for seminary: "Don't forget son, a wet bird never flies alone at night." He has never quite figured out what that meant or what his father was really trying to say.

What this or similar sayings do not convey is what may be most needed at the moment: a blessing that communicates unconditional love for a child, a recognition of their individual uniqueness, a wish for their success on the journey, an affirmation of the bond that will remain even after they have left, and a prayer for God's protection along the way. The blessing is a ritual recognition for both parents and children of God's promise to accompany them into an uncertain future.

---
o

Kirsten had packed her boxes. Jacque, my wife, had prepared Kirsten's favorite meal. In anticipation of this night I had written a special prayer, "A Guest at Our Table," to be used before the evening meal.

Emotions we'd stored up for weeks found their first expression in our family's tears as the prayer was read. The prayer offered, we brushed away the tears and enjoyed Kirsten's chosen meal of chicken fajitas.

After clearing the table—and her younger brother's unceremonial prompting of "Let's get on with this!"—we gathered at the fireplace. I lit a candle on the mantel and invited Kirsten to kneel. Each member of the family placed a hand upon her head. With voice cracking, I offered a blessing.

The blessing spoken, our emotions spilled out. Kirsten sat back on the couch, and all five of us piled on top and around her. Our hugs, kisses and tear-swollen faces turned to laughter as Beret, Kristen's sister, opined how silly we would look if someone were to come to the door [Quello, 1996, pp. 16–17].

○

Sometimes a blessing will occur spontaneously; other times it will come during a planned walk in the woods or, as for Kirsten, at the end of a farewell family dinner. However it is done, a blessing recognizes that change is imminent. It further celebrates an individual's uniqueness and confirms their separateness while affirming an enduring connectedness. It is a unique combination of the mythic and parabolic at a significant threshold moment in a much longer process that brings the divine narrative to bear in a young life. In some ways, such a blessing is thoroughly baptismal: a ritual admission that the child is ours but not ours, loved but not stifled, held on to even as we give her or him away. It is a ritual gesture and a transitional moment that should not be overlooked.

Promising Again in Marriage

Another moment in the development of a family that needs ritualization is the recommitment in relationship and marriage we call "promising again." Today people live longer and have fewer children, so the life span of a marriage more frequently survives the childbearing years. In some social contexts, divorce in the middle years has become a patterned, almost expected response to the transition that occurs when children leave. A more constructive alternative is promising again.

○

Kevin was born one year after Keith and Carla were married and one month after Keith finished law school. Joy and sorrow mixed together, because Kevin was born with severe disabilities. Keith and Carla decided to care for him at home and devoted their life to his well-being. When Kevin was eight, Keith and Carl had healthy twin girls. About a year after their birth, Kevin's behavior became demanding and aggressive. By the time he was twelve, Carla could no longer handle his violent outbursts, and Kevin was placed in a residential home. In his mind Keith had failed his son. The more dark and joyless Keith's world became, the more Carla invested in the twins. She and Keith became emotional strangers who shared a common bed. About eighteen months after Kevin was placed in the residential home, Keith and Carla attended a couples' retreat sponsored by their church. Keith was able to acknowledge out loud his fear of knowing how to be married to Carla without Kevin present. It was the beginning of an awareness that they needed to renew their promises to one another if the relationship was to endure.

o

One way to ritualize a recommitment is to renew one's wedding vows. This is a relatively common practice for couples who make a retreat, such as the one Keith and Carla attended, or who participate in a marriage encounter weekend. In some denominations, it is also traditional for a couple to renew the wedding vows publicly at major milestones in the relationship, such as a twenty-fifth or fiftieth wedding anniversary. There is a difference, however, between the public celebration of such a familial milestone and the private processes and ritualizations that may be required for ritual honesty at such public celebrations.

The weekend Keith and Carla spent together allowed feelings to be expressed and was the beginning of an awareness of their need for recommitment. Maybe a simple renewal of marriage vows might have been sufficient ritualization for them in this recommitment. It is possible, however, that more might be needed. Maybe Keith and Carla need to make a pilgrimage back through their memories, recall the grace and sin that marked their relationship, ask for and speak forgiveness to each other, and then seal this process with an exchange of vows.

Other couples have found that the process of promising again requires not the recovery of memory but the creation of a new memory that is not reliant upon the presence of children or parents or other significant individuals who may have been a wedge between them. Some parents, for example, reappropriate their home to suit their new relationship after children have moved away. One couple that we know bought a cottage that they had rented for several summers, even though they were financially quite stretched. The wife later observed, "I think this cottage is a symbol of renewed commitment in our marriage and of the need to provide sacred space and sacred time for us as a couple."

More often than not, promising again occurs in the midst of making other decisions, such as planning a special trip or turning what once was a child's bedroom into a sewing room or home office. Formally ritualizing the recommitment may occur after the fact. It may be implicit in the determination to meet for lunch once a week or the willingness to modify work patterns in order to provide time for nurturing the marital bond. However it occurs, promising again often requires painful negotiation, deliberate compromising, and hopeful waiting. It means holding in tension forgetting and remembering so that a new chapter in the story can sustain and endure the complexities of being married today. It is a renewal of the promise to be tending toward the other for the sake of the marriage. The myth and parable of this tension is only enhanced when it is spoken, symbolized, acknowledged, and brought to ritual.

○

There is a difference between worship and pastoral care. Worship focuses on the glorification of God and the sanctification of people. Pastoral care is concerned with helping people achieve wellness. At the same time, there is an intimate relationship between growth in holiness and wellness. The more individuals realize their full human potential and affirm their life as valuable and good, the more potential for responding to God's working in their own life. Our exploration of stories without rituals in this chapter has a therapeutic aspect to it. We acknowledge that enabling people who have experienced miscarriage or divorce to ritualize those situations in all of its complexity and ambiguity is healthy. The challenge for the pastoral minister, however, is to shape such ritualization so that it is not only healthy at the level of the human story but also redounds to the health and vitality of the divine story. Taking a holistic approach to pastoral care and worship as distinct but not separate facets of ministry is, to our way of thinking, essential for establishing the human and divine linkage. It is also essential for the integrity of our ministry.

We have not told every story in need of ritualization in this chapter. We have explored some of the more containable examples of stories without rituals. There are many more; some are quite distressing and exceedingly dangerous. We did not, for example, address the need for rituals of healing in the face of experiences of sexual abuse. This is not to ignore them but to recognize that they would have overwhelmed our attempt to set forth some general principles and map the terrain of stories without rituals. In addition, it is impossible to raise issues of sexual abuse without addressing the appalling reality that many official representatives of our churches have been perpetrators of this abuse or that abuse will continue as long as both the church and the society foster implicit forms of sexism. There has been significant systematic secret keeping about such abuse by our churches. How to bring this frightening story to ritual or how to integrate care and worship in the midst of horrific stories of abuse is an exceedingly complex agenda when the official ritualizers and leaders of worship may themselves be the victimizers.

The topic of abuse, like many others not treated here, requires our best efforts at storytelling and ritualization. As we have already noted, communities of faith rooted in the promise of baptism are spared the tyranny of being good. Having accepted that promise, that our value rests on God's grace alone, it is still difficult to fashion stories and rituals that include the presence of abuse or violence in human life without camouflaging evil or promoting premature reconciliation. Robin Green suggests it is worship that "puts us in touch with threatening and liberating truths" (Green, 1988, p. 32). There are many human situations in need of ritualization where we can only wait expectantly for God's presence in the midst of our anguish, at the center of our pain. In the end, the parabolic shatters any facile attempt to contain either our rituals or our narratives. They are too mighty; they are too dangerous.

8

REVITALIZING
RITUALS WITH STORIES

*There is great opportunity to celebrate the divine and the human
together in the public worship of Sunday assemblies that is too
often experienced as a ritual without human stories.*

○

OUR CONSIDERATION of the linkage of worship and pastoral care through
narrative and ritual has focused thus far on what are sometimes called
occasional services. These are worship events such as baptisms, marriages,
or funerals, which, although occurring regularly in the life of a faith community, are occasional experiences in most believers' lives. A worshiping
community may have twenty weddings a year, but the participants in these
weddings will come mostly from outside the local community. That practice varies, of course, according to geographic context and the character
of the congregation. A small-town location or churches with a strong
communitarian profile will often be more close knit and therefore generate higher participation by regular worshipers in occasional services. Generally, the particular and personal nature of the occasions that give rise to
such services will determine the ad hoc nature of their assemblies.

Baptismal planning, marriage preparation, and support for the grieving process are often moments of intense pastoral care and ritualization
in a faith community. As we stressed in Chapters Four through Six, attention to the storytelling and ritual making around these events is crucial
both for the individuals directly involved and for the community that provides their context. The ritual and narrative effectiveness of particular life-
cycle moments is enhanced by the intersection of worship and care that
is rehearsed in the ordinary cycle of a faith community's storytelling and

ritualizing. It is difficult to imagine that the worship and pastoral care around occasional services will be fully effective or transformative without the sustaining context of an equally effective and transformative cycle of regular worship.

One crucial place for the ongoing rehearsal of this linkage between a community's commitment to worship and pastoral care is the Sunday assembly. In particular, this connection is enacted in the Eucharist or Lord's Supper, which—according to Christian tradition and a growing consensus among the various Christian denominations—is a focal part of the Sunday assembly. The document *Baptism, Eucharist and Ministry* (1982), prepared under the auspices of the World Council of Churches Commission on Faith and Order, acknowledges the Eucharist as a pivotal Christian mystery and recommends that it should be celebrated "at least every Sunday" (paragraph 31). This growing ritual practice has not, however, increased the likelihood that human and divine narratives will intersect significantly in the assembly's worship together.

While there may be considerable theological agreement among Christian scholars that Eucharist is the appropriate ritual for Sunday worship, there is little compelling evidence that this theological consensus translates into a high level of personal or communal satisfaction for worshiping believers. Sociological studies generally show a decline in the number of church members who attend Sunday worship on a regular basis. Even without satisfaction, people continue to participate in Sunday gatherings of worship for many reasons, some of which have to do with God, and some do not. Andrew Greeley has observed that Roman Catholics continue to worship regularly "because of the stories" (Greeley, 1994, p. 38). We are inclined to believe Greeley is correct for Protestants and Catholics alike. If so, is it possible that the opposite is also true; namely, that people do not participate in worship regularly because the ritual is without stories?

The Problem of Inadequate Storytelling

A critical assessment of worship is sometimes offered as a reason for the decline in church attendance. People will say they get nothing out of the Sunday worship or that the preaching seems disconnected from life or the assembly is not friendly. The underlying concern of those criticisms, as caricatured by noted television critic Neil Postman, could be simply a yearning to be entertained. According to Postman (1985), television has not only presented us with entertaining subject matter, but it presents all subject matter as entertaining. Thus politics, education, and even religion as transmitted across the airwaves are intended and perceived as distinct but related forms of entertainment. The cumulative impact of this experience is that—even apart from television—we expect all experiences of politics, education, and religion to be entertaining.

○

Derek considered himself a good Catholic; it was just that he had stopped going to church. He started attending church again when he met Patrice, and now it was something he did regularly, although he said he didn't get much out of it. As Derek explained to me during our first meeting for marriage preparation, he thought he was a good Christian. He tried to live a moral life, was honest in his dealings with others, and even prayed to God from time to time. For as long as he could remember, church was boring. Therefore from the time he left for college until he met Patrice, the only time he saw the inside of a church was when he escorted his mother to midnight Mass on Christmas Eve. But now he was back, and he accepted attendance at worship as one of his obligations if he wanted to be married in the church. It was, however, still boring.

"And when you have children," I asked him, "what will you teach them about their obligation to worship on Sunday?" Without much reflection Derek answered, "I guess I'll teach them that when you belong to any organization you have certain responsibilities, some of which are more enjoyable than others. But if you want to join the club, you have to pay your dues."

○

While Derek might be more honest than some, his response to Sunday Eucharist is not untypical. The Sunday celebration of the Lord's Supper is officially heralded as the bedrock of Christian ritual and the cornerstone of the church year. Experientially, however, it is often much less than that. The desire to be entertained is surely one diminishing factor but not the only one. Faithful Christian people who regard worship as an obligation are regularly disappointed and unfed. They do not find themselves in the stories told and the rituals enacted in the Sunday gathering.

There are churches that have responded to reactions from people such as Derek by shaping worship according to entertainment principles. The move toward an entertaining style of Sunday worship is advocated by some who argue that providing people with worship forms that they enjoy is an important part of evangelization. Borrowing a market-wise philosophy, proponents of this approach ask "Who is our customer?" and

"What do our customers consider valuable?" (Truehart, 1996, p. 40). Evidence suggests that this has proven to be an effective strategy in drawing new members into church and gaining higher approval ratings from those who have become non-practicing believers. At the same time, a turn to market strategies and commercial models of entertainment raise serious questions about the nature of worship and the image of care in the community. How can Christians, for example, frame the central belief in the saving death of Jesus Christ in an entertaining way?

There is another way to respond to the concern that ordinary Sunday worship is irrelevant and boring besides turning to entertainment. This response begins with a different analysis of the root problem of Sunday worship. It may be that a basic difficulty with Sunday Eucharist is not that it is poor theater but that it is poor human storytelling and inadequate divine storytelling. While a solemn, well-planned Lord's Supper may proclaim loudly the great divine narrative, it often fails to make connections with the real stories of people's ordinary lives. Herbert Brokering (1974, p. 54) has observed this disjuncture in this way:

> Once there was a church
> where they couldn't find the bible
> one Sunday.
> The minister asked if anyone
> had good news from the Lord.
> No one admitted having any,
> so they all started leaving.
> One man said his wife
> had just had a baby this morning.
> The people decided that this
> wasn't a word from the Lord
> and they went home.
> The man stayed for a whole hour.
> He was sure that was good news
> from the Lord.

Our Sunday experience is seldom as blatant as Brokering's parabolic portrayal of one worshiping community's inability to acknowledge real-life narratives as worthy of being repeated in worship or even acknowledged as a divine word. It is nonetheless true that in preaching and in praying, between the opening hymn and the final benediction, the weekend church often demonstrates itself as inadequate and sometimes wholly incapable of honoring and integrating the stories of the faithful who week after week fill the pews. In this sense, much weekend worship might be characterized as ritual without story.

Ironically, the practice of Sunday worship was born in storytelling about transformative encounters between God and ordinary people in the person of Jesus the Christ. The New Testament is littered with these tales. The characters sound like people we know: a divorcee (John 4:7), grieving parents (Mark 5:40), a young man who doesn't know what to do with his life (Matt 19:16), a government official (Luke 7:2), an old women who has suffered through too many doctors (Mark 5:26), and a baffled clergyman (John 3:1). What is so fascinating about these tales of divine-human engagement is that the arena for these encounters is the human story.

In Chapter Three we stressed that ordinary people yearn for a union between their story and God's story. We suggested that such a union can be achieved in two ways. One is characterized by the Christian virtue of hope: we hope that—if not in this world, at least in the next—we will become part of God's story of glory and eternal peace. The other is more characterized by the Christian virtue of faith: we want to believe that God is very near and that God is even present in the story we are currently struggling to narrate.

It is true that the New Testament has a number of stories that give us hope to believe that by following Christ we will become part of God's eternal narrative of everlasting life. The resurrection accounts certainly fall into this category, as do certain passages that hint at future glory, like the story of Jesus' transfiguration or the raising of Lazarus. Most of the New Testament tales that interweave the human and the divine, however, fall into our second category: not hope that someday we will become part of God's story, but faith that God has broken into ours. Our human reality, our everyday stories become the vehicle for divine revelation. Ultimately, the Gospels reveal that the human story, be it a wedding or a funeral, focused on an adult or child, a tale of public gossip or secret keeping—is a privileged place for divine revelation.

While our faith tells us that God does not need us, that same faith announces that for some inexplicable reason God has chosen to reveal the Divine Self in and through our lives. Every human tale has the potential and even the need for divine coauthorship, if we are to be transformed into the new creation announced at our baptism. How ironic, therefore, that the events of our lives, which are a critical touchstone for the divine-human encounter, are so often ignored in the Sunday assembly. The power of these stories, like their Gospel antecedents, is frequently overlooked in abstract preaching and empty ceremonies. Worshipers are presented with the externals of traditional worship without the engagement of the personal and communal stories that give such rituals life.

> When the Guru sat down to worship each evening the ashram cat would get in the way and distract the worshipers. So he ordered that the cat be tied during evening worship. After the guru died the cat continued to be tied during evening worship. And when the cat expired, another cat was brought to the ashram so that it could be duly tied during evening worship. Centuries later learned treatises were written by the guru's scholarly disciples on the liturgical significance of tying up a cat while worship is performed [de Mello, 1994, p. 63].

There are ashramic cats in our sanctuaries. They are rituals without stories, divine narratives that overlook the human tale, and official prayer without careful attention to human stories that come from the way we care for one another in community. This is certainly not what Christians find in Jesus, who is a remembered as a master of storytelling and ritual making: a living integration of worship and care.

Jesus: A Storyteller with Bread

Labels such as storyteller and ritual maker may not be the first that come to mind when thinking about Jesus. Many, for example, first think of him as a great teacher or a healer, a miracle worker or gentle shepherd. For some he is simply the ultimate martyr. All of these titles are applicable. What we forget, however, is that his teaching, healing, miracles, gentleness, and even martyrdom were framed by ritual. In particular his public ministry was framed by the ritual meal: an intentional pattern of eating and drinking, or what is sometimes called his table ministry. It was especially in the context of those ritual moments that Jesus not only told the great stories of the reign of God but, we imagine, listened to the stories of the people who flocked to him and brought these two narrative streams into dangerous and transformative proximity to each other.

We become aware of Jesus as a ritualizer and a storyteller when we comprehend how much of his ministry is remembered through the food and dining metaphors that provide the vernacular for narrating the Jesus event. His food was the will of the one he called the Father, and this divine will, in turn, became the enduring banquet for any who dared to follow him. Jesus' ministry, his evangelizing, his legacy were so intimately linked to the ritual metaphors of dining and food that, in his fascinating book *Six Thousand Years of Bread* (1944), H. E. Jacob could title his chapter on Jesus as "Jesus Christ: The Bread God." Such metaphors are not lost on scripture scholars who often repeat the comment that, at least in the Gospel of Luke, Jesus must have weighed about three hundred pounds because he was either at a meal, going to a meal, or leaving a meal (Karris, 1985). Jesus literally ate his way through the Gospels. And, as remembered over and over again in the Gospels, they killed him because of the way he ate; that is, because he ate and drank with sinners.

Apart from the many table tales, the Gospels also remember that Jesus spoke in table metaphors. When he wasn't at a banquet he was telling a story about a banquet. When he wasn't teaching that bread can be a vehicle of God's presence, he was talking about bread as a way to discipleship for those who wished to live as his body in the world. Food language permeates every stratum of the Gospels. In Luke's version of the beatitudes, for example, Jesus proclaimed, "Blessed are you who hunger, you shall be filled . . . but woe to you who are full; you shall go hungry" (Luke 6:21, 25). In the Gospel of Matthew, when the disciples had forgotten bread that was needed on the voyage across the lake, Jesus used it as an occasion to put the disciples on guard against the yeast of the Pharisees and Sadducees. Even when he taught us how to pray, the first intercession he invited us to offer was for daily bread.

Jesus is so recognizable by his disciples as the Bread God that even after his resurrection, he was identifiable to those with whom he had spent so much time especially through the ritual act of eating and drinking. The paradigmatic story on this theme is found in Luke 24, in the story about the two disciples on the road to Emmaus. They are filled with emotion, sharing their information, and gossiping with a stranger. While they did not recognize their old teacher, they must have appreciated his teaching, for they pressed him to stay for dinner. It was at the table that Jesus taught them again, but this time with bread, not words; thus did they recognize him in the breaking of the bread, and he vanished from their sight. It should not be surprising to us that eating and telling stories are intimately connected human events where we also meet God.

It may be a caricature to think of Jesus as God with a food obsession, but he did appear to be God with a people obsession. One of the best ways to somebody's heart, as the old adage reminds us, is through their stomach. That is what Jesus seemed to be about: getting to people's hearts and to the heart of their stories. One of the ways the New Testament makes this point is by linking Jesus' table ministry with the forgiveness of sins. Over and over again, Jesus sits down at table with people who have a story of unfaithfulness. Often the Gospels report only the eating event and occasionally Jesus' words of forgiveness. If we listen between the lines, however, we can detect the personal tales of Levi, the Magdalene,

Zaccheus, and so many others who must have poured their hearts out to the Son of God in the midst of a simple meal or over a cup of wine.

The recollection of Jesus at table is not a memory of empty ritualism. There are no ashramic cats here, no magical mystery rites. Rather, at the heart of this eating and drinking was storytelling that led to forgiving: that unmistakable symbol that the human story has been heard, God's story has been proclaimed, and the two have met. There are many amazing things about the banquets that Jesus hosted: their frequency, their diversity, their visibility through every strand of the Gospels. Maybe more amazing than any of these, however, is the way they functioned as the critical symbol of God's willingness that the human story be the context for divine revelation, especially in forgiveness that was announced in the breaking of the bread.

In the memory of the early disciples, Jesus' table ministry was the ultimate enacted parable. It was the paradigm of storytelling and ritual making where the human and divine ultimately converged. Sharing a piece of bread, drinking from a common cup—both expressed and created the union they symbolized. Here was the center where the divine and the human tale merged in an awesome balance of the mythic and parabolic. Forgiveness was proclaimed, healing proffered, and the ultimate mythic resolution of life over death assured. Yet the assurance was only possible in parabolic mode: by admitting a need for forgiveness, acknowledging brokenness that required healing, and, like the grains of wheat that gave life to the bread at the heart of this ritual meal, accepting death as the way to life.

The paradigmatic place of Jesus' table ministry in and for the Christian imagination cannot be overemphasized. While it is true that Christians believe that Jesus' death and resurrection are the central tenets of their faith, the power of these pivotal events was anticipated and remembered in the meal. Long before Calvary, the Gospels reveal that Jesus rehearsed life and death with his disciples around a table. It was at table that old ways were challenged, enemies were embraced, outcasts were honored as teachers, and the fulfillment of the reign of God was previewed.

This rehearsal in eating and drinking culminates in the supper Christians distinguish as the "last" in Jesus' earthly life. It is remembered as the most sacred of meals in which his dying and rising were anticipated in a broken piece of bread and a shared cup of wine. Here earthly elements give up their previous way of life for a new, transformed existence. So too, were those who dared to share in these elements confronted with the challenge of a similar transformation. This meal, fashioned in the image of Jesus' whole ministry and recalled in every Christian Eucharist, is a place where death is sampled in a loaf of bread; where tasting wine imperils life as we know it. The mythic proportions of this supper cannot be denied, nor can the parabolic entrance requirements to such a meal be ignored. Here is where belief is tested and faith is forged.

Attention to authentic storytelling and ritual making in baptism and betrothal, vigil and burial is essential for ministry that is worthy of the name. Similarly, shaping ritual for those significant moments of our lives that lack an appropriate symbolization—what we characterize as stories without rituals—is a critical form of pastoral care. While ministry in these moments is critical, it is by definition occasional. Engaging individuals and communities in the practice of faith requires the occasional, but sustaining them in faith requires something more. The Sunday Eucharist, the story-telling and ritual vernacular of the Christian community, is that something more. It is here, Sunday after Sunday and season after season, that the divine and human story, the individual and community tale, in mythic and parabolic mode, must find ritual expression. Without weaving the human and the divine narratives into a single web, it is unlikely that any Christian community of faith can survive. In that way, we understand the Lord's Supper as the ultimate embodiment of the Christian's *mighty story*. And so it becomes our most *dangerous ritual*.

Embracing the Liturgy of the World

Unfortunately, for too many worshipers today, the Sunday ritual enactment of the Lord's Supper, born of such divine-human intimacy, is neither mighty nor dangerous. It has become an empty shell or irrelevant formality. The Eucharist is no longer the enactment of an ancient or timeless tale; rather, it is rather a meaningless repetition of a dead story. One of the crucial questions for faith communities is how this central worship event can be ritually resuscitated and narratively revived. How do we recover the dynamic between God's story, as embodied in Jesus, and the human stories through which we make sense of the world and fashion our identities? The answer, as intimated in the Gospel stories of Jesus, is related to the ritual's capacity to engage and honor the real-life narratives of ordinary people. This necessitates both the convergence of worship and pastoral care and the continuity between occasional service and sustaining worship. Both may be accomplished by the intersection of the worship in our sanctuaries with what Karl Rahner (1976) calls the "liturgy of the world."

According to Karl Rahner, the gift of God's gracious self-communication is not limited to a baptized few nor somehow dispensed within the confines of divinely sanctioned ritual or devotional activities. Rather,

God's self-communication and the divine call to salvation occur throughout the whole of human history. Rahner, like many other contemporary
theologians, believes that the world is permeated by the grace of God,
constantly and ceaselessly possessed by God's self-communication from
its innermost roots. This continuous self-communication of God through
all of human history is what Rahner calls the liturgy of the world. He
writes, "The world and its history are the terrible and sublime liturgy,
breathing of death and sacrifice, which God celebrates and causes to be
celebrated in and through human history in its freedom, this being something which [God] in turn sustains in grace by [God's] sovereign disposition" (Rahner, 1976, p. 169).

It is this liturgy, according to Rahner, that is fundamental and prior to
any particular notion of ecclesial practice or denominational forms of
worship. It is this liturgy in which, according to the Gospels, Jesus is
immersed. Despite some belief to the contrary, Jesus was not a Christian
and did not attend church. He was a good Jew, attended synagogue, and
from time to time worshiped at the temple. The image of worship embodied by the Jesus of the Gospels, however, was not one centered in build-
ings or focused on canonically prescribed rubrics. Rather, it was a
primordial example of the liturgy of the world, unfolding in people's
homes, town squares, and local pubs. It was ritual fashioned out of everyday encounters between Jesus and grieving widows, innocent children,
and skeptical onlookers. It was a liturgy of the world in which God's story
and the human narrative found common ground through the table parables of a carpenter from Nazareth.

The categories of worship and pastoral care employed through this book
would not have been familiar to Jesus of Nazareth. In particular, he would
not have understood the way they are often separated or wholly unrelated
in the practice of ministry today. His own integrity would have made that
impossible. The Gospel accounts provide an impressive array of stories
about Jesus' ritualizing as he tended to people's stories and needs. What
may be more telling than the sheer number of these stories, however, is
their integrity with each other and the whole of Jesus' life as evoked in
Gospel memory. This is especially clear in the way the Gospels recall the
many encounters between Jesus and the marginalized of his time.

While Jesus was not at the top of the social registry in first-century Palestine, he did attain a certain level of public recognition and respectability.
Thus the Gospels do recount that he was sought out by community leaders
such as Jairus and had some wealthy and distinguished disciples, such as
Joseph of Arimathea. Most of Jesus' encounters as recorded by the Gospels,
however, were with people of the lowest social standing. The Gospel writers do not seem concerned with playing up Jesus' relationships with the

upper class or the powerful; to the contrary, they seem to revel in his association with the outcasts and the unclean. And almost as a badge of honor, each of the Gospels repeats what could have only been a common criticism of Jesus: he eats and drinks with sinners.

The criticism here was not that Jesus preached a necessary word of conversion to tramps and prostitutes but that he spent so much time with them in intimate settings that he came to know and identify with their stories. He knew of their addictions, shattered relationships, and broken dreams. In turn, he shared that which possessed him: the life-giving relationship he had with the Holy One and the dream of a peaceable kingdom. In this mutual exchange, he became an intimate part of people's ordinary stories and a symbol of unusual integration of the human and the divine. Jesus not only spoke a word to them but became the Word; he not only proclaimed forgiveness but was their forgiveness; he not only provided nourishment but was their nourishment. The integrity of this care and engagement with people's real-life struggles culminates in table intimacy, which is not a substitute for engagement or an alternative to care but rather the source and symbolization of that care.

It is noteworthy that what the church eventually calls the Lord's Supper or Eucharist is not a story or ritual that took as its source the narrative and life of Jesus in the singular. Rather, the story-packed ritual of Eucharist emerged from the meeting of Jesus' story with that of fishermen, widows, tax collectors, and all the other alternately shady and respectable characters that populate the Gospels. Table ministry, while divinely initiated, also has a string of human coauthors. It is not God's story with a human audience. Rather, at its most primitive level, the practice of table ministry was an exchange of human and divine stories.

Jesus was not a bread dispenser or a wine pourer; neither was he a story giver or imparter of rituals. He was a dinner companion, a story partner, and a ritual friend. He did not demand that his table associates forget their lives or ignore their world in order to dine with him. He didn't overlook their lives or world in that dining, either. Rather, he savored each life and celebrated them all as the liturgy of the world. Ritual and care were one; story and symbol were united; God and people were coauthors. Moreover, the human story is primary in this ministry in that it is the first order of business at the table. The human story is heard first; only then is the divine narrative invoked. So was it at the beginning, and so it must be now if the Lord's Supper is to be the sustaining ritual that the Christian tradition reveals it to be. The Eucharist that we remember in our Sunday assemblies is undoubtedly the privileged place for announcing the divine narrative. Such divine narration and powerful ritualization, however, must never be at the expense of the human story.

Sunday's Myth, Monday's Parable: Redefining the Sacramental

Many people are able to discern something divine, even holy, in the special moments of our lives. Countless parents know the birth of a child as a miracle; many couples instinctively recognize their first sexual encounter as a step into mystery; the death of a loved one is often a close encounter with the eternal. Previous chapters in this book have played on this human instinct in an attempt to demonstrate how such sacred moments require appropriate narration and ritualization for both individual and community faith and wholeness. The turn to weekly worship, however, offers an unusual challenge, since by definition it is a corporate form of ritualization and narrative that is not generated by special moments or crisis.

Most Sunday worship occurs in what many liturgical calendars label as "ordinary time." While worshiping communities have high seasons, such as Christmas and Easter, and special festivities or crises that generate distinct prayer and care, these are the exception. This is demonstrated, for example, by the unusual church attendance that marks such high holidays as Christmas or Easter (Gallup, 1996). A community of faith, however, cannot survive on the spasmodic cycle of festivals or crises. Instead, it must be reconciled to living in the ordinary, engaging, everyday life as the saving parable and reconciling myth.

Admitting the sacred, even sacramental quality of the extraordinary moments of our lives is important but insufficient. It may also be self-defeating, because it raises the expectation that divine-human encounters only occur in such heightened moments of festivity or tragedy. From that perspective, however, most of us live in extended periods of divine drought. The option and the direction for living differently is to embrace the present human story as the only sacred one we have. Again Herbert Brokering has articulated this vision in poetic form (1974, p. 64).

> Once there was a teacher
> who knew lots of stories,
> and they were all true.
> The story she told best
> was always the one that was just going on
> or had just happened,
> and the class was always in it.
> Whenever they were learning,
> they talked about what was happening,
> so that it was a story.

It was always the only story
all of them could remember
and they knew it by heart.
Whenever things aren't going well
and they want to learn,
they think about the story that is going on,
and then what is happening is important.

The weekly Sunday gathering, regularly assembling around word and sacrament, is the way that faith communities embrace "the story that is going on." It is the way we are formed and sustained in the story of Jesus for our life in the world. Without this weekly embrace, the authentic story of God's self-communication in the ordinary events of life may simply pass us by, remaining as a divine invitation never heard and never heeded.

Espousing the everyday as potentially sacramental challenges us to admit and correct the mythic tendencies of Sunday worship. In a grand display of singing and Sunday best, our liturgical gatherings on the first day of the week too often specialize in announcing good news and promising that all will be better, if not in this world then in the next. As we have noted before, myths are necessary because they assure us that everything is going to be all right. They allow us to live into God's future, confident that it will be better than the present. But mythic worship without the balancing dimensions of parable is dangerous. It could strand us in a religious reality where we flounder hopelessly without a shared understanding of the world in which we live. For that reason, the myth of Sunday requires the parable of Monday; the proclamation of the divine story requires its integration with real human stories; and the public display of Sunday services demands attention to the cares of everyday life if it is to be a transforming ritual moment.

Worship is an occasion for care not only because it creates an environment for telling our stories: it is a way to make sense of our lives in relation to the Jesus story. Each human story is unique and the result of our common humanity. We hear familiar themes of failure and hope in the stories of unremarkable women and men of faith from the past and in the present. No matter how they regard themselves, they come to us as a gift. But, as Green (1988) states, "Christian liturgy also tells the story in a very particular way. It goes on retelling the story of Jesus because through that story we are to make sense of our own stories. [In the process], we discover something given and take hold of our own worth" (pp. 17, 19). This willingness to give and receive worth in the context of worship is possible because we have had an experience of God in our midst that liberates us from our illusions.

Inclusivity in Worship: Hearing All the Stories

There is considerable conversation and some debate today about inclusivity in religious thought and worship. Often, the debate focuses on gender. Inclusivity becomes a code, therefore, for the full and equal participation of women in the churches. In particular, the language of worship needs to be inclusive of all who gather for worship. While we wholeheartedly share the belief that our language needs to recognize the equal place for women in religious thought and practice, we also believe that inclusivity is a much larger issue. At its heart, inclusivity is a matter of stories or, more specifically, whose story gets heard and told in what we say and do as religious people.

○

Ana Maria spoke about how difficult it was for her growing up Catholic in a mostly Polish parish in Chicago, because she didn't see or hear about any saints in the church's prayer who were like her. Oh, there were some women, a few Roman saints, but none of them had brown skin. She always wondered as a little girl and through early adolescence whether there was a place in heaven for brown-skinned girls. And then, when a junior in high school, Ana Maria attended her first Guadalupe celebration with some Hispanic friends she had met in high school. To her amazement and utter delight she there discovered not only that there were young, brown-skinned girls that the church called saints, but that one of them was the Mother of God.

○

Ana Maria's story is one illustration of the many ways in which ordinary human stories are excluded from divine narrations and Sunday ritualizations. People whose ethnic heritage is a minority may not always feel their stories are part of the community's story. People who live alone are excluded when sermon illustrations are primarily about family living. People whose doubts are stronger than their beliefs may not always be included in the Sunday stories. Worship is catholic, as Robin Green has observed, "because it contains the whole of human experience which is now included in God" (Green, 1988, p. 139). Authentic inclusivity, however, provides a place for each human tale and ritual resonance in the ordinary rhythm of Sunday worship with the lives of all worshipers.

Achieving this goal is not so much the consequence of technique as it is a matter of attitude. In order to ensure that weekly worship is thoroughly inclusive of the people, leadership in communities of faith must be willing to admit and embrace the liturgy of the world as a place where the divine and human stories continue to be woven together. This shift in attitude presumes that the divine-human encounter may occur at any time or in any place in people's lives. The call to salvation is rehearsed in our sanctuaries and pulpits, but it is not necessarily realized there. Acknowledging that worship announces salvation but does not contain it is an important step toward embracing public worship both as myth and parable for communities of faith. It promises a reconciliation of all things in our lives without escaping into worship as the safe haven where that reconciliation takes place. Rather, worship in parabolic mode sends us out of church to struggle for reconciliation in the midst of daily life.

Even so, it matters what happens when the community gathers for worship. Establishing and sustaining a mutually respectful dialogue between official public liturgy and the liturgy of the world requires a second change in thinking about the worshiping assembly for leadership and laity alike. The people who are part of the worshiping assembly are not the "object" of the stories of salvation but participants and even coauthors in the work of a new narrative from human and divine stories. Unfortunately, presiders and preachers often communicate through word and deed that they themselves are the subjects, the doers, the actors in worship and that the assembly is the consumer who is the object of their action and leadership.

If worship is a privileged symbolic rehearsal of the divine-human dialogue, however, the assembly is not an object. Worshiping believers are subjects of both the official liturgy and the liturgy of the world. The people who gather are, in a true sense, the real sacramental agents. Presiders and preachers are not charged with engaging the community with themselves but facilitating the engagement of the community with God. Effective prayer leadership, therefore, means knowing how and when to facilitate and how and when to get out of the way.

A final transformation in attitude comes not only in recognizing that the self-communication of God is an everyday occurrence in the liturgy of the world but in admitting that the rituals we instinctively employ in that world are vehicles for divine revelation. For Christians this means that Jesus is not only present in baptisms, church weddings, or the weekly celebration of the Lord's Supper but in the bathing rituals between mother and child, the sexual intimacy of marital partners, and in the ordinary meals that punctuate our existence.

Preaching the Stories

There are many moments in Sunday worship when it possible to weave together human and divine narratives. It can happen when the music of a Sunday worship experience resonates deeply with the hopes or longings or memories of the human heart. Prayers of the people are an occasion when, in general ways, the stories of people's lives are the subject of intercession and form a chorus of supplication to God. It happens when the context of our lives connects with the words of a hymn in a new way. Three days before Joseph Cardinal Bernardin of Chicago died, one of us sang a hymn as part of the Sunday assembly that connected with our common experience of waiting for death to come. Here are two stanzas of that hymn:

> I know a sleep in Jesus' name,
> A rest from all toil and sorrow;
> Earth folds in its arms my weary frame
> And shelters it till the morrow;
> With God I am safe until that day
> When sorrow is gone forever.
>
> I know of a blessed eventide,
> And when I am faint and weary,
> At times with the journey sorely tried
> Through hours that are long and dreary,
> Then often I yearn to lay me down
> And sink into peaceful slumber.
> [*Lutheran Book of Worship*, no. 342]

The immediate connection of the hymn is with death. There are, however, many times when we are "faint and weary" from the struggles of living and from the "journey sorely tried." We long to rest in God. Narratives are deepened when human and divine stories meet in our worship song.

Music can touch deep into our emotions; architecture can invoke the wonder of the divine; and ritual can provide revelations and comfort beyond our words. It is, however, the preaching event, with all its narrative possibilities, that is perhaps the most potent vehicle for interweaving the human and the divine. Unfortunately, the narrative potential of our preaching is often overlooked or underutilized. Thus, instead of a dynamic center in Sunday worship, preaching becomes irrelevant—even oppressive.

---

o

Sunday held little promise of relief from the six-day heat wave. By the time 11:00 Mass began at St. Timothy's it was clear that the rising temperature and oppressive humidity would render the normally stoic congregation more listless than usual. The entrance rites and readings were quickly dispatched without much passion, but also with little complaint from the assembly. As the fans were temporarily silenced and the congregation sat in quiet resignation for the homily, however, they knew that neither season, temperature, nor dew-point reading would have any influence on the length or quality of Monsignor Carter's sermon.

The Gospel from the end of the thirteenth chapter of Matthew was a mystery to most worshipers, but Monsignor Carter was going to explain it to them. A brief excursus on the nature of parable soon gave way to a moralistic exposition of each of the three parables in the passage. For twenty-seven minutes the preacher explained to them that the great hidden treasure for them was their faith; that the pearl was the church; and that Mass was like a net thrown into the sea, catching fish of every kind. "But just coming to Mass is not going to save you," he chided, "because as the Gospel says, when the net was brought to shore, the disciples picked through the fish, saving the good and throwing out the bad. So will you be judged, says the Gospel, separated into evil and righteous by the angels at the last judgment. You know what you have to do to avoid condemnation: you adults stop sinning, children respect your parents, everyone pray the rosary, and be more faithful about coming to Mass. Maybe then, through God's mercy, you can hope to find yourself standing with the righteous at the last judgment. In the name of the Father, and of the Son . . ." the monsignor's voice trailed off, and the fans were restarted. As a slight breeze filled the air an almost audible sigh of relief rose from the assembly, grateful for this modicum of relief from what could only be considered a stifling environment [Foley, forthcoming].

---

o

The experience of the people at St. Timothy's is, sad to say, not unique. It is not that ministers such as Monsignor Carter are ill intentioned when it comes to preaching, but they are often ill informed. Preaching for them is often an exercise in moralizing, public exegesis, or doctrinal exposition. What these forms of preaching miss is the fact that preaching, like the whole of worship, is meant to be an encounter between God and believers. As noted earlier, in preaching as in worship, the assembly is not the object of the event but rather the subject. From this respect, preaching could be conceived as a ritual conversation between God and a worshiping community mediated by a preacher (Foley, 1997).

The assembly is the subject of preaching not because they literally say anything during the sermon, but rather because the sermon finds such resonance with their lives that it speaks their story. Of course, preaching not only speaks the human story but also announces and interprets the divine tale, especially as it has been proclaimed in the day's scripture readings. Worship preaching from this perspective is an unusual opportunity to weave together these two narrative strands. To do so, however, requires knowing and respecting both human and divine narratives.

To the extent that preachers err today, it is in overlooking the human story. We attend weddings and funerals and hear generic sermons that, by changing the name and a few sparse details, could be used for any number of believers. Specificity, which is an important gauge of our sensitivity to the human story, is often completely missing from such preaching. Similarly, our Sunday preaching is often so generic that it does not resonate in a particular community. As an antidote to the generic, preachers need to be engaged at the center of people's lives.

What are their tales of joy and stories of grief? Who have they loved and who have they lost? What kind of work do they do, what do they think of their employment, and how does the job shape their family and their faith? Knowing the people for whom we preach, cherishing their dreams and embracing their stories, may be the ultimate test and criterion for an effective liturgical preacher. Their lives are the particularization of Rahner's awesome liturgy of the world. Their struggles with family, employers, local government, and the church are the terrible and sublime liturgy, breathing of death and sacrifice, which Rahner insists God celebrates and causes to be celebrated.

One of the tasks of preaching is informed by the human need to be understood. When someone hears our story in a moment of pastoral care and is able to communicate that she or he has understood our story, we feel confirmed and validated. Preaching can also be such an experience if the homily is able to connect the hearer's story to the biblical story. We cannot solve all the human problems people bring to worship. Nor can we adjudicate every conflict or comfort every sorrow that preoccupies the hearers in the Sunday assembly. "But we can validate their experience by linking it with very real human stories in Scripture" (Anderson, 1991, p. 78). Locating our stories in the larger story of God's presence in the world is a religious act of validation.

Happily for us, the Jesus of the Gospels is an astounding model for any minister of the Word who recognizes the need to hear and embrace the ordinary stories of people's everyday lives. Over and over again Jesus enters into another's story: bringing a daughter back to life, forgiving sins, providing believers with a new life direction, or often simply sitting down to learn names and share a meal. The incarnation of the Word was a consummate story-hearer. Those who wish to proclaim that same Word today cannot be anything less.

9

RECONCILING STORIES
AND RITUALS

*In order to honor both human and divine narratives
in the stories we tell and the rituals we enact, we need
to foster a spirituality of reconciliation.*

○

STORIES AND RITUALS are both potential agents of reconciliation and
agents in need of reconciliation themselves. Telling our story honestly is
a necessary component of reconciliation and wholeness in human communities. We know that our stories need reconciling whenever we fabri-
cate an environment in which truth and falsehood are indistinguishable,
or our lives are governed by hiddenness and secret keeping. Stories may
be reconciled if they are honestly told, but telling stories does not necessarily bring resolution to the conflicts that separate us or the actions that
have wounded us.

Rituals have power to heal broken relationships or alter destructive patterns of human interaction when they are authentic enough to create an
atmosphere that opens up new possibilities. We can all recall situations
where so much tension or conflict was hidden beneath the surface of a
glitzy wedding or somber funeral that the power of these rituals to effect
change was severely limited. Because our stories are flawed and incomplete and our rituals fragile and inadequate, they need to be reconciled at
the same time that they function as agents of reconciliation.

Reconciliation as a Spirituality

Our turn to reconciliation in this final chapter does not add another particular set of stories or group of rituals to the practice of faithful living.

Rather, reconciliation is a way to speak about the fundamental challenge and promise of all the stories and rituals examined in this book. Throughout this text, we have explored various sets of polarities: myth and parable, individual and communal, public and private, moment and process. While certain modes of storytelling or ritualizing might emphasize one or more of these elements, we need to reckon with the tension that these various polarities point to in all stories and rituals. Our insistence on balancing the mythic and parabolic perspectives in narrative and ritual suggests that the mythic expectation of the permanent reconciliation of opposites is both possible and not possible. Similarly, we have stressed that both the human and divine narratives need to be ritualized and that an individual story must be told in a way that respects the larger communal stories in which the individual occurs without losing sight of human particularity.

This emphasis on honoring the polarities of faith and living with the ambiguities of life has come to have a certain urgency in our time. Although diversity has always been part of creation, it is now in our neighborhoods, our churches, and our families. Because we are committed to recognizing the uniqueness of the other who is different but close at hand, tension and conflict are more likely to be part of daily living. Polarization, scapegoating, and prejudice are all violations of the other that call for a new understanding of living together in our globalized villages. What makes it urgent that we learn to practice reconciled living is that bombs and handguns are so lethal and so pervasive that it is no longer enough just to think about reconciliation as a way of healing broken relationships and restoring people and communities shattered by violence. All of these factors make it necessary that we practice reconciliation as a way of living in order to foster understanding as well as restore brokenness.

Reckoning with this tension requires a particular disposition—what might be considered a spirituality—for respectful living in the midst of ambiguity. It presumes a way of being in the world that not only admits of the possibility of ambiguity and paradox but embraces their reality. In his writings on faith development, James W. Fowler (1981) reminds us that in the present practice of our faith, there are very few "naked" facts or truths. Everything is subject to interpretation, and not all interpretations are the same. Believers of every faith tradition are challenged to take into account multiple perspectives on truth, including paradoxical or opposing ones. Fowler concludes that this requires a "conjunctive faith," or the capacity to embrace polarities in one's life, alertness to paradox, and the ability to hold multiple interpretations of reality in view. This understanding of spirituality is particularly required of those who are willing to embrace mighty stories and practice dangerous rituals. It is a spirituality that allows us to practice reconciliation without resolution.

○

It was mid December 1972. The negotiations between the United States and North Vietnamese delegations in Paris had collapsed, and President Nixon had renewed the order for massive bombing of Hanoi and Haiphong. U.S. citizens, already horrified by the war, were stunned at the brutality of this sudden and violent reescalation. In one small church in Milwaukee, an interdenominational group of Christians gathered in a reconciliation service to pray for forgiveness and ask for absolution. The ritual that occurred that winter's eve, however, was like no other they had ever experienced.

"We beg for forgiveness," they prayed, "for our sin against humanity, and for the violence our country perpetrates in our name." A lone minister, obviously of oriental descent, garbed in alb and stole, answered back from the sanctuary, "Your words are empty; your actions betray you; the murdering continues."

"We are truly repentant," the assembly continued, "for our national arrogance, for our reliance on bombs rather than God, and for our thirst for war rather than peace." The minister replied, "Your words are easy, but they are hollow to the thousands of innocents you have savaged in the name of democracy."

"We ask for absolution," the people prayed. "Absolve us for the pain and destruction we rain on the people of North Vietnam, and for our inability to stop the leaders who commit these crimes in our name." A pause . . . and then frightful, unexpected words from the minister: "I deny you absolution; I withhold the consolation of the church from you; I refuse to collaborate in your search for spiritual comfort, for though you may be repentant, you have not been reconciled with your enemies."

○

This story, from the time of the war in Vietnam, is remembered because it raises poignant questions about the nature of reconciliation in the broadest sense of that term and because it suggests that reconciliation is not as easy or accessible as we would like it to be. The story shatters our expectations that absolution is automatic, even when repentance is authentic. Withholding absolution in response to public acts of repentance may have been intended to demonstrate the seriousness of the sin of that war, but the denial of absolution is a shocking experience. It was undoubtedly unsettling for the participants in that Milwaukee church who expected resolution. After the ordeal of seeking reconciliation, repentant religious people often think they deserve to be forgiven, especially after enduring the agony of admitting guilt and the embarrassment of public repentance. Minimally, at least, reconciliation is the polite thing to do.

Reconciliation, however, is more than politeness or a reward for sincere apology. We know that reconciliation is not achieved simply by declaring "I'm sorry," and yet we often hope those two words will be enough to repair a broken relationship. These expectations about reconciliation are not just the result of a need to resolve conflict or be righteous. Religious traditions have sometimes implied that saying the right formulas in the right way will bring peace of mind. Sometimes it is in the form of absolution; other times it is simply a reassuring word, psalm, or prayer. Whatever the mode, most of us count on organized religion and its properly designated representatives to deliver comfort and forgiveness when we have done wrong. Ultimately, that is because we expect absolution and forgiveness from God. It is a common way we weave the divine and human narratives: people sin, God forgives, and all is well in the world. Withholding reconciliation challenges our expectations of forgiveness as an entitlement.

The nature of reconciliation in its general sense is not always easily understood or appreciated. That may in part be because the nature of reconciliation in its more particular manifestations—as, for example, after the perpetration of some evil or violent act—might also not be adequately understood or appreciated. We have learned from the stories of countless women who have experienced sexual abuse or physical violence that insisting on premature reconciliation or a hasty peace simply furthers the abuse. In order to understand and appreciate something of the remarkable gift of reconciliation and the spirituality it engenders, we need to examine what reconciliation is not before exploring what it might be.

Reconciliation Is Not Just Forgetting

Reconciliation does not require amnesia. To forgive does not mean to forget. When we insist on forgetting, reconciliation is reduced to what Robert Schreiter (1992) calls a hasty peace. This false form of reconciliation attempts to suppress the memory of violence or wrongdoing in the faulty hope of putting the violent history behind us so that we can begin afresh. It is a move toward the mythic at the expense of the parabolic. This kind of reconciliation is often advocated by the perpetrators of violence who realize the consequences of their actions and want to erase them from view. The move to such a hasty peace is actually the opposite of reconciliation, for in forgetting the suffering "the victim is forgotten and the causes of suffering are never uncovered and confronted" (Schreiter, 1992, p. 19).

○

Michael Lapsley currently works as a chaplain to a trauma center for victims of violence and torture in Cape Town, South Africa. Born in New Zealand, he joined a missionary community and was transferred to South Africa the year of his ordination in 1973. Father Lapsley was expelled from South Africa four years later. He lived for a while as part of a community of exiles in Lesotho. He then moved to Zimbabwe, where during his first three years he lived with armed police guards, because Zimbabwean authorities had notified him that he was on a South African government hit list. In April of 1990, just two months after the announcement that Nelson Mandela was to be released from prison, he received a package from South Africa. When he opened it, a letter bomb hidden inside exploded, blowing off his hands, blinding him in one eye, and damaging his sight in the other.

Once when speaking about this experience, Father Lapsley said, "The question is not one of forgetting but rather it is the problem of how do we heal our memories. How do we stop our memories from destroying us? Forgiveness, yes—that is always the Christian calling— but no one should suggest that forgiveness is glib, cheap, or easy. What does it mean to forgive those who have not confessed, those who have not changed their lives, those who have no interest in making it up to the relatives of victims and the survivors of their crimes? If you forgive a murderer, does that mean that there should be no justice? . . . It is important for all the relatives of victims and for all survivors to tell their story—and for that story, often for the first time, to be acknowledged, reverenced, and recognized. This will help us to begin to create a shared memory" [Lapsley, 1997, pp. 21, 23].

○

Michael Lapsley's moving testimony confirms that true reconciliation is neither easy nor quick. Nor is it a matter of forgetting. The antidote to this false form of reconciliation, as Lapsley notes, is ample storytelling that allows the tale, maybe for the first time, to be acknowledged, reverenced, and recognized. When we forget, we create what Schreiter has identified as the "narrative of the lie," or storytelling that ignores or glosses over the injustice. One of the dangers of secret keeping, as we have noted earlier, is that it fosters a dishonest narrative. We are learning from the struggle of the people of South Africa who are healing the wounds of apartheid that reconciliation is possible only if all the stories are told. And we are more likely to tell all the stories for the sake of reconciliation if amnesty is granted and forgiveness extended.

The opposite of dishonesty, according to Robert Schreiter, is found in embracing a "redeeming narrative" that acknowledges and liberates the truth. A liberating narrative is often created by telling our story in the context of a larger salvific narrative. For all human beings this means telling an individual tale of violence in the context of a community narrative of care; for believers of every stripe this means telling of injustice in light of God's liberating story; and for Christians, this means relating a personal story of death and destruction to story of the violent death and liberating resurrection of Jesus. Myth and parable converge with unusual power in this redeeming narrative. As Schreiter (forthcoming) states,

> The whole question of remembering past pain and forgiving the wrongdoer might better be phrased in this way: in forgiving, we do not forget; we remember in a different way. We cannot forget what has happened to us. To erase part of our memory is to erase part of our very identity as persons. But we can remember in a different way after we have experienced reconciliation and after we have extended forgiveness. We remember in a way that does not carry rancor for what has been done. We remember now from God's perspective, thanks to the grace of reconciliation.

Ritual is a privileged place for appropriating this redeeming narrative because it honors diverse stories within a community of shared values. It also provides a setting in which to explore the darkness and name the demons without mythologizing or secret keeping. Such communal gatherings have a particular capacity for embracing personal tales of violence and destruction. Meetings of Alcoholics Anonymous rehearse an exceedingly simple but nonetheless effective example of such a liberating ritual every time a member of the group says, "Hi, my name is John, and I am an alcoholic." With great simplicity this ritual introduction names the destructive force of addiction within the community of recovery. Each time a new member summons the courage or receives the grace to admit publicly her or his addiction by attending a meeting of AA and joining in this introductory ritual, the narrative of the lie is shattered, and the possibility for a redemptive narrative arises.

The privileged place for this convergence of stories—the individual with the communal, the human with the divine—is the arena of public worship. Weddings, funerals, baptisms, and even the ordinary cycle of Sunday Eucharist are moments of unusual promise for proclaiming a redemptive narrative capable of embracing multiple stories of sin and destruction. Like other rituals, however, liturgy can perpetrate the lie, keep secrets, and ultimately oppress rather than liberate the participants. Marjorie Procter-Smith identified this ritual malpractice in her consideration of liturgy and domestic violence. She writes, "Christian liturgy, like any other 'form created,' can disguise and mystify domestic violence and its roots, making the abuse seem not only acceptable, but even divinely sanctioned. . . . Exploring the intersection of liturgy and domestic violence is painful, wrenching, and costly. It is painful to acknowledge the depth of the social sin of sexism which expresses itself in violence against women, and the extent to which the church in its liturgy has abetted that violence" (Procter-Smith, 1987, pp. 18, 26).

The fact that public worship is affirmed as a privileged place for narrating the story of God's redeeming love does not ensure that redemption will always happen. Public ritual in the service of authentic reconciliation is neither hasty, glib, nor facile; nor is it automatic. It cannot be presumptuous of its virtue nor uncritical of its message. There is no bypassing the parabolic even in the privileged realm of worship in order to pursue an expeditious road to mythic resolutions. Rather, public worship, like personal narration, must encourage and confront the full and authentic memory of the violated, sometimes with terrifying honesty. Furthermore, it must amply ritualize the injustice. Our aim is not to forget wrongs that have been done but learn to remember in God's way. In extreme situations, that may even mean denying a repentant community, like the one that gathered in Milwaukee in 1972, absolution that announces reconciliation prematurely.

Reconciliation Is Not Bargaining

In an earlier chapter, we noted that those who are dying fear incompleteness. As a result of that fear, they often make bargains with God for more time. Individuals facing the end of life will promise "a life dedicated to God" or "a life in the service of the church" in exchange for some additional time to "get Jerry through college" or attend daughter Sally's second wedding or be present when Elaine's baby is born. The pattern of bargaining for more time, which Elizabeth Kübler-Ross identified as a stage in the dying process (Kübler-Ross, 1969) actually happens in less intense ways all through life and permeates many of our religious practices.

While the practice of bargaining with God is common, it is odd. Bargaining usually presumes that each party has something that the other party wants or needs. True bargaining requires a certain degree of leverage for each of the parties. It is the give-and-take through the application of such leverage that ultimately leads to what might appear to be reconciliation. Revealing bargaining for what it really is—the mutual application of leverage for the purpose of a mutually agreeable resolution—also demonstrates how problematic it is in relation to God. Robert Schreiter characterizes this type of false reconciliation as a managed process of conflict mediation.

> Reconciliation of this type is seen as being brought about by a disciplined process in which a skilled mediator helps the conflicting parties recognize the issues at conflict as representing different interests and values that have to be negotiated. Reconciliation then becomes a process of bargaining in which both sides are expected to accede some of their interests in order to reach an end to conflict. The process acknowledges that both sides have legitimate interests, but that both sets of interests cannot be met in a finite world. Consequently a balancing process must be undertaken that will require both sides to give something up, but not give up so much that the conflict flares up again [Schreiter, 1992, p. 25].

Rather than liberation, however, this form of reconciliation is actually a conspiracy of leverage. The act of balancing, which Schreiter notes as essential to this understanding of reconciliation, is also a trap. Stories are held in check; certain episodes are not mentioned; ordinary meetings that might precipitate conflict are avoided; and sacrifice is seldom perceived by both sides to be equal. Rituals of reconciliation mask the disappointment or anger that often festers around lost ground and lost leverage of power.

Recall, for example, the so-called "historic handshake" between Chairman Yasir Arafat and Israeli Prime Minister Yitzhak Rabin that took place on September 13, 1993. The occasion was the signing of an unprecedented accord between the Palestinian Liberation Organization and Israel on the White House lawn. The signing of this treaty on Palestinian self-rule in the Gaza Strip and Jericho was supposed to signal the end of years of acrimony and tension between the PLO and Israel. Some heralded the event as an important moment of reconciliation between these enemies and the dawn of real peace. The perfunctory three-second handshake that capped the treaty signing, orchestrated by President Clinton, who stood between Arafat and Rabin, underscored the staged nature of the whole process. The handshake itself was not a spontaneous ritual gesture but a clearly managed moment in which Clinton physically prodded Rabin and Arafat toward each other. This closely controlled ritual betrayed the fact that opposing forces were balanced so precariously that any shift in leverage from one side to the other could undue the entire process. When Rabin was assassinated a short time later, the delicately arrived-at peace between Palestinians and Israelis was upset, and the conflict had to be managed all over again.

Authentic reconciliation is not a balancing act. True peace is neither managed nor bartered. It is not achieved by establishing a sufficient amount of power so that the other can be either held at bay or contained through some leveraged position. Rather, reconciliation is about unbridled generosity that catches us off guard, upsets our calculated responses, and creates the possibility for transformation. For Christians, the crucifixion and death of Jesus is a paradigm of reconciliation at the other end of the spectrum from managed bargaining or conflict mediation. The result is a graciousness that must either be divine or insane. John Shea (1977) acknowledges the ambiguous line between the character of divine love and what may seem like insanity to us in his "Prayer for the Lady Who Forgave Us."

> There is a long-suffering lady
> with thin hands
> who stands on the corner of Delphia and Lawrence
> and forgives you.
> "You are forgiven," she smiles.
> The neighborhood is embarrassed.
> It is sure it has done nothing wrong
> yet everyday, in a small voice
> it is forgiven.
> On the way to the Jewel Food Store
> housewives pass her with hard looks
> then whisper in the cereal section.
> Stan Dumke asked her right out
> what she was up to
> and she forgave him.
> A group who care about the neighborhood
> agree that if she was old it would be harmless
> or if she was religious it would be understandable
> but as it is . . . they asked her to move on.
> Like all things with eternal purposes
> she stayed.
> And she was informed upon.
> On a most unforgiving day of snow and slush
> while she was reconciling a reluctant passerby
> the State People
> whose business is sanity,
> persuaded her into a car.
> She is gone.
> We are reduced to forgetting [Shea, 1977, pp. 24–25]

Reconciliation is not the result of forgetting or bargaining because it is finally the work of God. Strategies are necessary in order to create truth-telling communities in which we might experience the grace of reconciliation and discover what God has already done. But our strategies do not effect reconciliation. The heart of Christian belief is that the world has already been reconciled in the work of Christ. Although repentance and forgiveness are necessary responses to shattered relationships in human life, they are the consequence of, rather than the condition for, reconciliation. The complexity of human life and the pervasiveness of human conflict is a further reminder that reconciliation requires more than human effort. It can only be the work of God within us.

Reconciliation Is Not Revenge

Models of false reconciliation are not only apparent in contemporary political maneuvering or economic and therapeutic bargaining. They also permeate the icons of popular culture. For example, films produced in the United States frequently convey messages about reconciliation in authentic and unauthentic modes. Revenge—specifically, what might be termed "justifiable revenge"—is one of the more prevalent movie themes today. It is often the motivation behind westerns, war movies, martial arts stories, or murder mysteries.

This theme of justifiable revenge has received a particular cinematic twist in recent years. Not only is the rancher seeking revenge on the rustlers who stole his cattle and the young martial arts expert retaliating against the gang that killed his mentor. Revenge is no longer just the prerogative of cop husbands who have lost their wives because of drug violence or members of the CIA whose child was kidnapped by a ring of international terrorists. Rather, in a growing number of movies, spurned wives, abused girlfriends, and oppressed female employees who have suffered injustice at the hands of their husbands, lovers, or bosses are gaining center stage.

The popularity of the "revenge movie" is understandable. We enjoy seeing the oppressor, the perpetrator, or the villain receive their comeuppance. We delight in watching the underdog take on the people at the top. We also celebrate when people who have been victims for most of their lives no longer act as victims. It is not surprising that movie audiences erupt in approval, for example, when the character of Bernadine in *Waiting to Exhale* wreaks incendiary revenge on the belongings of her husband, who dumped her for another woman. In this moment in our history, when there is such growing social awareness regarding the continued harassment and abuse of women at home and in the workplace, the popularity of the "woman's revenge movie" is particularly understandable.

The equation of revenge with reconciliation is also reflected in the growing demand for the death penalty from families of violent crime victims and their insistence on being present at the execution in order to bring closure to their grieving. For some families, revenging a violent death becomes an all-consuming passion; their grief is not resolved until the perpetrator has been brought to "justice." If justice is primarily understood as retribution, as it often is, the cycle of violence continues, and nothing changes. Retribution creates new victims and new demands for revenge. Justice turns to revenge when it does not seek truth. Reconciliation, as Schreiter outlines it, is rather about truth, and truth dictates its own kind of justice. Moreover, truth is a prelude to justice because it undoes the lies of the evildoer. Robin Green has made a similar observation in his book *A Step Too Far* (1990): "It is really impossible to address questions of reconciliation until we have started to reflect on the nature of self-deception" (p. 29). Reconciliation is a new creation, born in truth, that seeks to reestablish authentic relations with God, with self, and with others.

In one sense, movies of revenge and the demands for retribution through the law are hopeful because they demonstrate ways that individuals can liberate themselves from the power of systemic evil or affirm that as individuals we are not powerless in the face of violent crime. At the same time, they communicate a flawed subtext about reconciliation. From this perspective, reconciliation requires that the oppressor have a real experience of oppression and that he (or she) experience something of the pain of the victim in order that the victim and/or survivors might experience emotional liberation.

The problem with revenge is that it is predicated on the assumption that reconciliation comes by replicating experience rather than by cultivating empathy. Instead of inviting the oppressor to imagine the pain of the victim, the oppressor is given his or her own pain. Instead of engaging the perpetrator in the story of the victim, the perpetrator is provided with his own alternate story of hurt or destruction. Having a parallel experience of violence or destruction is not true reconciliation, just as having any parallel experience is not the same as entering the story of another. Understanding the whole truth of any situation comes from speaking and listening for the truth. It also comes from the capacity to listen empathically to the other side.

Empathy might be characterized as "your pain in my heart." We understand the pain of others by listening carefully to their stories. Empathy is a process by which we think and feel ourselves into the place of another and then by vicarious introspection imagine the experience of another as if it were our own in order to arrive at an appreciation of the world of another. The possibility of empathy not only requires attentive listening; it presumes the exercise of imagination. Empathy is what Alfred Margulies calls an "imaginative projection of one's consciousness into another being" (Margulies, 1989, p. 16). It is not, therefore, supplying the other with an equally devastating or painful experience. Rather, it is the intent of both victim and oppressor to enter the world of the other. When that can occur, there is the possibility of reconciliation without the expectation of facile resolution. The fallacy of revenge is that it may "even the score" by replicating the pain, but it does not eliminate pain or alter the story of suffering.

Empathy is a matter of imaginative seeing and attending with the heart. The Sufi mystic Jalal ad-Din Muhammad Dinar-Rumi alludes to such attending in his verse "When Things Are Heard," when he writes "if words do not reach the ear in the chest, nothing happens" (Barks and Bly, 1981). This stunning metaphor goes to the center of empathy, which is not about sharing an experience but entering the experience of another. When the practice of reconciliation is governed by the desire to understand the world of another, even someone who may have seriously wounded me or violently damaged me, their first task is to let the other's story reach "the ear in [my] chest." That kind of imagining another's story enables us to discover reconciliation beyond amnesia, beyond bargaining, and beyond revenge.

There is more to reconciliation than empathy, but hearing the other's story as fully and as accurately as possible is a necessary beginning. Reconciliation is possible only when the truth is told and clearly heard. It is essential, therefore, that we learn how to include the alienating event as part of the process of reconciliation. In order to do that, we will need to alter our expectations of who or what we must be. Self-righteousness is an impediment to reconciliation. So is blaming. At the same time, the acknowledgment of responsibility is a necessary part of the process. Restitution without revenge or some effort at restoration may also be necessary for a broken relationship to be repaired, because it demonstrates that the offender takes the consequences of the sin seriously.

A Spirituality of Reconciliation

Reconciliation is many things. It is the work of God, discovered in moments of victimization or vulnerability, that enables us to locate our story in a larger narrative. For the Christian, this means that the difficult memories of the past and painful experiences of the present are transformed by being placed in the story of Christ's passion and death. Reconciliation is also something that we do. It is our response to abuse and violence in our lives. Although we often think of reconciliation as overcoming alienation for the sake of returning to a previously known peaceable state, Christian reconciliation does not reconstitute things as they were before. Rather, reconciliation takes us to a new place (Schreiter, 1992). Whatever expression reconciliation might take, it is always something more than forgetting or bargaining or revenge. It is a process with many moments that allows time for repair and enables us to heal the hurt without forgetting the harm. Reconciliation is about a new creation in which "our struggles are yoked to God's design for the world" (Schreiter, forthcoming).

In addition to being a gift from God and a strategy for human living, reconciliation is also a spirituality that includes at least the following characteristics: embracing contradiction, honoring the other, showing hospitality to strangers, and being surprised by grace. Reconciliation is not simply about righting wrongs or canceling debts but a way of being that transforms all human narrative and ritual. This is not always an easy place in which to be: a place devoid of tension and free of pain. On the contrary, it is uncharted territory that promises its own terror in our new-found vulnerability. It is the terror of transformation and change. In this new world we are promised death and threatened with resurrection.

Our aim in exploring reconciliation at the conclusion of this book is not to introduce more ritual or narrative forms. Rather, we are proposing a spirituality of reconciliation that transforms the stories we tell and the rituals we make into occasions for weaving human and divine narratives in a more inclusive way. The spirituality we are proposing is not a prescription for victims or oppressors; rather, it is a perspective for telling stories and making rituals, for living in a time with more diversity and fewer absolutes.

Reconciliation: Embracing Contradiction

The spirit of reconciliation, which enables us to enter a world of contradiction, is the same disposition that allows us to embrace paradox without needing to resolve it. This is a spirituality that thrives only in paradox, between the mythic and parabolic, around the human and the divine story, and in the tension of the individual and communal. It is a spirituality that is nourished by the ambiguity of mighty stories and dangerous rituals. This experience of ambiguity is inevitable because pluralistic living is a permanent part of contemporary human society. If we are to flourish in this society, we need to learn how to tolerate opposing forces, both within and without.

Living with contradiction is, however, more than social necessity. For Christians, Parker Palmer has observed, it means living with contradiction because we follow the way of the cross. "The cross speaks of the greatest paradox of all: That to live we have to die" (Palmer, 1980, p. 38). The cross is a symbol that suggests the oppositions of life. It is the divine-human, death-life paradox of God in Jesus Christ that shapes us and beckons us. Moreover, in order to reach the depth of human living we long for, we must learn to live the contradictions as fully as possible. We are willing to tell our stories and plan our rituals knowing full well they are filled with paradox and contradiction.

Throughout this book, we have sought to embody this spirit of reconciliation by acknowledging contradictions such as myth and parable, individual and communal, public and private. We have done so from the conviction that these contradictions hold the deepest and most enduring truths of life. The impulse to absolutize stories or rituals is therefore alien to a spirituality of reconciliation that invites us to love the contradictions in the hope that we will thereby discover the redeeming paradox.

Reconciliation: Honoring the Other

David Malouf's powerful novel, *Remembering Babylon* (1993), tells the tale of Gemmy, a British cabin boy who survived a shipwreck in the late 1800s, is washed ashore in the far north of Australia, and cared for by Aborigines. After a number of years Gemmy finds his way into a white settlement, where there is great concern about his arrival. There is no harm in him, it is said, "but he is a danger just the same." What made Gemmy so disturbing was the "mixture of monstrous strangeness and unwelcome likeness" which is always the problem of the proximate other. Gemmy comes to live with the McIvor family, and his presence changes members of that family. A year after Gemmy's arrival, Jock McIvor reflects on this change in relation to his friends and family:

> Was he changed? He saw now that he must be, since they were as they had always been and he could not agree with them. . . . It was as if he had seen the world till now not through his own eyes out of some singular self, but through the eyes of a fellow who was always in company, even when he was alone; a sociable self, wrapped always in a communal warmth that protected it from dark matters and all the

blinding light of things, but also from the knowledge that there was a place out there where the self might stand alone. Wading through waist-high grass, he was surprised to see all the tips beaded with green, as if some new growth had come into the world that till now he had never seen or heard of [Malouf, 1993, pp. 106–107].

Learning to honor the other, whoever that might be, is a characteristic of Fowler's conjunctive faith and a prerequisite for authentic reconciliation. It is not always easy to see the world of the other as a gift instead of a threat. When we are able, however, our world is enlarged through our engagement with the world of the other. That is what happened when Jock McIvor met Gemmy. It is what happens often whenever a spirituality of reconciliation fosters true respect for the other and invites us to show hospitality to the stranger.

Reconciliation: Hospitality to the Stranger

The stranger is our future waiting to happen; the other is the parable and myth that looms on our horizon. They are sources of anxiety, fear, and sometimes violence. They are also necessary, for without the other, without the stranger, we are bereft of the distance we need to discover the God who is wholly other and even to glimpse ourselves more clearly. In the words of the poet Rainer Maria Rilke, "Once the realization is accepted that even between the closest human beings infinite distances continue to exist, a wonderful living side by side can grow up, if they succeed in loving the distance between them, which makes it possible for each to see the other whole against a wide sky" (Mood, 1975, p. 28).

The other is dangerous, and difference is challenging—but the presence of the other is unsettling also because I am reminded that I too am a stranger. When I walk an unfamiliar neighborhood, turn off the freeway too early, or walk into the wrong meeting room, I discover that the stranger is myself. The experience of the other, or myself as other in unfamiliar settings, also reminds me that sometimes I am a stranger to family and friends, an outsider to my own home or place of work. Ultimately, of course, this experience of the stranger rehearses at close range that sometimes I am a stranger even to myself. Thus we sometimes find ourselves feeling what St. Paul writes, "I do not understand my own action, for I do not do what I want but I do the very things I hate" (Rom. 7:15). A more contemporary prophet, the songwriter Billy Joel, says something similar in his song "The Stranger" when he asks whether you ever see the stranger in yourself.

The Gospel story that underscores most powerfully the grace of the stranger is not one in which Jesus meets a stranger but rather one in which Jesus himself is encountered as the stranger. It is the well-known story mentioned earlier of the two disciples on the road to Emmaus in Luke 24. The two are discussing the crucifixion and death of Jesus, who appears to them on the road, but they do not recognize him. As the story unfolds it is the stranger who opens the disciples' hearts to the scriptures and interprets the events for them. When they reach their destination they press Jesus to stay and join them for a meal. It was at this ritual meal that they recognize him in the breaking of the bread. This early Eucharistic story underscores in a particularly pointed way that Eucharist is not possible without the stranger, without the other, without the different.

Showing hospitality, as Schreiter has observed, is a prelude to reconciliation because it sets up an environment in which trust, kindness, and safety prevail. "Kindness reaffirms that violence is now past and that the vulnerability that healing requires can count on a place to operate. Safety is the other side of trust [that] allows the bonds of trust to be rebuilt" (Schreiter, forthcoming). Hospitality is part of a spirituality of reconciliation because it prepares damaged souls to discover the healing grace of God in their lives.

Reconciliation: The Courage to Be Surprised by Grace

Learning to embrace the other and honor the stranger is stepping into the unexplored world of reconciliation. It is a world unexplored because once the other is embraced and the stranger honored, we are in a place in which we have never before been. Jock McIvor was surprised to see all the tips of grass beaded with green. He had been among the tall grass before, and yet it was as if he was seeing it for the first time. McIvor's friends and family were not the same, either. The ordinary is transformed in our seeing, and the familiar is quite new and different when our vision has been transformed. We are surprised by what we discover in the uncharted territory that reconciliation creates.

In order to embody a spirituality of reconciliation, we need the courage to be surprised. If we are willing to live toward reconciliation as victims of violence or abuse, we will find instances of healing grace in unlikely places from unlikely people. When we experience ourselves being forgiven, we will in turn be surprised by the ways God works forgiveness in the lives of others. Our stories and God's stories intersect unexpectedly. Ultimately it is in the stories we tell and the rituals we enact that the great paradox is exposed: to live we have to die. In the meantime, we look for enough courage to love the questions and live the contradictions of the stories and rituals that bring them to life. To do so in a spirit of reconciliation does not demand resolution but allows transformation as we never imagined it and grace where we least expect it.

○

Father Lawrence Jenko was an American Roman Catholic priest held hostage in Beirut, Lebanon, for 564 days in the 1980s. He was secluded in various apartments and was most often chained blindfolded to a radiator. (In the Arab world, if you see your captors you must die.) When he was moved he was gagged with a dirty rag in his mouth, wrapped like a mummy, placed under the chassis of a truck, and driven around for an hour or two to a new location. He often feared suffocation in the moves.

Because of the constant blindfold, he never knew when he was being touched whether it was a touch of violence or a touch of compassion. His glasses were taken from him, so he could not read anything. In the beginning he was imprisoned alone, but later he was held with William Buckley, Ben Weir (a Presbyterian minister), John Jacobsen (a CNN reporter), and Terry Anderson. He watched William Buckley die from lack of needed medication. After that the Lebanese kidnapped a Jewish doctor and made him care for the rest of them.

Both the heat and the cold were unbearable. There was torture and abuse. He was allowed to leave the cell once a day, to go to the bathroom, when his captors felt like it. John Jacobsen eventually escaped. After Jenko was released, Terry Anderson was held another four years. Jenko said that he survived by repeating over and over several phrases. One is an old Jewish proverb: "When violence happens, first you cry, then you sing, and then you remain silent." He also said to himself during periods of torture, "I am a person of dignity. I am loved, I am worthy, and I do have a destiny." He offered the Eucharist every day, even when all he had to offer was a small pile of dust from the floor.

His guards were often cruel. Sometimes, however, they would ask if he needed anything. His little joke with them was "only a little money for a taxicab to Damascus." On the day of his release, the cruelest of the guards slipped something into his pocket. Then once again he was bound, gagged, and blindfolded, driven two hours under the truck to the outskirts of Damascus, where he was dumped by the side of the road. When he finally freed himself, removed the blindfold and gag, he found in his pocket enough money to take a taxicab to the center of the city.

○

EPILOGUE

IT IS DIFFICULT for two practical theologians to share a significant experience without reflecting upon it. Writing this book has been such an experience for us, and an important episode in our personal and professional lives. In the Preface we indicated that this book was born in friendship between two very different individuals. Coauthoring this volume has revealed to us, however, just how different we are from each other. Writing together has been both a mighty and a dangerous experience for our friendship. It has also, in many ways, been an occasion for struggling together with many of the paradoxes and principles contained in this book.

Throughout the book, we have explored the need and the challenge to balance the human and divine perspective, the individual and the communal, or the public and the private. While we were writing about that balance, we were struggling with our own ability to balance two very strong, yet sometimes divergent perspectives, about narrative and ritual, liturgy and pastoral care. We have learned again and again through this process that these differences were reflective not only of dissimilar ways of thinking but more especially of two very different personal stories that we were weaving together to make a book with one narrative.

It would have been possible, and certainly easier, simply to divide the task of writing the chapters equally in order to honor those differences and respect one another's autonomy in the common project. While the project began that way, in the redrafting phase we plunged into a more radical form of coauthorship. We critiqued, redesigned, and rewrote each other's chapters. The mythic hope of a single unified book was only possible, we discovered, through a painful parabolic process of coauthorship. While the success of the effort can, in one sense, only be judged by the reader, our ultimate satisfaction with the process is manifest in our difficulty at the end in recognizing, and even remembering, who wrote which passage.

The clash and convergence of the authors' own stories also revealed similarities and differences in our understanding of the divine narrative. Many times our conversations about a particularly problematic idea or passage revealed our own uncertainty or disagreement about God's role in our personal lives or the church or the world. Accommodation about beliefs is never easy. Trying to weave together our very human stories meant confronting the place of the divine in our lives. So we talked: often no longer about the book but about faith and doctrine and our very different experiences and interpretations of the God story.

At the end of this process, as we write this Epilogue, we are still friends. But the friendship has been forever altered. We have known one another well for twelve years. But because of the stories we have told to each other and our joint engagement in this book-writing ritual, we are now more flawed in the other's eye, more vulnerable, less mythic, more complex. There is more room and more need for ongoing reconciliation between us. Not reconciliation in the sense of hasty peace over our disagreements or quick resolution of our differences but continued and deepened friendship in the midst of those differences and disagreements. We have learned for ourselves, through this process, what we wrote about the ongoing need for a spirituality of reconciliation in a world in which difference is increasingly nearby.

We finish this book in the midst of the Easter season. Through the good auspices of one of the Lotti granddaughters, we are the recipients of one of the famous *calzone* featured in Chapter Two. We will share that resurrection food at the end of this project. While we will toast the completion of a book, we will also drink to a friendship that, though not perfect, endures and continues to be life-giving. And we will feast in thanksgiving for the pain and the privilege of having shared in this mighty story and dangerous ritual.

REFERENCES

Anderson, H. "Preaching as Validation: The Christmas Story and Family Birth Story." *New Theology Review*, 1991, 4(4), 78–83.

Anderson, H. "Belated Grief for a Miscarriage." *New Theology Review*, 1995, 8(2), 76–78.

Anderson, H., and Fite, R. C. *Becoming Married*. Louisville, Ky.: Westminster/John Knox, 1993.

Attig, T. *How We Grieve: Relearning the World*. New York: Oxford University Press, 1996.

Barks, C., and Bly, R. (eds.). *Night & Sleep*. Cambridge, Mass.: Yellow Moon Press, 1981.

Brokering, H. *"I" Opener: 80 Parables*. St. Louis, Mo.: Concordia Publishing House, 1974.

Brueggemann, W. *Power, Providence and Personality*. Louisville, Ky.: Westminster/John Knox Press, 1990.

Buechner, F. *Godric*. New York: Atheneum, 1981.

Chopp, R. *Saving Work: Feminist Practices of Theological Education*. Louisville, Ky.: Westminster, John Knox Press, 1995.

Churchill, L. "The Human Experience of Dying." *Soundings*, 1979, 62, 24–37.

Close, H. T. "An Adoption Ceremony." *Journal of Pastoral Care*, 1993, 47(4), 382–386.

Cococh, R. *Ritual in Industrial Society*. London: Allen and Unwin, 1974.

Cox, H. *The Feast of Fools: A Theological Essay on Festivity and Fantasy*. Cambridge, Mass.: Harvard University Press, 1969.

Crossan, J. D. *The Dark Interval: Towards a Theology of Story*. Niles, Ill.: Argus, 1975.

de Mello, A. *The Song of the Bird*. Garden City, N.Y.: Image Books, 1984.

Dillard, A. *Holy the Firm*. New York: HarperCollins, 1977.

Driver, T. F. *The Magic of Ritual*. San Francisco: Harper San Francisco, 1991.

Erikson, E. H. *Toys and Reasons: Stages in the Ritualization of Experience*. New York: Norton, 1977.

Estes, C. P. *The Gift of Story: A Wise Tale About What Is Enough*. New York: Ballantine, 1993.

Foley, E. *The Chicago Guide to Preaching*. Chicago: Liturgy Training Publications, 1997.

Foley, E. "Preaching About Dignity, or Preaching with Dignity?" In R. Duffy (ed.), *Human Dignity*, forthcoming.

Fowler, J. W. *Stages of Faith*. San Francisco: Harper San Francisco, 1981.

Friedman, J., and Combs, G. *Narrative Therapy*. New York: Norton, 1996.

Gallup, G. H. *Religion in America 1996*. Princeton, N.J.: Princeton Religion Research Center, 1996.

Gerkin, C. *Widening the Horizons: Pastoral Responses to a Fragmented Society*. Philadelphia: Westminster Press, 1986.

Gibran, K. *The Prophet*. New York: Knopf, 1923.

Greeley, A. "Why Do Catholics Stay in the Church?" *The New York Times Magazine*, July 10, 1994, pp. 38–41.

Green, R. *Intimate Mystery: Our Need to Worship*. Cambridge, Mass.: Cowley, 1988.

Grimes, R. L. *Beginning in Ritual Studies*. Lanham, Md.: University Press of America, 1982.

Grimes, R. L. *Reading, Writing and Ritualizing: Ritual in Fictive, Liturgical and Public Places*. Washington, D.C.: Pastoral Press, 1993.

Grimes, R. L. *Marrying and Burying: Rites of Passage in a Man's Life*. Boulder, Colo.: Westview Press, 1995.

Hamilton, D.S.M. *Through the Waters: Baptism and the Christian Life*. Edinburgh, Scotland: T. and T. Clark, 1990.

Hefner, P. "Focusing the Spectrum: Mythic and Ritual Resources for the Current Crisis in American Praxis." *Currents*, 1993, *20*(5), 335–344.

Hersey, J. "The Announcement." *Atlantic Monthly*, Dec. 1981, pp. 88–92.

Jacob, H. E. *Six Thousand Years of Bread*. (R. Winston and C. Winston, trans.). New York: Doubleday, 1944.

Karris, R. *Luke: Artist and Theologian*. Mahwah, N.J.: Paulist Press, 1985.

Keene, J. A. *A Winter's Song: A Liturgy for Women Seeking Healing from Sexual Abuse in Childhood*. New York: Pilgrim Press, 1991.

Kelleher, M. M. "Liturgical Theology: A Task and a Method." *Worship*, 1988, *62*(1), 2–25.

Kübler-Ross, E. *On Death and Dying*. Old Tappan, N.J.: Macmillan, 1969.

Lapsley, M. "My Journey of Reconciliation in South Africa—From Fighter to Healer." *New Theology Review*, 1997, *10*(2), 21–23.

Littell, M. S., and Gutman, S. W. (eds.). *Liturgies on the Holocaust: An Interfaith Anthology*. Valley Forge, Pa.: Trinity Press International, 1996.

Luther, M. "Large Catechism." In T. G. Tappert (ed. and trans.), *The Book of Concord*. Philadelphia: Muhlenberg Press, 1959. (Originally published 1538.)

Lutheran Book of Worship. Minneapolis: Augsburg Fortress, 1978.

Malouf, D. *Remembering Babylon.* New York: Pantheon Books, 1993.

Margulies, A. *The Empathic Imagination.* New York: Norton, 1989.

McAdams, D. *The Stories We Live By: Personal Myths and the Making of the Self.* New York: Morrow, 1993.

McDargh, J. "Telling Our Stories of God: The Contributions of a Psychoanalytic Perspective." In C. Simpkinson and A. Simpkinson (eds.), *Sacred Stories: The Celebration of the Power of Stories to Transform and Heal.* San Francisco: Harper San Francisco, 1993.

McKenna, J. H. "Infant Baptism: Theological Reflections." *Worship,* 1996, *70*(3), 194–210.

Mead, M. "Ritual and Social Crisis." In J. Shaughnessy (ed.), *Roots of Ritual.* Grand Rapids, Mich.: Eerdmans, 1973.

Mitchell, K. R., and Anderson, H. *All Our Losses, All Our Griefs.* Philadelphia: Westminster Press, 1983.

Mood, J. (ed.). *Rilke on Love and other Difficulties.* New York: Norton, 1975.

Nouwen, H.J.M. *A Letter of Consolation.* San Francisco: Harper San Francisco, 1982.

Nussbaum, M. M. "Sleeping on the Wing." *Assembly,* 1995, *21*(5), 696–697, 702.

O'Connor, F. *Everything That Rises Must Converge.* New York: Noonday Press, 1965.

Palmer, P. *The Promise of Paradox: A Celebration of Contradictions in the Christian Life.* Notre Dame, Ind.: Ave Maria Press, 1980.

Postman, N. *Amusing Ourselves to Death.* New York: Penguin Books, 1985.

Price, J. "New Divorce Rituals." *Family Therapy Networker,* 1989, *13*(4), 45.

Procter-Smith, M. "'Reorganizing Victimization': The Intersection Between Liturgy and Domestic Violence." *Perkins Journal,* 1987, *40,* 17–27.

Quello, D. Y. "A Blessing for Kirsten." *The Lutheran,* Aug. 1996, pp. 16–17.

Rahner, K. *On the Theology of Death.* (C. H. Henkey, trans.). New York: Herder and Herder, 1961.

Rahner, K. *Theological Investigations XIV.* (D. Bourke, trans.). New York: Seabury Press, 1976.

Ramshaw, E. *Ritual and Pastoral Care.* Philadelphia: Fortress Press, 1987.

Rosenthal, T. *How Could I Not Be Among You?* New York: Braziller, 1973.

Schreiter, R. *Constructing Local Theologies.* Maryknoll, N.Y.: Orbis Books, 1985.

Schreiter, R. *Reconciliation: Mission and Ministry in a Changing Social Order.* Maryknoll, N.Y.: Orbis Books, 1992.

Schreiter, R. *Healing Wounds: Reconciliation as Spirituality and Strategy.* Maryknoll, N.Y.: Orbis Books, forthcoming.

Schwartz, M. *Letting Go: Morrie's Reflections on Living While Dying.* New York: Walker, 1996.

Shannon, T. A., and Faso, C. N. *Let Them Go Free: A Family Prayer Service to Assist in the Withdrawal of Life Support Systems*. Kansas City, Mo.: Sheed and Ward, 1987.

Shea, J. *The Hour of the Unexpected*. Niles, Ill.: Argus Communications, 1977.

Smith, M., and O'Loughlin, F. *Go Forth Faithful Christian: Prayer Services for Withdrawal of Life Support Systems and Donation of Bodily Organs*. Melbourne, Australia: Diocesan Liturgical Centre, 1991.

Stevenson, K. *To Join Together: The Rite of Marriage*. New York: Pueblo Publishing, 1987.

Tolstoy, L. *The Death of Ivan Illich*. (L. Solotaroll, trans.). New York: Bantam Books, 1981. (Originally published 1886.)

Trokan, J. "Ministry to Marriage: Pastoral Praxis and Theological Assumptions." In M. G. Lawler and W. P. Roberts (eds.), *Christian Marriage and Family*. Collegeville, Md.: Liturgical Press, 1996.

Trueheart, C. "Welcome to the Next Church." *Atlantic Monthly*, Aug. 1996, pp. 37–58.

United States Catholic Conference. *Pastoral Care of the Sick: Liturgy Documentary Series 3*. Washington, D.C.: Office of Publishing Services, 1983.

Walker, B. G. *Women's Rituals: A Sourcebook*. San Francisco: Harper San Francisco, 1990.

Walsh, F., and McGoldrick, M. *Living Beyond Loss: Death in the Family*. New York: Norton, 1991.

Whitehead, E. E., and Whitehead, J. D. *Marrying Well: Stages on the Journey of Christian Marriage*. New York: Image Books, 1983.

Wiesel, E. *The Gates of the Forest*. (F. Frenaye, trans.). Austin, Tex.: Holt, Rinehart and Winston, 1966.

Wiltshire, S. F. *Seasons of Grief and Grace: A Sister's Story of AIDS*. Nashville, Tenn.: Vanderbilt University Press, 1994.

Winquist, C. E. *Practical Hermeneutics: A Revised Agenda for the Ministry*. Chico, Calif.: Scholars Press, 1980.

World Council of Churches. *Baptism, Eucharist and Ministry*. Faith and Order Paper no. 111. Geneva: World Council of Churches, 1982.

FURTHER READING

CHAPTER ONE

Bateson, M. C. *Composing a Life.* New York: Plume, 1989.

Gerkin, C. *The Living Human Document: Re-Visioning Pastoral Counseling in a Hermeneutical Mode.* Nashville, Tenn.: Abingdon Press, 1984.

Tilley, T. W. *Story Theology.* Collegeville, Minn.: The Liturgical Press, 1990.

CHAPTER TWO

Bell, C. *Ritual Theology, Ritual Practice.* New York: Oxford University Press, 1992.

Douglas, M. *Natural Symbols.* New York: Vintage Books, 1973.

Shaughnessy, J. (ed.). *The Roots of Ritual.* Grand Rapids, Mich.: Eerdmans, 1973.

Turner, V. *The Ritual Process: Structure and Anti-Structure.* Hawthorne, N.Y.: Aldine de Gruyter, 1969.

CHAPTER THREE

Underwood, R. L. *Pastoral Care and the Means of Grace.* Minneapolis: Augsburg Fortress, 1993.

Willimon, W. H. *Worship as Pastoral Care.* Nashville, Tenn.: Abingdon Press, 1979.

Wimberly, E. P. *Using Scripture in Pastoral Counseling.* Nashville, Tenn.: Abingdon Press, 1994.

Worgul, G. *From Magic to Metaphor.* Mahwah, N.J.: Paulist Press, 1980.

CHAPTER FOUR

Fitzgerald, T. *Infant Baptism: A Parish Celebration.* Chicago: Liturgy Training Publications, 1994.

Lathrop, G. (ed.). *Open Questions in Worship: What Is Changing in Baptismal Practice?* Minneapolis: Augsbury Fortress, 1995.

Searle, M. *Alternative Futures for Worship Volume 2: Baptism and Confirmation.* Collegeville, Minn.: Liturgical Press, 1987.

CHAPTER FIVE

Cooke, B. (ed.). *Alternative Futures for Worship, Volume Five: Marriage*. Collegeville, Minn.: The Liturgical Press, 1987.

Stevenson, K. "Van Gennup and Marriage: Strange Bedfellows?" *Ephemerides Liturgicae* 100 (1986), 138–151.

Whitehead, E., and Whitehead, J. *Marrying Well: Stages on the Journey of a Christian Marriage*. Garden City, N.Y.: Image Books, 1983.

CHAPTER SIX

Begman, L., and Thiermann, L. *First Person Mortal: Personal Narratives of Illness, Dying and Grief*. New York: Paragon House, 1995.

Nuland, S. B. *How We Die: Reflections on Life's Final Chapter*. New York: Knopf, 1994.

Rutherford, R. *The Death of a Christian: The Rite of Funerals* (rev. ed.). Collegeville, Minn.: Liturgical Press, 1990.

CHAPTER SEVEN

Hines, V. "Self-Generated Ritual: Trend or Fad?" *Worship* 55 (1981), 404–419.

Imber-Black, E., and Roberts, J. *Rituals for Our Time: Celebrating, Healing, and Changing Our Relationships*. New York: HarperCollins, 1992.

Ostdick, G. "Human Situations in Need of Ritualization." *New Theology Review,* 1990, 3(1), 36–50.

CHAPTER EIGHT

Lathrop, G. *Holy Things: A Liturgical Theology*. Minneapolis: Augsburg Fortress, 1993.

LaVerdiere, E. *Dining in the Kingdom of God*. Chicago: Liturgy Training, 1994.

Moloney, F. *A Body Broken for a Broken People*. Melbourne, Australia: Collins Dove, 1990.

CHAPTER NINE

Fink, P. (ed.). *Alternative Futures for Worship, Volume Four: Reconciliation*. Collegeville, Minn.: The Liturgical Press, 1987.

Kennedy, R. (ed.). *Reconciliation: The Continuing Agenda*. Collegeville, Minn.: The Liturgical Press, 1988.

Patton, J. *Is Human Forgiveness Possible? A Pastoral Care Perspective*. Nashville, Tenn.: Abingdon Press, 1985.

INDEX

A

Abandonment, dying person's fear of, 106–107

Abduction, 126. *See also* Missing persons

Abuse: Christian liturgy and, 173; forgetting versus reconciliation of, 170–171; forgiveness versus reconciliation of, 170; and grace, 182–183; ritual for healing of, 129, 147–148

Agnostics, 116–117

Alcoholics Anonymous meetings, 172

Alzheimer's disease: creating good-bye rituals for, 136–139; and mourning of death, 112–113

Ambiguity, and spirituality of reconciliation, 168–176, 179–180. *See also* Paradox; Reconciliation

"Americo" story, 106–107

"Ana Maria" story, 162

Anderson, H., 53, 81, 93, 132, 166

Anderson, T., 183

Animals, ritual of, 22, 25–26

Anointing of the Sick, 109

Antiritual, 135–136

Apology, and reconciliation, 169–170. *See also* Reconciliation

Arafat, Y., 174

Arlington National Cemetery, 21

Attig, T., 114

Authenticity: in narrative, 18–19, 171–173; and reconciliation, 167, 171–179; in ritual, 35, 128–129; in wedding preparation, 91; in worship, 172–173. *See also* Ritual-narrative honesty

Autonomy/differentiation: birth stories and, 60–61; family stories and, 79–81; leaving home and, 85; marriage and, 79–83, 85; parental expectations' influence on, 62; uniqueness of children and, 61–62. *See also* Leaving home; Marriage

B

Baptism, 71–74; and death, 110, 112, 122; death-resurrection story and, 65–66, 73; parabolic narrating of, 64–66, 72–74; and pastoral care, 66–72; prebaptismal catechesis for, 69–71; renewal of vows of, by dying person, 110; shift in theological focus in, 69–70; and stillbirth, 133–134. *See also* Birth

Baptism, Eucharist and Ministry (World Council of Churches), 65–66, 70, 150

Bargaining: and dying, 104, 173; versus reconciliation, 173–176

Barks, C., 178

Beauty and the Beast, 13, 16

Becoming Married (Anderson and Fite), 81

Bella figura, 88

Bernardin, J., 164

"Bernice" story, 112–113

Biko, S., 128

Birth, 57–74; baptism narrative and, 64–66; baptism rituals and, 69–72; and death, 68–69, 73, 112, 122; and miscarriage and stillbirth, 131–134; parables of, 62, 64–66,